The Siege of Dunkirk 1944/45

THE SIEGE OF DUNKIRK 1944/45

AND THE CAPTURE OF THE CHANNEL PORTS

Graham A Thomas

Pen & Sword
MILITARY

An imprint of
Pen & Sword Books Ltd
Yorkshire – Philadelphia

Pen & Sword
MILITARY

First published in Great Britain in 2025 by
Pen and Sword Military
An imprint of
Pen & Sword Books Ltd
Yorkshire – Philadelphia

Copyright © Graham A. Thomas

ISBN 9 781 39908 060 6

The right of Graham A. Thomas to be identified as Author of this work has been asserted by him in accordance with the Copyright, Designs and Patents Act 1988.

A CIP catalogue record for this book is available from the British Library.

All rights reserved. No part of this book may be reproduced, transmitted, downloaded, decompiled or reverse engineered in any form or by any means, electronic or mechanical including photocopying, recording or by any information storage and retrieval system, without permission from the Publisher in writing. No part of this book may be used or reproduced in any manner for the purpose of training artificial intelligence technologies or systems.

Typeset by Lapiz Digital
Printed and bound in the UK by CPI Group (UK) Ltd, Croydon, CR0 4YY.

The Publisher's authorised representative in the EU for product safety is
Authorised Rep Compliance Ltd., Ground Floor, 71 Lower Baggot Street, Dublin D02 P593, Ireland.
www.arccompliance.com

For a complete list of Pen & Sword titles please contact

PEN & SWORD BOOKS LIMITED
47 Church Street, Barnsley, South Yorkshire, S70 2AS, England
E-mail: enquiries@pen-and-sword.co.uk
Website: www.pen-and-sword.co.uk

or

PEN AND SWORD BOOKS
1950 Lawrence Road, Havertown, PA 19083, USA
E-mail: uspen-and-sword@casematepublishers.com
Website: www.penandswordbooks.com

Contents

List of Plates vii
Author's Note xi
Maps xiii

Chapter 1	Overview	1
Chapter 2	The Situation at 30 June 1944	8
Chapter 3	Operation TOTALIZE: Caen	19
Chapter 4	Operation TRACTABLE: The Capture of Falaise	30
Chapter 5	In Pursuit	42
Chapter 6	Crossing the Seine	47
Chapter 7	Operation ASTONIA: Liberating Le Havre	51
Chapter 8	Operation WELLHIT: Boulogne Liberated	70
Chapter 9	Operation UNDERGO: Calais Liberated	98
Chapter 10	The Siege of Dunkirk Begins	120
Chapter 11	The Siege of Dunkirk: 1st Czech Independent Armoured Brigade Group	144
Chapter 12	The Siege of Dunkirk: 7th Royal Tank Regiment War Diary	154
Chapter 13	The Air Campaign and Epilogue	180

Notes 191
Bibliography 207
Index 209

List of Plates

1. Churchill tanks and a bridgelayer of 34th Tank Brigade during the assault on Le Havre, 13 September 1944. (No. 5 Army Film & Photographic Unit, Sergeant Wilkes, IWM, Wikimedia Commons, Released)
2. A Churchill AVRE advances in support of an assault on the German garrison at Le Havre, 10 September 1944. (Sergeant Collins, No. 5 Army Film & Photographic Unit, IWM, Wikimedia Commons, Released)
3. Churchill tank crews of 34th Tank Brigade watch the RAF bombing the defences of Le Havre, 10 September 1944. (No. 5 Army Film & Photographic Unit, Sergeant Wilkes, IWM, Wikimedia Commons, Released)
4. Churchill tanks and infantry in action during the assault on Le Havre by Canadian 1st Corps, 10 September 1944. (No. 5 Army Film & Photographic Unit, IWM, Wikimedia Commons, Released)
5. Churchill tanks of 7th Royal Tank Regiment form up for the assault on Le Havre by Canadian 1st Corps, 10 September 1944. (No. 5 Army Film & Photographic Unit, IWM, Wikimedia Commons, Released)
6. A Churchill tank leads a troop of Sherman Flail tanks of the specialized British 79th Armoured Division during the assault on Boulogne, September 1944. (IWM Wikimedia Commons, Released)
7. German prisoners marching through Boulogne after its liberation by the Allies. (Crown copyright, Archives of Canada 136333, Wikimedia Commons, Public Domain)
8. Dunkirk was one of the last German outposts to surrender. Note signs painted on the roofs of some buildings by Allied prisoners of war to show their location to Allied aircraft. (Flying Office W. Moss Royal Air Force official photographer, IWM CL 2620, Wikimedia Commons, Released)
9. Churchill tanks of 7th Royal Tank Regiment advance during the assault on Le Havre by Canadian 1st Corps, 10 September 1944. (No. 5 Army Film & Photographic Unit, IWM BU 1193, Wikimedia Commons, Released)
10. A Churchill tank of 'B' Squadron, 107th Regiment Royal Armoured Corps, 34th Tank Brigade, Odon Valley, Normandy, 17 July 1944. (No. 5 Army Film & Photographic Unit, IWM B7639, Wikimedia Commons, Released)
11. An RAF Typhoon landing at a forward airstrip, as supply lorries pass in the foreground, 26 July 1944. (No. 5 Army Film & Photographic Unit, IWM B8146, Wikimedia Commons, Released)
12. British and German troops man a checkpoint at Dunkirk during a truce to allow refugees to enter British lines, 4 October 1944. (Captain E.G. Malindine,

No. 5 Army Film & Photographic Unit, IWM B10500, Wikimedia Commons, Released)

13. Bombardier C. Bailey of the 5th Duke of Wellington Regiment (600th Regt RA) sets out on a 'recce' patrol in the Dunkirk perimeter, 3 March 1945. Photo: Sergeant Hewitt, No.5 Army Film & Photographic Unit, IWM B15109, Wikimedia Commons, Released.

14. Churchill AVREs of 79th Armoured Division moving into Caen, 10 July 1944. (Sergeant Christie, No. 5 Army Film & Photographic Unit, IWM B6901, Wikimedia Commons, Released)

15. Churchill Crocodile flamethrower tank, 79th Armoured Division, 13 February 1944. Photo: Sergeant Brown, War Office Official Photographer, No. 5 Army Film & Photographic Unit, IWM H35809 Wikimedia Commons, Released.

16. Churchill AVRE laying carpet from a bobbin, 79th Armoured Division experimental trials, 26 April 1944. (Sergeant J. Mapham, War Office official photographer, No. 5 Army Film & Photographic Unit, IWM H37860 Wikimedia Commons, Released)

17. Sherman Crab Flail tank under test, 79th Armoured Division, 27 April 1944. (Sergeant J. Mapham, War Office official photographer, No. 5 Army Film & Photographic Unit, IWM H37860 Wikimedia Commons, Released)

18. Two Sherman tanks are pictured on a beach with the tide out. In the distance, are two more Shermans, next to an army truck. (C.A. Russell, IWM LD5562, Wikimedia Commons, Released)

19. 'Winnie', one of two 14in guns emplaced at St Margaret's near Dover, 10 March 1941. (Mr Puttnam, War Office official photographer, IWM H7918, Wikimedia Commons, Released)

20. Squadron Leader K.K. Majumdar of 268 Squadron RAF waits in the cockpit of his Hawker Typhoon FR Mark 1B for the take-off signal at Fort Rouge in France, autumn 1944. (Pilot Officer T. Lea, RAF official photographer, IWM CL 1176, Wikimedia Commons, Released)

21. A road near Chambois, south-east of Trun, Normandy, filled with wrecked vehicles and the bodies of retreating German soldiers following an attack by Hawker Typhoons of 83 Group. (Flying Officer N.S. Clark, RAF official photographer, IWM CL910, Wikimedia Commons, Released)

22. Airmen of No. 419 Repair and Salvage Unit, aided by an AEC mobile crane, remove a damaged Hawker Typhoon Mark IB, MN413 'I8-T', of 440 Squadron RCAF from the landing strip, following a wheels-up landing at Lantheuil, Normandy, on 1 August 1944. (Pilot Officer R.R. Broom, RAF official photographer, IWM CL652, Wikimedia Commons, Released)

23. The aftermath of an attack by Hawker Typhoons of 121 Wing on German armoured vehicles which had massed at Roncey, south-east of Coutances, Normandy, to counter-attack American forces on 29 July 1944. (Flying Officer N.S. Clark, RAF official photographer, IWM CL631, Wikimedia Commons, Released)

24. Clouds of dust are raised as a Hawker Typhoon Mark IB, MN529 'BR-N' of 184 Squadron RAF, takes to the air from Bazenville, Normandy for another sortie against German ground targets. (Flying Officer A. Goodchild, RAF official photographer, IWM CL147, Wikimedia Commons, Released)
25. This photo by RAF Bomber Command shows Cap Gris Nez before Operation UNDERGO on 26 September 1944. (RAF Bomber Command, Wikimedia Commons, Released)
26. The vehicles shown are British Armoured Recovery Vehicle conversion of Sherman IIIs (M4A2), REME, 79th Armoured Division, summer 1944. (Library and Archives Canada, ID 4233174, Wikimedia Commons, Released)
27. Ready for another sortie over France, Hawker Typhoon 1B, MN304 'FJ-N' of 164 Squadron RAF, runs up its engines in preparation for take-off at Thorney Island, Hampshire. (Flying Officer B. Bridge, RAF official photographer, IWM CH13344, Wikimedia Commons, Released)
28. Sherman and Stuart tanks of the Guards Armoured Division advance towards the German positions at Arras on 1 September 1944. This image is an example of the way the Allies advanced into France and towards the Channel ports. (Sergeant Hewitt, No. 5 Army Film & Photographic Unit, IWM BU270, Wikimedia Commons, Released)
29. Pictured are vehicles of 3rd Canadian Division advancing on German positions at Bretteville-le-Rabet towards Falaise to cut off the German retreat, 14 August 1944. (Library and Archives of Canada ID3396206, Wikimedia Commons, Released)

Author's Note

I initially came across the Siege of Dunkirk while I was conducting research for my book *Attack On The Scheldt*. At the time, I didn't feel that it was relevant for that book so I filed it away as something I had to look into at a later date.

When I started researching for my next book *The Dieppe Raid: The German Perspective*, I searched through the same files I had put aside while working on the previous book. Indeed, I thought this research would be relevant for the Dieppe book but as I began writing I realized that, once again, I needed to store away the files on the Siege of Dunkirk for another project. I did some more digging to see how many other books had been written about this episode in the war and it seems as if this subject is not that well documented. Hence, I give you this book, designed to give the audience as complete a picture as possible of these extraordinary events.

But this book is not just a narrative of events: it is meant to show the futility of war and the cost in blood and treasure that all nations suffer when they go to war. We no longer have to look back to the past, we can see the futility of war in the conflict in Ukraine. While the cost is high in personnel, including civilians, it is also very high in rebuilding nations. The rebuilding of the Channel ports, of Dunkirk and of Germany as a whole was a bill that everyone had to fulfil. I suspect the same will be true of Ukraine.

Because of the nature of the research and the events that took place in 1944 in terms of clearing the Channel ports there is a strong emphasis on the Canadian armies. However, I have tried to ensure that other Allied units are mentioned as fairly as research allowed.

It is my hope that this book provides the reader with an insight as to why no nation should ever consider going to war.

Graham A. Thomas
Warminster, Wiltshire, 2024

Maps

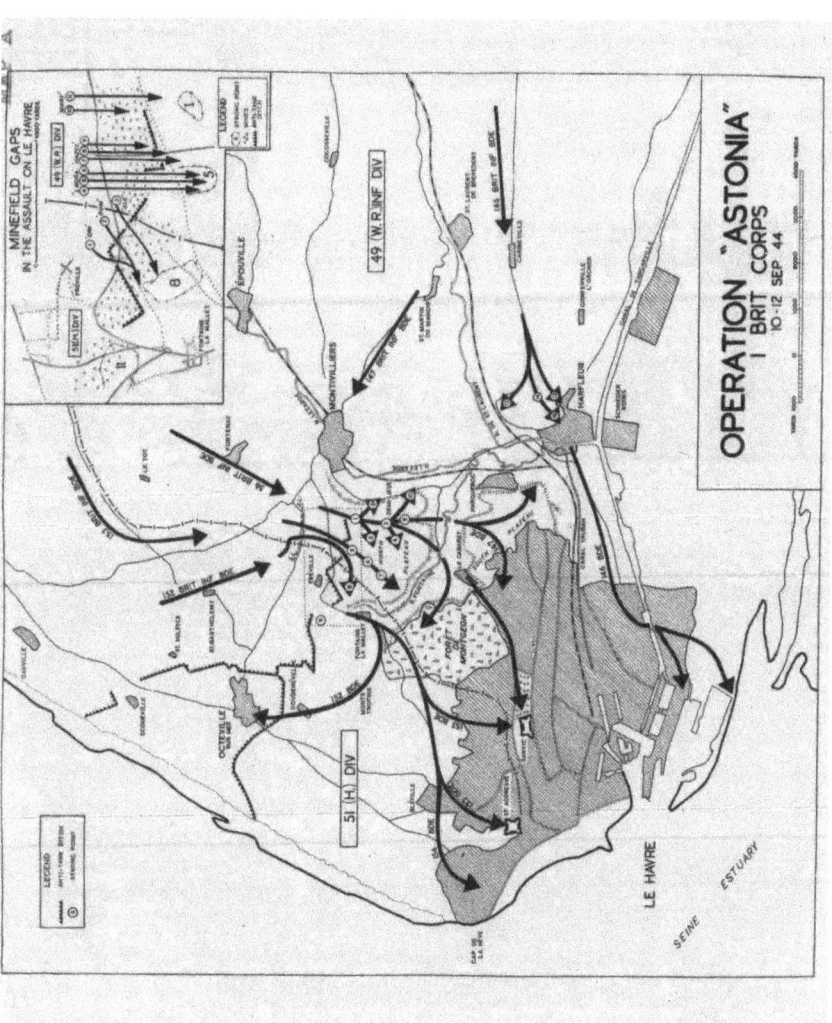

Map A:
This map shows Operation ASTONIA, the Liberation of Le Havre, from the perspective of 1 British Corps. (Report No 184, Historical Section, Canadian Military Headquarters: Canadian Participation in the Operations in North-West Europe 1944, Part V: Clearing the Channel Ports 3 Sep 44 – 6 Feb 45)

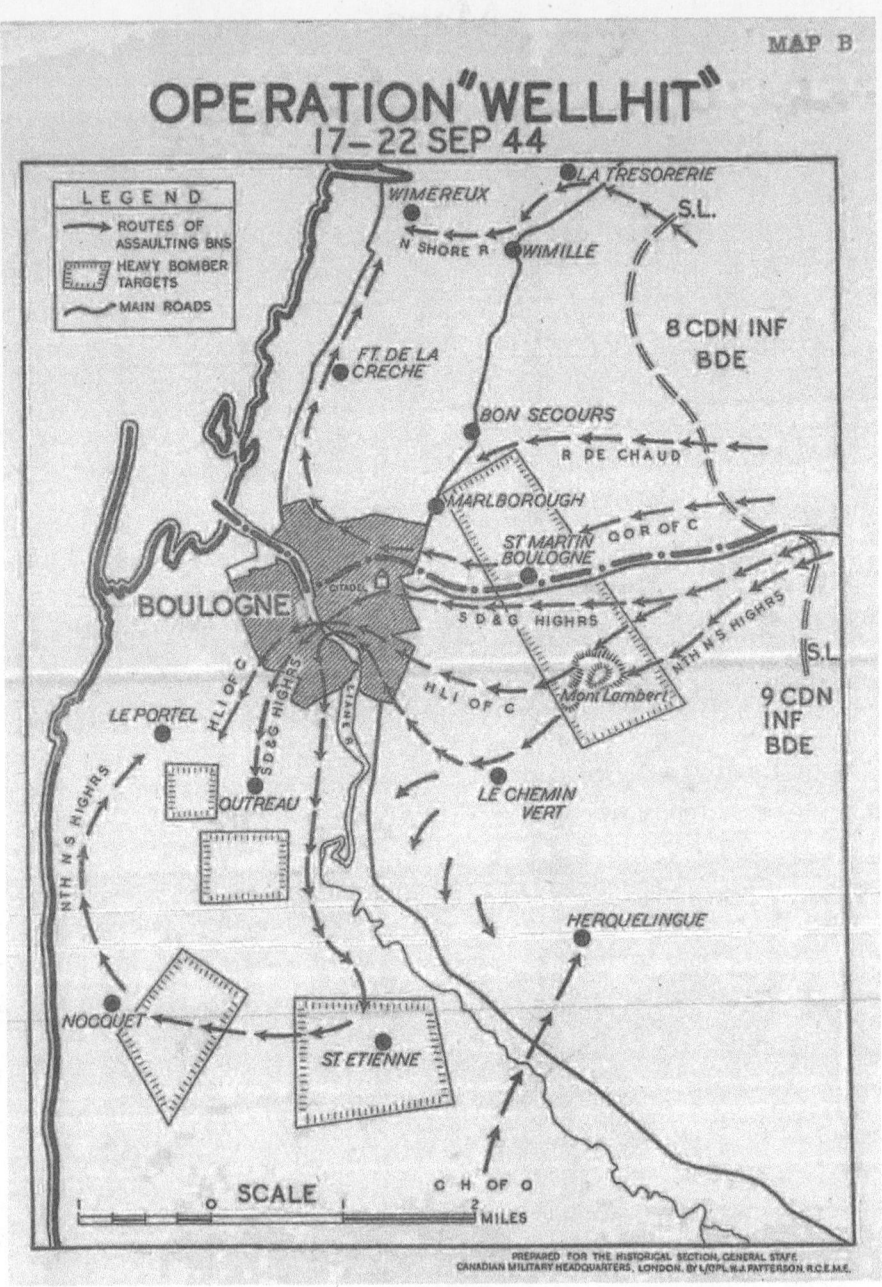

Map B:
This map illustrates the movement of the Allies during Operation WELLHIT, the liberation of Boulogne, from the perspective of the Canadian forces involved in this operation. (See Report No. 184, Map B)

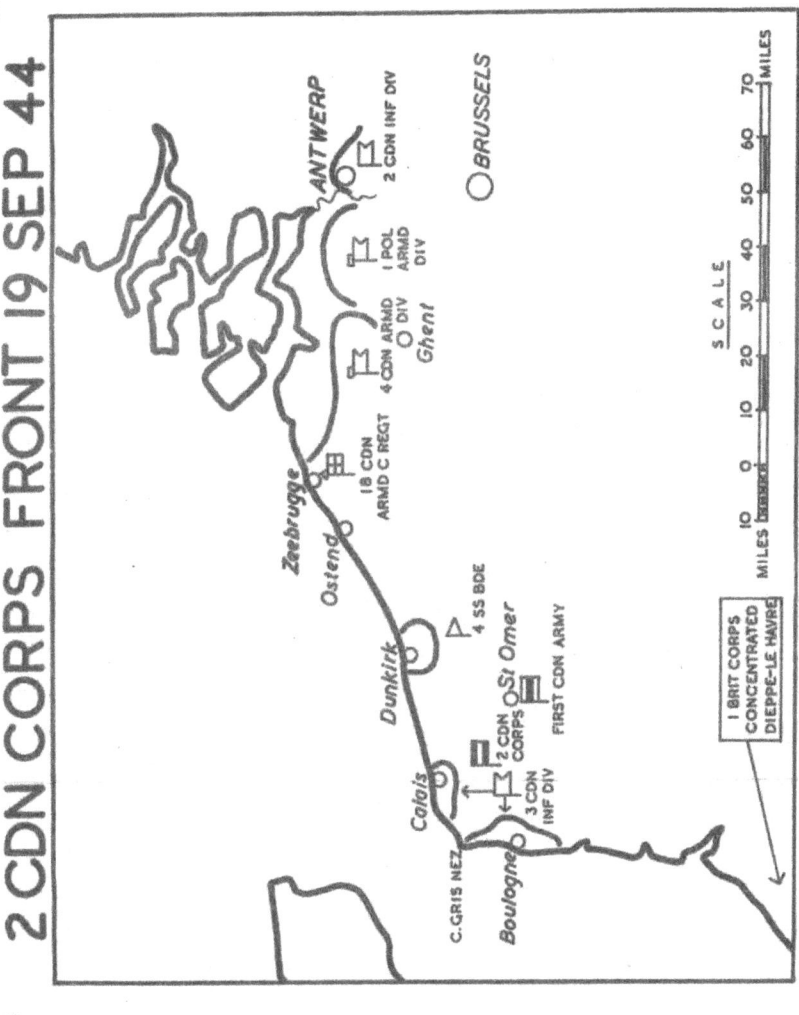

Map C:
Here we see the 2nd Canadian Corps front as it was just before the launch of Operation UNDERGO, the liberation of Calais. (See Report No. 184, Map C)

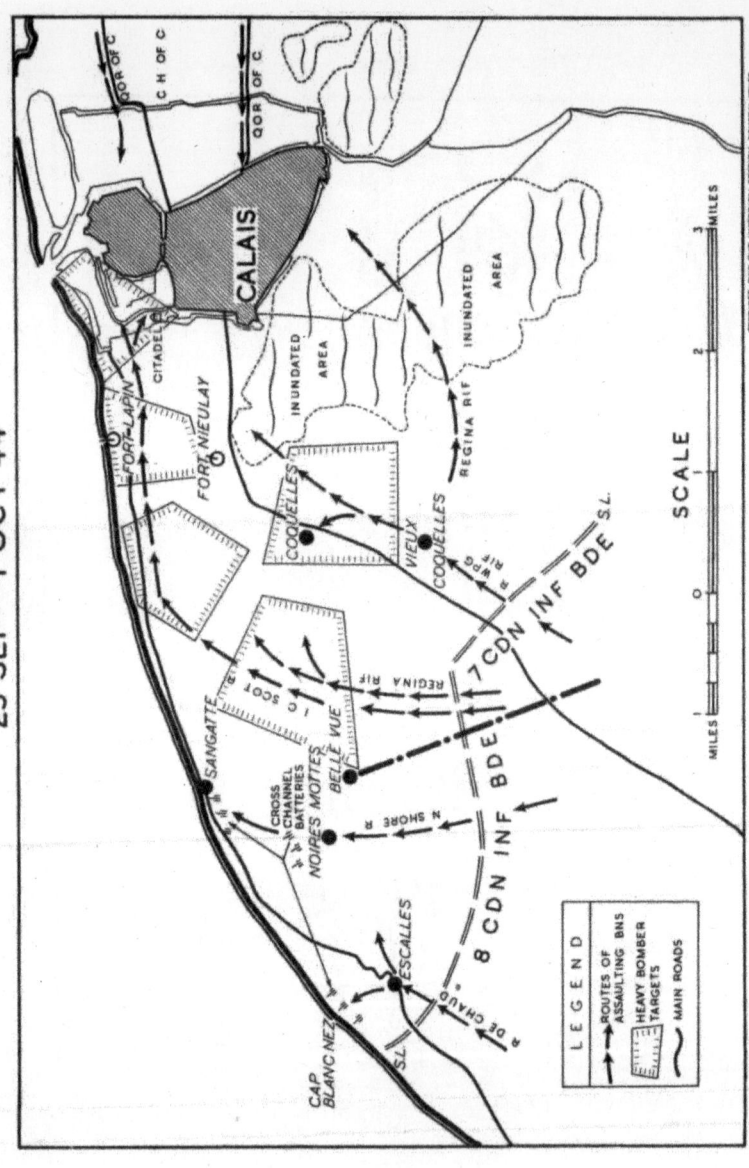

Map D:
This map is a much closer view than the previous one of Operation UNDERGO and shows the disposition of Allied troops for this attack. (See Report No. 184, Map D)

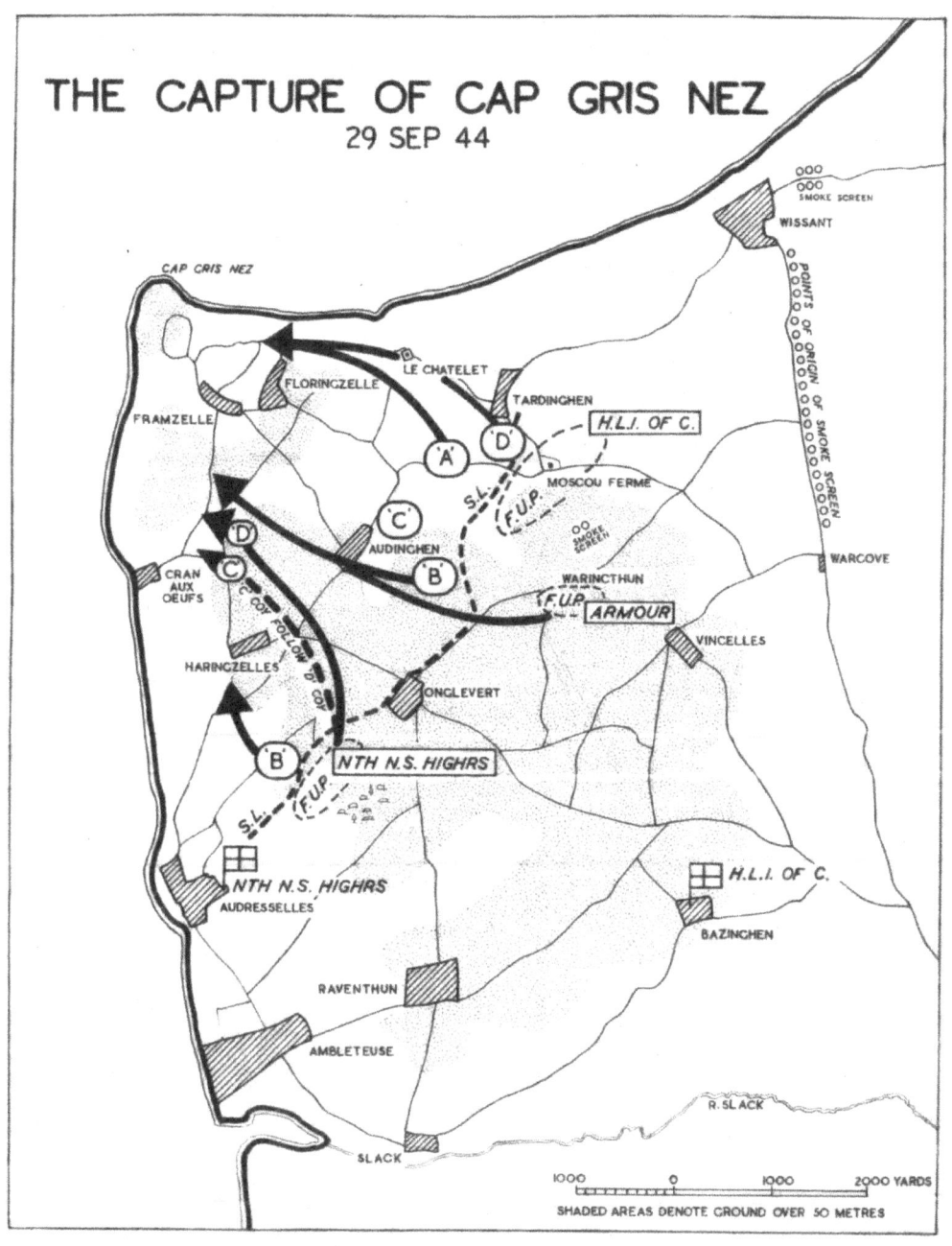

Map E:
This map drills down into Operation UNDERGO and shows the Allied operations against the German positions and the capture of those positions on Cap Gris Nez. Most of the German defences and big guns were concentrated on the tip of the peninsula. (See Report No. 184, Map E)

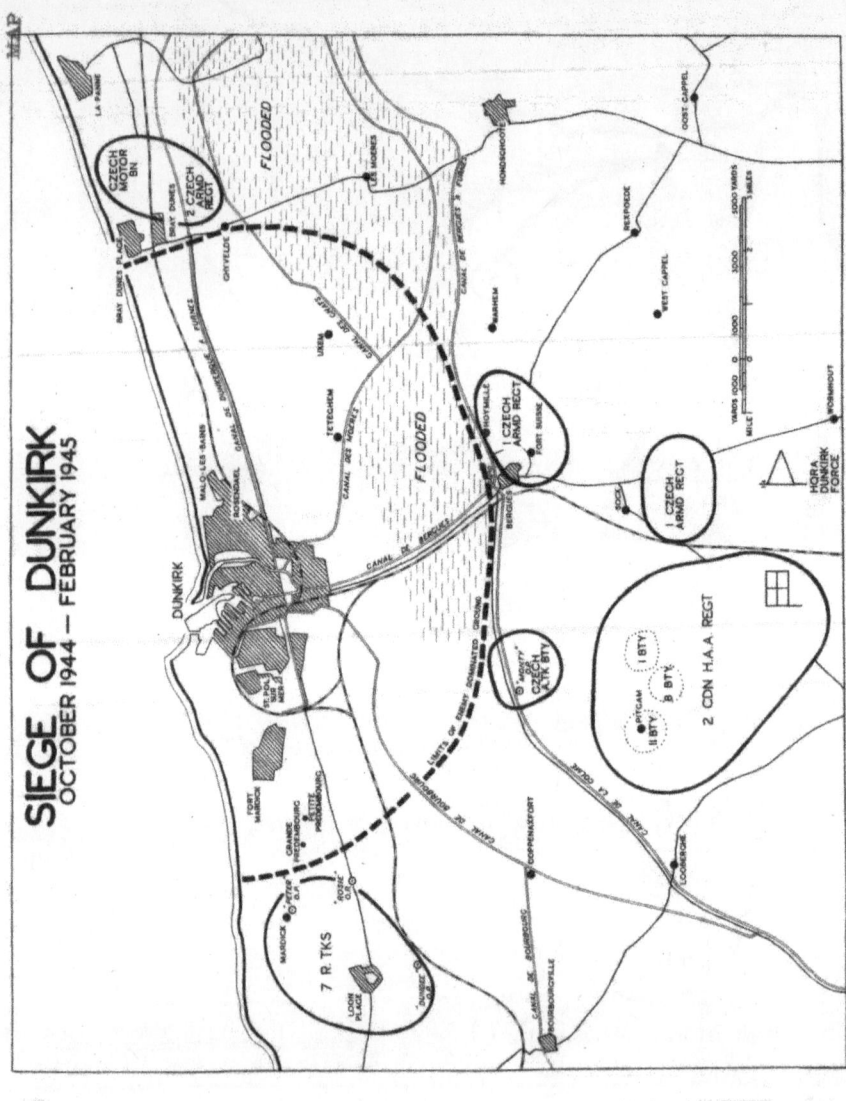

Map F:
This final map is the most important as it shows the Allied siege of German defences at Dunkirk. We can see the siege line that rings the city. This was the German defensive line that the Allies whittled away at bit by bit. (See Report No. 184, Map 5)

Chapter 1

Overview

In the early summer of 1940 the Allies, particularly the British Army, were stranded on the beaches of Dunkirk, their backs to the sea. Surrounded on all sides by the victorious German Army they were pounded mercilessly by the Luftwaffe and artillery fire. It was only the Royal Navy and 'the little ships' that saved the British Army from extinction and managed to get them back to Britain.

In September 1944, the tables had turned. Now it was the Germans who were surrounded by the Allies at Dunkirk, with their backs to the sea. However, the Germans had fortified Dunkirk and the other major French ports so instead of waiting on the beaches as the British had done in 1940, they were ensconced in the fortified towns of Le Havre, Boulogne, Calais and Dunkirk itself. But for the Germans, there was no Royal Navy to come along and take them to safety. Instead, they had to endure the Allied pounding through air power, artillery, armour and infantry attacks on the Channel ports and the siege surrounding Dunkirk. The siege lasted up until the German garrison there surrendered in early May 1945.

Primarily, it was the 2nd Canadian Division that initially surrounded the town as the clearance of the other Channel ports got under way. However, many Allied units were rotated through as the siege continued into the winter of 1944 and then subsequently into 1945 until the end of the war. For the Allies, opening the port of Antwerp as soon as possible was much more important as it had modern facilities and was a huge port. Its facilities were also largely untouched by the Germans and could be quickly put back into operating order by the Allies. Many of the Channel ports had been badly damaged and would take time for the Allies to get them up and running. Time was something the Allies couldn't afford to waste, they needed supplies and they needed to keep the momentum going.

Capturing Antwerp would immensely improve the Allies' supply problems, enabling them to land large amounts of military personnel and materiel, far more than they had been able to do up to that point using the temporary Mulberry harbours that still remained on the beaches of Normandy.

Because Antwerp was so important to the Allies, the commander of the 21st Army Group, Field Marshal Montgomery, whose responsibility it was to capture Antwerp and get it up and running again, decided that the German garrison in Dunkirk could be contained instead of captured. He did not want to lose precious personnel, materiel and ammunition trying to capture the heavily defended city. Instead, the Allies would lay siege to it in a similar way as the Germans had done four years earlier.

Several British and Canadian units were involved in the initial siege until the responsibility for containing the Germans in Dunkirk fell upon the 1st Czechoslovak Independent Armoured Brigade Group whose task was to control the Allied siege, probe the German lines, attack and harass them wherever possible but keep them pinned in their defensive positions and then gradually force them to contract those positions. These German units managed to withstand probing attacks by the Allies and remained in situ until the commander, Admiral Friedrich Frisius, surrendered on 9 May 1945 to the Czechoslovak brigade group commanded by Brigadier General Alois Liska.

D-Day had taken place on 6 June 1944 when thousands of Allied troops landed on the beaches of Normandy but by September, the Allied advance inland was beginning to slow as German resistance grew. The Battle of Normandy was a gruelling slog as the Germans threw more and more troops and armour at the Allied advance in order to slow it down, stop it and push them back to the sea. By late August 1944, supplies for the Allies were still primarily from the Normandy beachhead from temporary harbours. The supply lines were hundreds of miles long as the Allied armies continued to advance. This meant that the Channel ports had to be captured and cleared of German troops, with the port facilities up and running as soon as possible. The situation for the Allies would begin to change in September and early October 1944 as each of the Channel ports fell.

Montgomery gave the task of clearing the ports to the First Canadian Army, who then ordered the 2nd Canadian Division, under its command, to take on the responsibility. Several different plans were made by the Allies on what operations would be needed to achieve this. However, it soon became evident that capturing Antwerp intact was more important than clearing the

Channel ports. The reason for this was because Antwerp had the largest harbour and its port facilities were intact. Eisenhower, the Supreme Allied Commander directed Montgomery to open Antwerp as quickly as possible. 'Early use of Antwerp so urgent that I am prepared to give up operations against Calais and Dunkirk.'[1] Montgomery wrote to General Henry Crerar, the commander of the First Canadian Army. 'Dunkirk will be left to be dealt with later, for the present it will be merely masked.'[2]

However, operations to capture and clear the port of Calais continued under Operation UNDERGO. This might have been in part because the German heavy artillery batteries situated near the town had to be silenced. Those gun batteries on Cap Gris Nez were capable of firing across to England and also attacking shipping heading up the Channel towards the Scheldt Estuary and the port of Antwerp. The rest of the Allied forces that might have been used to take Dunkirk were, instead, released to take part in the Battle of the Scheldt, which would result in the Allies gaining the largely undamaged port of Antwerp. Under these conditions, the Allies used a smaller force to ring the city of Dunkirk and keep the Germans within it contained.

To achieve this containment, units such as the British 4th Special Service Brigade (4SSB) who relieved the 5th Canadian Infantry Brigade, were rotated through the siege. The British 154th Infantry Brigade relieved 4SSB but in October 1944, this rotation ended when the 1st Czechoslovak Independent Armoured Brigade Group arrived and took on the task until the final surrender.

But what of the Germans inside the fortress? The garrison was made up of personnel from the Navy, Luftwaffe, Army and special fortress units. In addition, there was a large detachment of Waffen-SS personnel numbering upwards of 2,000 men. The total strength of the German garrison was more than 10,000 men. Many of these were remnants of five army divisions which had been mauled during the Normandy campaign and had retreated to Dunkirk. The town itself was heavily fortified and well-supplied for a lengthy siege.[3]

The outer perimeter of the German garrison in Dunkirk stretched roughly 13km from the city, running through the villages of Mardyck, Loon-Plage, Spycker, Bergues and Bray-Dunes.[4] Bourbourg was captured by the 5th Canadian Infantry Brigade on 7–8 September while Loon-Plage was attacked by the Calgary Highlanders on 7 September. German opposition in this town was very heavy and the Highlanders suffered significant casualties. They captured the village as the Germans withdrew on 9 September.

The following towns were taken by the Canadians over the next ten days, Coppenaxfort, Mardyck, Bergues, Veurne, Nieuwpoort and La Panne (De Panne). Also, villages east of Dunkirk were also taken during this time – Bray-Dunes and Ghyvelde.

Also, in Belgium, nearby Ostend (Oostende) had fallen when the Germans withdrew, retreating to fortified Dunkirk. At this point, the Allies realized that it would be impossible to clear the Germans out of Dunkirk without a major assault that would use up men and material badly needed elsewhere. Dunkirk itself had been heavily damaged and as such, the port was of limited use from a logistics point of view. Since Ostend had been captured the port there was in better condition and it was opened on 28 September 1944. This eased the supply problems for the Allies while they worked towards capturing Antwerp. Dunkirk became less important and not worth the cost in blood and treasure.

Dunkirk was the most resilient of the Channel ports in terms of the German defences as it was the only one that held on until the end of the war. The German garrison was relentlessly pounded by artillery and air bombardment as well as being flooded with propaganda leaflets dropped from the air. One of the Allied objectives of the siege was to ensure the German supply routes predominantly from the sea (E-boats and submarines) and from the air were completely cut off. Despite this, the Canadian probing attacks against the German defenders were thwarted with astonishing aggression, sufficient enough to dissuade the Canadians from mounting a full-scale assault.[5]

The British 4th Special Service Brigade relieved the 2nd Canadian Infantry Division on 16 September and ten days later the 4SSB were relieved by the 154th Infantry Brigade.

The Germans attempted to take advantage of the change with sorties against the 7th Black Watch in Ghyvelde and against 7th Argylls at nearby Bray-Dunes Plage. Both attacks were repulsed but only after the Argyll headquarters had been partially occupied and houses in Ghyvelde had been destroyed.[6]

The 1st Czechoslovak Independent Armoured Brigade Group arrived at the Allied lines on 9 October where they took over the siege permanently. They mounted several attacks and harassing raids against the German defenders in the perimeter towns with the objective of taking as many prisoners as they could, forcing the Germans to either reinforce or withdraw from those positions. On 28 October the Czechs attacked German positions in the eastern suburbs of Dunkirk, taking more than 300 prisoners. November saw several attacks and counter-attacks in the eastern sector. Bit by bit the Czechs were wearing down the Germans.

Conditions on both sides were difficult in the winter. The low-lying ground outside the city had been flooded to form part of the defences and adjacent land easily became waterlogged, hampering movement and making life unpleasant. Canadian gunners reported that gun-pits needed to be bailed out, the sides of dugouts collapsed and transport became mired.[7]

As the siege wore on the Germans began suffering with poor food and health while the Czechs were able to maintain their moral by granting leave to nearby towns such as Lille. The Germans, however, were running out of food and medical supplies, their moral slowly beginning to crumble.

However, twice during the early months of 1945 the Germans were partly resupplied by some of their midget submarines, those that were still operational and manned. These submarines, known as *Seehund* (Seal), carried special food containers (nicknamed 'butter torpedoes') instead of torpedoes, and on the return voyage used the containers to carry mail from the Dunkirk garrison. However, it was not enough and in early May the Allies dropped flyers over the German positions at Dunkirk:

> WARNING! To the German troops at Dunkirk! Your last opportunity to join Army Group Montgomery will soon be over. Show white flags over your positions! To discuss the handover, Admiral Frisius or a certified representative is allowed through the Allied lines. ZG 130.[8]

On 9 May 1945, the German garrison besieged at Dunkirk surrendered unconditionally to the Allies. This was two days after the overall surrender of Nazi Germany had been signed and one day after it came into effect.

Units involved in the Siege of Dunkirk:

The Allies:
- 5th Canadian Infantry Brigade (relieved 18 September)
- The Black Watch (Royal Highland Regiment) of Canada
- Le Regiment de Maisonneuve
- The Calgary Highlanders

- 5th Canadian Infantry Brigade Ground Defence Platoon (Lorne Scots)
- British 4th Special Service Brigade (relieved 26 September)
- British 154th Infantry Brigade (26 September–9 October)
- 7th Battalion Argyll and Sutherland Highlanders
- 1st and 7th Battalions Black Watch
- 1st Czechoslovak Armoured Brigade Group (9 October–9 May 1945)
  - 1st Czech Tank Battalion
  - 2nd Czech Tank Battalion
  - 1st Czech Motorized Infantry Battalion (two companies)
  - Field Artillery Regiment
  - Anti-tank battalion
  - Armoured Reconnaissance Squadron
  - Field Engineers Company
  - Attached British, French and Canadian units
  - 7th Royal Tank Regiment
  - 2nd Canadian Heavy Anti-aircraft Regiment
  - 109th Heavy Anti-aircraft Regiment, Royal Artillery
  - 125th Light Anti-aircraft Regiment, Royal Artillery
  - French 51st Infantry Regiment formed from the French Forces of the Interior [9]

The Germans: Elements From:
- 49th Infantry Division
- 226th Infantry Division
- 346th Infantry Division
- 711th Infantry Division
- 97th Infantry Division
- 26th Fortress Battalion
- 104th Fortress Battalion
- Waffen-SS Reineck group[10]

This is a brief overview of the Allied Siege of Dunkirk. What follows now is a deep dive into the details. However, even this 'deep dive' is not the entire definitive picture of the events that took place in the liberation of the Channel ports and the Siege of Dunkirk. A much deeper look would likely provide greater detail, possibly even day to day detail on this period of the war. For instance, it would be interesting to know what the Germans felt about the siege from their perspective as defenders. In this book, there are glimpses of this viewpoint from the garrison commanders who were taken prisoner but further research might uncover much more. Of course this depends upon additional research being readily available.

At any rate, this book is designed to give the reader as detailed a look as possible in the events leading up to, and the subsequent events of, the Siege of Dunkirk in late 1944 and 1945.

Chapter 2

The Situation at 30 June 1944

The end of June saw the Allies now with a foothold in France. In these early days, it was believed by the Allies, particularly the British, that capturing Caen was the key to success as they could pivot away from that city, which was strategically located, and move inland from there. The Second British Army continued piling on the pressure against the Germans in that sector. The Cherbourg Peninsula was all but cleared of German troops since the capture of the port on 26 June. The last of the German units still holding out in the north-west tip of the peninsula were being mopped up by 7th US Corps.

The Second British Army's 8th Corps had, by 28 June, created a bridgehead across the Odon River south of Tourville that enabled 11th Armoured Division to pass through the bridgehead and take up positions south of the river. This was in readiness for a move south-east by the British and Canadians to bypass the city of Caen. 'This penetration was to produce a most violent enemy reaction' – in the words of an official communique of 30 June – 'the most powerful counter-attack yet launched'.[1]

> Up the Villiers Bocage – Caen road in the latter part of June had come the tanks of 2 SS Panzer Division (Das Reich). Following in swift succession appeared 'a galaxy of talent' from – 1 SS Panzer Division (Adolf Hitler), 9 SS Panzer Division (Frundsberg) recently from Russia, and 10 SS Panzer Division (Hoehenstaufen) – formations constituting the reserve which Field-Marshal Rommel had been assembling behind the immediate battle area.[2]

It was estimated at the time that the Germans had between 300 and 400 tanks ready for battle in the Caen sector but, although their attacks were heavy and difficult, they were erratic. The Germans feared there would be another Allied invasion somewhere in the Pas de Calais area and so did not throw the full weight of their strength, infantry and armour, into the Caen battles. Some divisions were held back in the north in case of such an invasion.

In addition to this, the Caen sector terrain was not conducive to large-scale tank attacks. Indeed, the fields in the Bocage area were too small for such attacks and 'it was impossible for more than a few tanks to be in view of each other at the same time. The physical effort of advancing, even without opposition, was prodigious. It was necessary to make frequent dismounted reconnaissance to find tank runs, and to bump and jolt across banks and ditches, clinging on for dear life, with one's head swept by the low branches of thickly planted orchards.'[3] Around Caen and Carpiquet the flat wheat fields should have enabled quick easy access for mass armour attacks but the country was littered with small farms and copses providing excellent cover for anti-tank guns. The result was slow, agonizing advances with small formations of tanks supporting infantry.

> Hence German divisions were sent into the battle piecemeal not as elements in a 'planned and concerted manoeuvre of war' but as makeshifts to plug holes. Small groups of tanks backed by infantry were thrown successfully into the fight to blunt a spearhead which was already beginning to threaten the whole German defence system south of the Odon and east of the Orne.[4]

While it's true the British and Canadians failed to achieve a quick breakthrough at Caen, this operation had the effect of eating up German armour and infantry in costly local counter-attacks.

While the attacks and counter-attacks were costly on both sides they were far more so for the Germans who had to keep reinforcing their divisions in the Caen sector. Nevertheless, their strength was slowly diminishing while that of the Allies was increasing. By the end of June 1944, the Allies had four armoured divisions and eighteen infantry divisions in France. In addition to this, there were 'twelve British and twelve American air-landing grounds operating in Normandy, and, although the Luftwaffe offered spasmodic resistance, Allied command of the air remained firm'.[5]

Part of the reason why the Allies had such a command of the air was that in addition to the bombers and fighters, the RAF were increasingly using rocket-firing Typhoon fighters and Typhoon fighter-bombers. These machines spread panic and destruction on German armour, strongpoints, observation posts and vehicle concentrations amongst other targets.

> While our move and counter-move pass unhindered, every German action is subject to interference in varying degree from the air. Strategically, his arms are harried with a ferocity never before believed possible; tactically any large scale concentration suffers the same fate. This, perhaps, is one of the many reasons for a complete absence of any similarity between the German attacks of 1940 and 1944.[6]

Allied operations in North-West Europe in July 1944 could be divided into three steps, or phases. Phase 1, running from 28 June to 10 July, was marked by the Allied capture of Caen and the beginning of the American offensive in the southern part of the Cherbourg Peninsula. Phase 2, 11 to 24 July, saw the British and Canadians attack east of Caen while the Americans attacked and captured Saint-Lô. The final phase of the July operations, the 25th to 30th, saw a failed advance by the British and Canadians along the Caen–Falaise road while the Americans were able to break-out west of Saint-Lô.

On 4 July the Canadians began Operation WINDSOR, the bid to capture Carpiquet. The units involved in this operation included 8th Canadian Infantry Brigade with support from the Royal Winnipeg Rifles and the 10th Canadian Infantry Brigade as well as a 'tremendous weight of artillery'. In addition to this, the Canadian force also had 16 Field Company Royal Calgary Engineers, while armour support consisted of one squadron of mine-clearing Flail tanks (primarily converted Sherman tanks), one of Crocodiles (flame-throwers, mostly converted Churchill tanks), a squadron of AVREs,[7] and a large number of anti-tank guns.[8]

Naval power was also involved in this operation. It included a monitor (smaller vessels with disproportionately large guns, such as 15in guns, taken from other battleships, used for shore support and bombardment), and the battleship HMS *Rodney*. Including the guns on the ships more than 760 guns took part, with more than 428 guns firing between 30 and 250 shells.[9]

The Germans, however, were not idle and once fire had been opened by the Allies they laid down an immediate counter-barrage of artillery and mortar fire, but it was not enough. The Canadians, using the Flails, flamethrowers, AVREs and anti-tank guns, broke the German defenders and rolled forward, consolidating their positions in the village of Carpiquet at 0700hrs.

The Royal Winnipeg Rifles' objectives were the hangars at the south end of the Carpiquet airfield, which they managed to reach. Once they did they came under intense fire from units of 12th SS Panzer Division and were forced to withdraw. This was in part because 43rd Division on the Rifles' right flank had not been able to hold onto their positions in Verson and were evacuated on 5 July. This had a knock on effect to the rest of the operation. Verson was not captured until four days later as part of the major Allied attack on Caen. This meant that the Queen's Own Calgary Regiment were not able to capture and hold their objectives on the east end of the airfield. Their objectives were the administration buildings and these were finally taken on 9 July. 'In short, against heavy artillery fire and frequent infantry/tank counter-attacks, 8 Cdn Inf Bde had to fight hard to hold its newly-won and almost isolated position on the Carpiquet feature.'[10]

While this book is about the clearing of the Channel ports and the subsequent Siege of Dunkirk, the capture of Caen under Operation CHARNWOOD was definitely an important step for the Allies in the successful liberation of the ports. Much has been written about the battle of Caen and its capture so we will not go into great detail here.

1st British Corps launched CHARNWOOD on 8 July at 0430hrs with the aim of capturing the city of Caen. Involved in this operation were several units that included 3rd Canadian, 59th and 3rd British Divisions plus 2nd Canadian, 27th and 33rd Armoured Brigades all under the command of 1st British Corps. The plan for CHARNWOOD also included the arrival of 34th Armoured Brigade and 2nd Canadian Infantry Division around 11 or 12 July, which were to go into Army Reserve. Part of the overall plan included 3rd Canadian Infantry Division to come into the line on the same days and take on the responsibility of the Caen sector even if 1st British Corps had been unsuccessful in its attacks. The plan also called for a bridgehead to be established over the Orne River once Caen had been taken by the Allies. This would lead to consolidation of 2nd Canadian and 3rd Canadian Infantry Brigades into 2nd Canadian Corps including 2nd Canadian and 33rd British Armoured Brigades once the 4th Canadian Armoured Division had arrived in France.

On 8 July the British and Canadians began their advance south towards Caen with 3rd and 59th British Divisions and 3rd Canadian Division. Buron, Gruchy and Authie were taken with little resistance by 9th Canadian Infantry Brigade. They then continued their advance, taking Franqueville and arriving at the outskirts of Carpiquet. Cussy and Ardenne were captured by 7th Canadian Infantry Brigade but were heavily pounded by German mortars and artillery on their left flank where 59th Division had been unable to capture Hitot. The northern outskirts of Caen were reached by 3rd British Division as daylight was waning.[11]

The Allies assumed that most of the Germans had left the city but that there would still be some enemy units, specifically snipers, that would cause them delays and severe difficulties in their advance. 7th Canadian Recce Regiment was ordered to move into the city and capture any bridges that were still intact. To avoid heavy casualties only armoured cars were used for this operation. As they moved forward, with the help of the French civilians and Resistance they bypassed those known German defensive positions slowly working their way forward. They discovered that every bridge save one had been destroyed. This one bridge was covered by strong German positions on the far bank so the armoured cars came to a halt and waited for the infantry to arrive.

By 9 July most of the remaining German defences in Caen had been destroyed and the S D & G Highlanders (Stormont, Dundas & Glengarry Highlanders (Canadian)) were able to advance directly into the city. They encountered little resistance from the Germans. Behind the Highlanders came the remaining elements of 9th Canadian Infantry Brigade. In the north-east of the city 7th Canadian Infantry Brigade remained in reserve, just in case. This improved situation enabled the last parts of the operation to be completed as the Canadians now occupied the whole of Carpiquet and the surrounding areas. This also meant the Canadians were able to help 43rd Division to clear the area south-east of Caen towards the Orne.

July 10th saw some fierce fighting around Caen while the Allies cleared remaining German positions in the city itself. This procedure was done using patrols which would concentrate their fire on German patrols on the south bank of the Orne. In the meantime, on the right flank of 3rd Canadian Infantry Division, 43rd Division worked its way around the city 'towards the confluence of the Oden and Orne rivers'.[12]

> The ultimate effort, however, was directed to the south and west and towards the high ground on which ran the Evrency road and which included Maltot and Esquay. Although this advance met with heavy opposition, especially on the left, none the less, 43 Div

were able to move ahead some two miles along the whole front, occupying the area between Esquay and Maltot.[13]

However, the Germans reacted with such ferocity that 43rd Division was forced to withdraw from Maltot but were able to hold the high ground west of the village.

Although the Allies had captured Caen it was still under observation and heavy fire from the Germans, mostly from the east bank of the Orne River. West of the Orne, the Germans had set up strong defences around Faubourg de Vaugelles using infantry, armour and artillery. The Second British Army then began a series of attacks into this area. 'While 43 Div drew off enemy armour by thrusting south-east towards the Orne, 49 and 59 Divisions on the left flank of 30 Corps, and 53 and 15 Divisions on the right flank of the Odon salient attacked south and south-west towards Moyers – Evrency.'[14]

The morning of 15 July saw 12th Corps thrust south in order to attempt to retake the high ground between Caen and Evrency while also drawing out the German troops and armour from their positions in the East to the West of the Orne. When night fell the British had captured Esquay and by 0600hrs the following morning they had two brigades covering the high ground beyond Esquay.

The stage was now set for Operation ATLANTIC (the Canadian part of the Allied plan to capture Caen)[15] to begin. The plan for this operation was to clear the Caen sector south and east of the Orne River while pulling German units away from the American First Army. This was to start on 18 July with a large attack southwards.[16]

The Allies knew that the Germans were well dug into their defensive positions, but they assumed that the Germans lacked the necessary resources, especially infantry personnel and troops to man their heavy weapons. As a result, the British decided that by using armour, heavy aerial bombardment and artillery fire they could achieve a quick breakthrough and cut the German lines, rendering them ineffective.

Five British and Canadian corps made up the bulk of Operation ATLANTIC – on the British side they were 1st, 8th, 12th and 30th Corps with 2nd Canadian Corps as well.

> According to the plan, 8 Corps would cross the River Orne north of Caen, attack southwards and occupy the general areas:

Bretteville-sur-Liase/Vinoht/Argences/Fallais. To delude the Germans as far as possible, the impression was to be given that 8 Corps intended to attack through 12 and 30 Corps to capture crossings over the Orne, from (and including) Amay-sur-Orne to Etavaux. 1 Corps was to maintain a firm base for 8 Corps in its present area, and simultaneously with the advance of 8 Corps, was to occupy the general area Toufreveill/Bammeville/La Campagne/Enienville, in order protect the left flank of 8 Corps.[17]

The role of 2nd Canadian Corps in Operation ATLANTIC, as a subset of the Second British Army, was to bridge the Orne after capturing Faubourg de Vaucelles and then capture and use the high ground in the area around Verrières.

Operation ATLANTIC called for the extensive use of medium and heavy bombers. The Allies had set aside 6,000 aircraft, 2,500 of which were heavy bombers. The idea was to pound German gun batteries and obliterate any opposition that tried to stop Allied armour from crossing the River Orne.

On 17 July the British and Canadians were positioned on the Second British Army's left flank, waiting for the 'Go' order that would come the following morning. The concentration of force on this left flank comprised 2nd Canadian Corps and 8th and 1st British Corps. For this operation, 2nd Canadian Infantry Division had moved into the Caen area on the right of 3rd Canadian Infantry Division where it was flanked by British 43rd Division. Other divisions were involved in this operation in one way or another. For example, 7th Canadian Recce Regiment had been given responsibility for the front along the north bank of the Orne, stretching from Caen to Herouville after relieving 7th Canadian Infantry Brigade on the 17th.

While all this movement was taking place in preparation for Operation ATLANTIC, the Germans had continued to pound Allied positions in Caen with artillery and mortar fire, especially at night. It was not just one way however; the artillery of 3rd Canadian Division kept up a barrage on German positions and on the evening of the 17th pounded a large fuel and ammunition dump in Vaucelles, setting off a huge explosion. At the same time, German air action increased over the entire Allied staging area but the RAF, along with divisional anti-aircraft fire, 'gave faithful protection against the inquisitive Luftwaffe, as well as enabling the Canadians to get the maximum of rest'.[18]

The general Allied attack began on 18 July at 0745hrs with British 8th Corps' 11th Armoured Division up front, in the centre of the attack advancing southwards, flanked on the right by 3rd Canadian Division and on the left by 3rd British Infantry Division. Initially, the tanks made fast progress reaching the Hubert/Folie/La Hogue line by 1200hrs but were unable to hold on to some of their gains as the infantry and armoured support was unable to keep up with them. Near Benouville, 3rd Canadian Infantry Brigade crossed the Orne and continued south. Leading the attack southwards down the narrow corridor on the Orne River's east bank was 8th Canadian Infantry Brigade closely followed by 9th Canadian Infantry Brigade. However, at 1030hrs the attack began to falter as the Allies ran into heavy German resistance around the chateau at Colombelles where it temporarily ground to a halt. The advance was quickly under way again as the area around the chateau was bypassed by elements of the Queen's Own Rifles of Canada who swung left capturing Giberville. Vaucelle was occupied by the Regina Rifles who had crossed the Orne from Caen while the North Shore Rifles attacked several factory buildings at Colombelles. As far as the Canadians were concerned, by the end of the day, the area around Colombelles to Giberville had been captured by 8th Canadian Infantry Brigade while 9th Canadian Infantry Brigade held Mondeville and part of Colombelles. Later in the day, elements of 2nd Canadian Infantry Division managed to advance south towards Fleury-sur-Orne, meeting strong German defences as they did.[19]

Despite the advance halting briefly in the area around the chateau at Colombelles, the attack had achieved its objectives.

> The enemy had been clearly outwitted since, from all appearances, he did not expect the main assault to come from the obvious quarter it did. Moreover, despite the tenacity of his armoured divisions, it was evident that the 'thin skin' of German infantry contained a good deal of low-grade material from the south of France.[20]

By the morning of 19 July the area of Vaucelles/Mondeville/Giberville was firmly held by the Canadians who began the lengthy tasks of mine-clearance and mopping-up operations to clear this sector of German hold-outs. At the same time, 9th Canadian Infantry Brigade captured Faubourg de Vaucelles while at 1745hrs, the Royal Winnipeg Rifles took Colombelles, while both the river and canal near Herouville had been bridged by the divisional engineers.

In the middle of the general attack by the Allies, British 8th Corps continued its advance, heading towards Bourguébus. 8th Corps had three armoured divisions, and by 1600hrs on 19 July, one of those divisions, 11th Armoured, managed to reach the general area of Hubert Folie/Bras against increasingly heavy German fire. Behind them came the Guards Armoured Division which captured the Caghy/Frenouville area. 7th Armoured Division had also occupied the line Soliers/Four. In the meantime, on 8th Corps' left, 3rd British Infantry Division, heading towards Troarn, swung south and captured the area around Emeville/Troarn.[21]

Once these positions had been consolidated, 3rd Canadian Infantry Division was ordered to rest and reorganize to build themselves back up to maximum readiness for more operations. An analysis of the offensive by the War Office showed that it had only achieved a limited break-through of the German lines. However, this analysis stated that the Allied offensive had 'yielded substantial dividends by firmly securing the left flank of the Allied bridgehead and by continuing to contain practically the whole weight of the German Armour'.[22]

Bad weather kept Allied air operations to a minimum for almost a week after 19 July. This also had the effect of ensuring that the armour stayed on metalled roads otherwise the tanks and armoured vehicles would become bogged down in the mud. Indeed, this bad weather prevented the Allies from mounting any further major operations but it also allowed the Germans to bring up more artillery and armour. Yet, while the bad weather prevented the Allies from continuing to advance, it was also a godsend as it allowed them to move their heavy armour across the Orne and set up in positions ready for the next offensive once the weather cleared.

On 22 July, the Allies held a conference where the last stages of their operations against the Germans in the Caen sector were finalized. This was Operation SPRING which was to start on the 25th. SPRING's main objective was to punch a gap using two infantry divisions through which the Allied armour could move and take the high ground south of Caen in the Fontenay-le-Marmion/Roquancourt/La Bruyère area. 'Thence it was planned to clear the eastern flank by the capture of the woods, and further exploit southwards along the road Caen – Falaise.'[23]

The operation was to be undertaken by 2nd Canadian Corps with the right flank consisting of 2nd Canadian Infantry Division and the left of 3rd

Canadian Infantry Division. Also under command for this operation were British Guards and 7th Armoured Division along with 27th Armoured Brigade of 3rd British Division.

Operation SPRING was to be carried out in two stages. The first was the capture and hold of the German line running from May-sur-Orne to Verrières to Tilly-la-Campagne. This was in order to ensure that Allied armour had an appropriate-sized starting line and assembly area for further attacks. The second stage of Operation SPRING was for the Allies to attack and hold the line running from Fontenay-le-Marmion to Roquancourt, which was then to be followed up by the capture of Cramesnil near La Bruyère.

On the evening of 23 July, at 1800hrs, the Allies began a harassing campaign against German gun, mortar, artillery and infantry positions. Leading elements of 2nd Canadian Infantry Division had, by midnight of the following day, moved up to a start line running from St Andre-sur-Orne to Hubert La Folie. A little later that evening, at 2130hrs, the forest south-east of Bourguébus was pounded by Allied medium bombers. A heavy concentration of bombs fell during this operation, half of which had been set to explode at 0630hrs the following morning.[24] The Germans, however, were not idle and they attacked the armoured assembly areas, cutting 3rd Canadian Division's line of communications with light and anti-personnel bombs.

Early in the morning of 25 July 1944, at 0330hrs, the North Nova Scotia Highlanders attacked German positions at Tilly-la-Campagne. They were supported on their right by 2nd Canadian Infantry Division. The Canadians used searchlights in this operation designed to blind the enemy as well as mark the way forward. It was not, however, as successful as it could have been. Despite this, the Canadians managed to enter the town of Tilly-la-Campagne but were unable to secure it against fierce German fire from infantry, tanks, anti-tank guns and mortars. The Canadians were now on the back foot but held out for several hours before withdrawing the following day despite being supported by a squadron of tanks from 7th Armoured Division and 27th Canadian Armoured Regiment. This meant that Allied armour was unable to break out.

May-sur-Orne and Verrières had been captured by elements of 2nd Canadian Infantry Division while the British 7th Armoured Division had arrived at their starting positions ready to mount the second stage of the operation.

> Unhappily, as a consequence of stiffening resistance on the part of enemy infantry as well as hull-down tanks, guns and mortars, the advance did not progress much more than half a mile. All the efforts of 7 Armoured Division and 5 Canadian Infantry Brigade to break through were of no avail.[25]

The Germans mounted counter-attack after counter-attack, forcing the Allies to stop the advance, which meant they were unable to reach their objectives. Before they could develop the momentum in the operation, many Allied units were stopped by heavy fire from German armour, guns and infantry.

> The Brigade War Diary contains a grim note with respect to the Black Watch 'the rifle companies got only as far as the ridge overlooking the town Fontenay Le Marmion, when they came under very heavy fire and so far are "missing".' Two days later there was still no sign of the missing companies.[26]

As a result of these setbacks, 2nd Canadian Corps had to retire to the ground it achieved on the first day of Operation SPRING – the line from Verrières to St Andre-sur-Orne that they were to hold no matter what the cost. At this point, the Allies were now on the defensive as Operation SPRING had failed. Any intention of mounting offensive operations were completely abandoned. However, it was not a complete failure; SPRING had achieved one thing. It had forced the Germans to concentrate most of their armour in one place, on one front, which had enabled the Americans to mount an offensive west of Saint-Lô. Thus, they were able to drive quickly towards Countances, Gavray and Brehal.

Operation SPRING was one part of a much larger operation mounted by 21st Army Group since D-Day on 6 June. It took the Canadians a month before they were able to take Caen but that month absorbed huge amounts of German armour: '... the area that we had, that was most valuable to him (the enemy) was Caen; every foot of ground he lost at Caen was like losing ten miles anywhere else.'[27]

By the end of July, the Americans had broken through on the right flank and reached Avranches, pushing their western flank down the coast by 30 miles.

Chapter 3

Operation TOTALIZE: Caen

In order to provide some clarity, it is worth looking at the events leading up to the situation the Allies were in at the end of July 1944.

> The basic plan for the Normandy campaign had been to land an American Army on the right and a British Army on the left, to capture local bridgeheads, secure a firm lodgement area with sufficient room to assemble large forces and the requisite administrative installations, and then capture the Cherbourg Peninsula.[1]

First Canadian Army assumed command of 2nd Canadian Corps at 1200hrs on 31 July. This also included all Canadian troops in the North-west European theatre, thus completing the build-up of the army on the Continent as an operational force. Seven weeks after D-Day Second British Army had all Canadian formations in France under their command while the Canadians reorganized. This was mostly due to the narrow amount of space in the bridgehead. On 17 June the Tactical Headquarters of First Canadian Army had been set up at Amblie but the establishment of the Main and Rear HQs was deferred until the end of July.[2]

By the end of July, the front held by First Canadian Army ran east and north from the Orne River to the sea. In this area, Allied forward defences ran from St Andre-sur-Orne to Bourguébus through Frenouville, west of Troarn, Les Mesnil to Sallenelles. Situated on the right side of this sector was 2nd Canadian Corps with the following under its command – 2nd Canadian Infantry Division, 3rd Canadian Infantry Division, 4th Canadian Armoured Division, 2nd Canadian Armoured Brigade and 4th British Armoured Brigade. Stretching from Caen–Mezidon Railway to the sea on the left side was 1st British Corps with formations of 3rd British Infantry Division, 51st (N) Infantry Division, 49th (FR) Infantry Division and 6th Airborne Division.

Once Cherbourg and its port had been captured, the Americans on the right flank were to move south to capture the Brittany Peninsula then, in a large turning movement, sweep east to the River Seine and its outer flank, the River Loire.

In the event, this is generally what happened. From the landings on 6 June 1944 throughout the rest of the month and through July these operations took place without much deviation from the original plan. However, in the accomplishment of their objectives, there was considerable delay that impacted the Allied timeline.[3] 'This great door that the Americans to the west were charged with forcing inwards was hinged at Caen.'[4]

By 1 August Second British Army had reached the general line of Beny-Bocage/Evrency and beyond to its joining-up point with First Canadian Army at the Orne River. Swinging eastwards, the forward elements of First US Army pushed along from Avranches–Villedieu-les-Poêles–Tessey-sur-Vire–St Martin-des-Besaces where they were able to form up with elements of the Second British Army. At the same time, the Third US Army took on the task of clearing the Brest Peninsula of enemy positions and troops then began what would be known as the 'Right Hook' along from the Loire to Alençon and Argentan.

First Canadian Army took on responsibility for the front held by 21st Army Group east of the Orne in the Caen sector, which was still strongly held by the Germans. Indeed, facing 1st British Corps positioned north of the Caen–Mezidon rail line were three German infantry divisions. These divisions were holding defensive positions in the Dives Valley, a natural obstacle that made major offensive operations very difficult. From the same rail line across to the Orne River were German armoured formations – 12th SS Panzer Division (Hitler Jugend), 1st SS Panzer (Liebenstandarte Adolf Hitler) and 9th SS Panzer (Hohenstaufen).[5]

The reaction of the Germans to the American breakthrough at Avranches was to move their best Panzer divisions into the area in order to pound the American flank. This they did, but the divisions they moved were taken from the line facing the Second British and First Canadian Armies. First US Army reached Mortain on 5 August and it was to this destination that the Germans were sending their armoured units.[6] Of course, this had the effect of weakening the British and Canadian front. '9 Panzer Division and 1 SS Division had been transferred across the ORNE from the Canadian Front.

Only one Panzer formation remained in the area – the badly battered Hitler Youth Division (12 SS Panzer Div.).[7]

The Germans now had a dilemma. These units that had been transferred to the American front had to be replaced and so they were. The key question for the hard-pressed Germans was where would these replacements come from? First of the replacements was 89th Infantry Division that took up positions on the German left. On the German right, elements of 272nd Infantry Division took up their positions near Troarn, filling the gap left by the Adolf Hitler Division that had also been transferred south. In addition to these units, the Germans also quickly pulled in 85th Infantry Division from across the Seine River into the British and Canadian sector to cover the loss of the Panzers.[8] Supporting these formations was a strong concentration of self-propelled guns, 88mm Flak guns converted to anti-tank weapons and hull-down tanks.

Early in the Normandy Campaign the Germans failed to grasp the real Allied intention for the Normandy battle. They believed, according to reports, that the Allies would follow up the landings on 6 June with another invasion somewhere along the coast between Le Havre and Boulogne. 'He [the Germans] therefore kept his forces north of the SEINE intact, holding them there while his position in Normandy steadily deteriorated.'[9]

Once the Germans realized that there was not going to be another Allied invasion they finally began to pull these units into the Normandy battle, which by that time they had already lost. These formations the Germans transferred from the northern area of the Seine River encountered harsh and difficult conditions, chief amongst these was their complete lack of air cover. Air superiority lay firmly with the Allies. Before D-Day many of the bridges over the Seine had been destroyed by Allied bombing. This meant that the Germans had to move most of their reserves and supplies by road by day and

> ... in the short nights could cover only short distances. It meant that his [the Germans] guns and H.Q. and his positions were always subject to new attack. Finally, it meant that the morale of the troops was sorely affected. Field Marshal von Kluge describes on the 31 July with impressive eloquence – 'the enemy's [Allies] air superiority is terrific and smothers almost every one of our movements. Every movement of the enemy, however, is prepared and protected by his air force. Losses in men and equipment are

extraordinary. The morale of the troops has suffered heavily under constant murderous enemy fire.'[10]

The Germans also had a key problem in lack of transport. The only motorized formations were their armoured formations. The rest moved either by bicycle, horse-drawn transport or on foot. German prisoners captured by the Allies on 9 August told how they had cycled for ten days from Abbeville, moving only at night because Allied air power forced them to find cover during the day.[11]

Therefore, the Germans were never really able to seize the initiative with their reserve formations. Reinforcements were thrown into the battle at the last minute. Generally, the first German units into the battle area were their reconnaissance elements and armoured formations that they committed as 'a matter of expedience rather than for any tactical advantage'.[12] In the first week of August, German infantry units began to arrive in their defensive lines south of Caen and it was at this point that the Germans were able to use some of their armoured formations for a very long-awaited counter-attack in the west.

On 4 August, General Montgomery ordered the Allies to begin a major offensive against the Germans by 8 August. This operation was vital to the Allied effort and was considered to be urgent. First Canadian Army was given the job of attacking towards Falaise from the Caen sector as their immediate task, as it was designed to destroy the German armies in Normandy. This operation, known as TOTALIZE, had three main objectives – break through German positions south of Caen, capture as much ground as possible around Falaise in order to cut the Germans off who were facing Second British Army and to destroy as much equipment and personnel as possible.[13]

> I firmly believe that a highly successful, large scale operation, now carried out by one of the Armies of the Allied Expeditionary Force, favourably placed for that purpose, will result in the crushing conviction to the Germans, even of the SS variety, that general defeat of the German Armies on all parts has become an inescapable fact. A quick termination to the war will follow. On that count, our responsibility is a proud as well as a great one, and I have no doubt but that we shall make the 8 Aug 44 an even blacker day for the

German Armies that is recorded against that same date twenty-six years ago.[14]

The German defences in the area were not weak, rather the opposite. Defeating them would be no mean feat and so Lieutenant General Crerar, commander of First Canadian Army, laid down a tactical plan that he believed was necessary for the Allies to beat the Germans in Normandy.

> My basic tactical plan required that, even in view of the obvious requirements of the military situation, it was impossible to disguise our general intentions from the enemy, the attack should secure the maximum of surprise as to means and methods employed. A further important requirement was that the technique of the attack should be such as largely to neutralize the long range and great strength of the enemy's anti-tank defence and to ensure that our infantry got through and beyond the enemy's zone of dense defensive fire, developed mainly by his mortars and machine guns, without heavy casualties.[15]

The difficulty was, however, how the Allies were going to achieve the main objectives laid out by Crerar. The solutions they came up with were straightforward. Surprise was to be achieved by attacking a night under the cover of darkness and by moving troops at the same time as the fire support began. The Germans should have their heads down under heavy bombardment while the troops attacked. Heavy bombers would be added into the artillery and land-based barrage in order to provide the most devastating fire programme they could. Finally, the infantry would be transported through the German fire zones in heavy armoured vehicles in order to afford them the maximum protection.

The Allies decided they would combine attacking armour with the bombardment from the heavy bombers at night in order to closely support the infantry attack. Moving the tanks under the cover of darkness meant that the Germans would not have clear visibility of the advance, thus nullifying their ability to hit advancing Allied armour. While the Germans would be unable to see where the Allies were, the Allies, in the darkness of night, would be blind as well, and would have difficulty following the direction of the advance. Dust thrown up by the heavy bombers pounding the ground around the German positions would also hamper the Allies ability to move forward.

The Allies devised several aids that would help the armour navigate through the darkness and the dust.

> It was decided to have the positions and bearing of thrust lines fixed by survey for the leading tanks; to provide wireless directional beams along the axis of the advance, operation to No 19 wireless sets; to employ Bofors guns firing tracer along each flank of the attack; during the progress of the operation to have thrust lines marked with light by AVREs and to use searchlights as artificial supplement to moonlight.[16]

The night targets for the heavy bombers had to be lit by 25-pounder red and green marker shells fired from artillery positions situated behind the start line. The Allies realized that with such a massive bombardment there would be cratering that would make the movement on the ground difficult for troops and armour. To get around this, the Allies understood that they needed to isolate a crater-free corridor for the infantry to move forward. As the troops were supposed to move forwards with the heavy bombing from the air the noise would be terrific. As such, a special aircraft was laid on to fly bales of cotton wool from England to be used as ear plugs for the troops.[17]

The other factor in the overall plan was; how to transport the infantry through German machine-gun and mortar zones safely. The Allies decided that M7 Priest/Kangaroo self-propelled guns would be used for this purpose (without the standard 105mm gun) along with M14 half-track armoured personnel carriers. This was the first time the Allies used the Priests as armoured troop carriers. Because the gun had been removed they were originally called 'Unfrocked Priests' by the infantry and were later officially named Kangaroos.

There were three phases to Operation TOTALIZE. The first was the night break into the German lines to seize and hold the Fontenay-le-Marmion area. The second was to see the Allies smash through the German lines at Haut Mensil-St Sylvain and the final phase was for them to continue the advance and capture their objectives 'in depth'.

TOTALIZE began on the evening of 7/8 August 1944 at 2300hrs when the heavy bombers roared overhead and began their bombing runs. At the same time, 2nd Canadian Infantry Division and 51st (H) Division began rolling forwards crossing the start line just as the Bofors guns began their directional firing along the attack axis. Fifteen minutes past H-Hour (2330hrs), sixteen searchlights suddenly beamed their bright lights along the avenue of advance, lighting the way forward. In order to gain an element of surprise the plan had been that there would be no artillery bombardment prior to the attack. With the armour moving forward and the bombing operation underway, the artillery began its bombardment of German positions at 2345hrs. The leading Allied troops picked up their artillery fire and watched it fall as they moved forward without difficulty. The Germans, it seems, were taken by surprise.[18]

The only reaction from the Germans at this juncture was some shelling and direct fire from tanks and self-propelled guns.

> Through clouds of dust that at times quite neutralized the artificial and natural moonlight, the eight columns of armour, each with its vehicles four abreast packed tightly nose and tail, rolled forward towards their objectives.[19]

The Germans reacted by laying a dense smokescreen not long after midnight that momentarily threw some of the Allied columns off course. The Germans then opened up from tanks and self-propelled guns setting several Allied vehicles on fire. However, the advance continued to rumble on and, as the reports suggest, the Germans, despite hitting several vehicles were firing blind into the darkness and had no idea of the magnitude of the attack that was rolling past them.

By first light a thick ground mist lay over the area, enabling the Canadians and the British to carry out consolidation and reorganization without the Germans able to do much about it. As daylight arrived, it was clear that the Canadians, had achieved all the objectives of the first phase except for 6th Canadian Infantry Brigade.

The 6th had run into difficulty when they began mop up operations of German resistance bypassed by the advancing armour. The infantry from South Saskatchewan Regiment moved slowly along the avenue between the tanks around 0300hrs and took Roquancourt easily enough but it was the two villages, May-sur-Orne and Fontenay-le-Marmion, that caused the Canadians much grief. Despite the heavy bombing both villages had suffered they were still held by the Germans. It transpired that there were caves and tunnels that connected these villages with old quarries in the Caen area. By hiding in these caves and tunnels the Germans were able to avoid taking casualties during the aerial bombardment. By late afternoon on 8 August both villages were finally taken by the Canadians using flamethrowing Crocodile tanks.

51st (H) Division, British, attacked on the left side of the Allied front for Operation TOTALIZE. During the night, the RAF hammered German positions in La Hogue and Garcelles-Secquenville enabling both villages to be easily taken. Indeed, these villages plus St Aignan-de-Cramesnil were taken at 0600hrs by armoured columns of 33rd British Armoured Division carrying 154th Infantry Brigade. However, to do this, they bypassed Tilly-la-Campagne, a scene of stubborn German resistance. The Germans mounted a counter-attack using elements of 89th Infantry Division but once this was broken a battalion of the Seaforth Highlanders of 152nd Infantry Brigade entered the village supported by tanks and captured it just after 1100hrs. By dusk, the village of Secquenville-la-Campagne had been captured by elements of 153rd Infantry Brigade.

The first phase of Operation TOTALIZE was successful. The Allies had pushed through strong German defences up to five miles in total, capturing villages and towns in the process and mopping up any lingering defenders. A thousand[20] Germans had been taken prisoner while the Canadians suffered 400 casualties in total, dead, wounded and missing. This phase had given the Allies a spring board for more offensive operations. This operation into German held territory by the British and Canadians had caught the Germans by surprise. 'It remained to be seen how effectively we could pursue our initial advantages before he should have time to recover his balance and strengthen his rear defences.'[21]

The second phase of Operation TOTALIZE saw the air campaign make some serious targeting mistakes. A large formation of Flying Fortresses and medium bombers from the US Eighth Air Force set off at the designated time and arrived over their targets on time where they bombed Bretteville-sur-Laize, St Sylvain and the area around Haut Mensil-Cauvicourt. However, several bombs missed the targets altogether with some hitting Mondeville and Cormelles behind the line. In these instances, several bombs slammed into 3rd Canadian Infantry Division Tactical Headquarters, wounding Major-General R.F.L. Keller, CBE, the Divisional Commander.

The air bombardment ended at 1355hrs, immediately setting off Phase 2 ground operations. 4th Canadian Armoured Division on the right, with 1st Polish Armoured Division on the left, began rolling forward launching the second phase of Operation TOTALIZE. The objective for this phase of the operation was to break through the second line of German defences and secure the high ground around Potigny.

A three-mile long ridge at Fontaine-Le-Pin that paralleled the Caen–Falaise highway just north of Potigny was to be taken and held by 4th Canadian Armoured Division. There were three main high points along the ridge that the Canadians were ordered to secure. At first, things went well. Nightfall on 8 August saw the Canadians, having smashed through heavy German defences at Cintheaux, destroying several German self-propelled guns and 88mm anti-tank guns. The following morning, heavy fighting raged around Bretteville and the Canadians took the town with the Germans suffering heavy losses trying to defend it. Behind the armour came the infantry who also met with some success capturing Cintheaux, Haut Mensil, Langannerie and Grainville-Langannerie. 10th Infantry Brigade firmly held this area as darkness fell.[22]

Yet the Canadians had not taken the ridge – their main objective. The Germans were dug in and poured heavy, accurate fire on the Canadians each time they tried to advance to capture the high points. According to the reports, the Allied armour had advanced too slowly for it to be effective against the German defenders. Indeed, they had created an anti-tank screen stretching in a crescent around three sides of the ridge.[23]

The German line of defence ran from Bray-en-Cinglais–Fontaine-le-Pin–Aisy–Quesnay Wood and comprised mostly self-propelled guns, heavy mortars, 88mm anti-tank guns, tanks and infantry. In an attempt to move around the German defences and get at them from another point, 28th Canadian Armoured Regiment went too far to the east where they ran into very strong German resistance and suffered several casualties and losing forty-seven tanks.[24]

Finally, by noon on 10 August, the Canadians managed to move forward and gain a foothold on the ridge.[25] Under heavy fire from the German armour, mortars and 88mm anti-tank guns the Canadians managed to hang on to this precious piece of ground.[26]

Elsewhere, during the night of 10 August, an attempt to clear the Germans in the Quesnay Wood failed and the two Canadian battalions that attacked these positions suffered heavy casualties. 'It was now apparent, and reports from the Polish sector gave confirmation, that a new German defence system had been established too strong for an armoured division to penetrate.'27

On the left of the Allied front, as Phase II started, 1st Polish Division made limited progress. In the St Aignan-De-Cranesnil area, on the first day, the Poles had encountered large groups of German Panther and Tiger tanks that destroyed several of their tanks. Even more were knocked out by the German 88mm anti-tank guns. By the morning of 9 August they were still a long way from their objectives Estrees-La-Campagne and the surrounding high ground. However, they were only mile from the forward elements of 51st Infantry Division (British).[28] The Polish divisional commander, Major General S. Maczek, believed that the reason they could not make any further headway was because their (Polish) front was too narrow and many areas within their front had been left uncleared before the attack began.

However, by nightfall on 9 August, the Poles had managed to move forward with the Polish armoured brigade attacking their objective at Estrees. Elsewhere, 10th Polish Motor Rifle Regiment, an armoured reconnaissance unit, had rolled into Soignolles where they were to secure the division's left flank. Cauvicourt and St Sylvain had been captured and secured by Polish Infantry by 10 August.

They could go no further. The Germans had organized their defensive positions so that they had become almost impregnable. Supported by tanks, mortars, 88mm anti-tank guns and infantry these newly-organized positions stretched across the Polish front running from the Quesnay Wood southeast of St Sylvain to Fier-la-Campagne. For two days the Polish Armoured Division held their positions under constant German artillery and mortar fire until they were relieved by the 7th Canadian Infantry Brigade on the night of 11 August.[29]

Due to heavy German defensive fire the Allied armoured divisions had been unable to complete their tasks for Phase II of Operation TOTALIZE. However, two infantry divisions had managed to complete their tasks of securing the Allied flanks. On the right, elements of 2nd Canadian Infantry Division held positions between the Caen–Falaise Road and the Laize River from the Orne to Bretteville-sur-Laize that had been captured on 8 May by 5th Canadian Infantry Brigade.

On the left, the British in the form of 51st Highland Division had moved steadily forward. Against light German resistance they captured and held Sequeville-la-Campagne and St Aignan-de-Cramesnil in Phase I then moved on and secured Conteville and Poussy-la-Campagne on 9 August. On this day, 1st British Corps brought 33rd British Armoured Brigade and 51st Highland Division under its command. This change of command now meant the British line ran from Tilly-la-Campagne down the Caen–Falaise Road to Gaumesnil through Cauvicourt and Soignolle to the Laison River which was all part of the 2nd Canadian Corps command.

TOTALIZE was not the success that the Allies hoped it would be. While Phase I had been hugely successful the failure of the tanks to rapidly move forward and reach their objectives in Phase II on the afternoon of 8 August had given the Germans time to bring their SS defenders back into this sector of the Normandy campaign.

> But a shattering blow had been struck at the hinge of the enemy's entire defence system in Normandy. We had advanced a distance of eight miles through strong positions that he had deemed almost impregnable. We had inflicted on him heavy casualties some 1200 prisoners being captured from his 89th Division alone.[30]

Chapter 4

Operation TRACTABLE:
The Capture of Falaise

The Allied strategy had, in all essentials, proceeded according to plan, and strong American forces were now advancing eastwards while the weight of the German Army was being retained by our pressure opposite Caen and in the bocage country south of Vire.[1]

Allied operations to capture Brest and Brittainy were now underway. The Americans were advancing rapidly and the Germans, in their haste to stop them, seemed unaware of the threats their divisions faced in the area around Falaise. In the Mortain area, the Germans had created a strong counter-attack to try to stop the advance and break through to Avranches, deploying upwards of six armoured divisions: 1st SS Panzer, 2nd SS Panzer, 10th SS Panzer, 2nd Panzer, 116th Panzer and 9th Panzer. Their aim for this determined counter-attack was to break the lines of communications between US forces in the Cherbourg Peninsula and those in Brittany.

August 11th saw the Allies in a strong position and the Germans in a much more tenuous one. From the south, the Americans, under General Patton, were advancing on Le Mans against limited resistance. The determined German counter-attack, mentioned above, had stalled and was held by General Omar Bradley's forces (American), along the Domfront-Mortain line in the west while General N.C. Dempsey's Second British Army was attacking the Germans from the north between Vire and the Orne River. The Canadians had taken up a position less than seven miles from Falaise.

West of the line from Le Mans to Caen lay the vast majority of the Germans' forces. The gap between Falaise in the north and Alençon in the south was the only escape route the Germans had as the Allies relentlessly narrowed it. Indeed, this was also the gap or channel through which all of the Germans' supplies and reinforcements had to pass and it was being squeezed hard. In overall command of the Allied operations in Normandy was General Montgomery commanding 21st Army Group and 12th US Army Group. He now issued orders for the gap to be slammed shut and the Germans trapped within it.[2]

The operation for closing the gap was called Operation TRACTABLE and the plan was for it to begin on 14 August with the 12th US Army Group swinging right, forward from Le Mans, advance up to Alençon then, from there, push on to the line running from Sees to Carouges. At the same time, Second British Army was to advance on its left flank towards Falaise then begin operations west and south of the town. With the Canadians less than seven miles from Falaise their task was to immediately capture the town and then secure a front from the sea to the town. They were to ensure they faced eastwards and then drive forwards to take Argentan.

On 11 August, at 2400hrs, Second British Army thrust forward towards Barbery, Moulines and Tournebu with the aim of joining up with elements of the First Canadian Army. On the 12th, 2nd Canadian Infantry Division attacked German defensive positions in Barbery and Moulines with a thrust designed to weaken the German positions north of Falaise. By the afternoon of the 12th, Barbery had been taken and occupied by the Allies. After heavy and confused fighting the following day, Moulines and Tournebu fell to the Allies.[3]

> On 8 August, Allied ground forces commander General Bernard Montgomery ordered the Allied armies to converge on the Falaise–Chambois area to envelop Army Group B (German), with the First US Army forming the southern arm, the British the base, and the Canadians the northern arm of the encirclement. The Germans began to withdraw on 17 August, and on 19 August the Allies linked up in Chambois. Gaps were forced in the Allied lines by German counter-attacks. The biggest was a corridor forced past the 1st Polish Armoured Division on Hill 262, a commanding position at the pocket mouth. By the evening of 21 August, the pocket had been sealed, with est. 50,000 Germans trapped inside. Many Germans escaped, but losses were huge. The Allied Liberation of Paris came a few days later, and on 30 August the remnants of Army Group B retreated across the Seine, completing Operation Overlord.[4]

The role of 2nd Canadian Corps in Operation TRACTABLE was to attack the Germans with two divisions, 3rd Canadian Infantry Division on the right and 4th Canadian Armoured Division on the left. The plan was for the Allies to capture and hold the roads running east out of the town of Falaise to ensure that the Germans were unable to escape from the pocket they found themselves in. The Germans were squeezed between British and Canadian troops in the north and the Americans further south pushing north to Falaise from Argentan. 2nd Canadian Infantry Division was to continue its attack against German positions in and around Falaise in order to capture and secure the town. Once the high ground above Falaise was in Allied hands taking the town itself would pose little difficulty.[5]

The Germans had set up their defensive positions that roughly followed along the line of the Laison River east of Potigny. In this area, the Germans were very strong in anti-tank weapons but weak in top-notch infantry troops. A series of infantry positions had been set up by the Germans roughly 1,500 yards north of the river. The troops manning these positions had been reorganized so that they were under command of 1st SS Panzer Corps and were a hodgepodge of talent from 85th, 89th and 271st Infantry Divisions. Two battle groups from 12th SS Panzer Division supported the line and consisted SS Panzer Grenadiers using assault guns and tanks.[6]

The Allies discovered later that the Germans had captured an operational order on the evening of 13 August that stated the full Allied plan for the coming operations. There was a 12-hour period before H-Hour and the Germans were able to use this time to rapidly reorganize their defences. The following day, the Allies managed to capture documents during the attack that showed the German dispositions and a new anti-tank battery of 88mm guns they'd brought up and placed directly along the line of the Allied advance.[7] 'Between the main Caen-Falaise road to the west and the town of Maizières (1749) to the east, which were roughly the flanks of the corps attack, he had at least ninety 88mm guns in anti-tank positions.'[8]

Two major problems faced the Allied planners of TRACTABLE: how could they punch through German forward defences in depth and how could they get their tanks behind German 88mm anti-tank guns and destroy them? Heavy bombardment was out of the question because it would warn the Germans of the impending attack and give them time to bring down their bombardment on the Allied forming-up positions. It also meant that the Germans would have time to concentrate their reserves to meet the Allied breakthrough attempt. Another decision would have to be made. It was General Guy Simonds (Canadian) who decided that the best way to punch through the German lines and circle round behind their guns was by using a smokescreen. This would blind the German gunners and tank crews so they would be unable to see where the Allies were.

The way this was to be done was that each divisional column would form up with their respective armoured brigades along as wide a front as possible. In order to get as many tanks as possible through the German defences as quickly as they could the tanks were to position themselves at approximately 15 yards apart. The objective was the high ground around Versainville and the Allies were to advance straight across the Laison River to get to it. Behind the armour, the infantry was to advance in armoured personnel carriers such as Kangaroos and half-tracks. Once they'd crossed the river line, elements of the infantry were to clear both right and left of the river bank, then they were to cross the river, push south and clear out German defensive positions not destroyed or engaged by the armour. Once over the river, 3rd Canadian Infantry Division was to pass through the leading Allied infantry positions and head for their objectives at Épany. The time for the beginning of the attack, when the first units would cross the start line, was set at 1200hrs on 14 August.[9]

Artillery support consisted of providing the smokescreen and counter-battery work, particularly using medium guns against the German 88mm anti-tank positions. The plan called for the smoke barrage of thick mist to move ahead of the advance in 500-yard increments along the Laison's south bank, while a thick blinding smokescreen was to be laid down along the flanks of the attack enabling the formation of a corridor for the armour and infantry to move through.

Air support was also involved in this operation. RAF 83 and 84 Group fighter-bombers were to attack targets in the Laison valley, Montboint, Rouvres and Naiziers. For two hours starting at H-plus-2hrs RAF heavy bombers were to continually pound German positions opposite 2nd Canadian Infantry Division situated on the right of the Allied front. This was to be a highly destructive bombardment centring on targets around Potigny, Quesnay Wood, Bons-Tassily, Hamel and Fontaine-le-Pin. It was this area that the Allies had been unable to break through during Operation

TOTALIZE because of the strength of the German defences. Now ground forces were to bypass them altogether and they were to be left to the bombers to destroy.[10]

The reorganization and regrouping of units in preparation of the attack by the Allies went off without incident. Indeed, a message from the GOC-in-C was sent to all commanding officers of First Canadian Army as the final preparations were being undertaken that read: 'Hit him first, hit him hard and keep on hitting him. We can contribute in a major degree to speedy Allied victory by our actions today.'[11]

At exactly 1200hrs two columns of Allied tanks and infantry rushed across the start line, pushing towards the Laison River supported by AVREs and Sherman Flail tanks. These armoured vehicles from 79th Armoured Division were to deal with minefields and help the main force cross the river. As the columns drove forward in the Laison Valley towards the river the Allies laid down the smokescreen. However, the forward elements of the advance encountered heavy mortar and anti-tank fire from German positions north of the river. Several Allied tanks were destroyed from this fire as well as being blown up as they rolled over mines. Indeed, Brigadier E.L. Booth was fatally wounded when his tank was knocked out by a mine.[12]

While the smokescreen helped to mask the forward armoured units from accurate German fire it also blinded them from recognizing any landmarks to help them find their way towards their objectives. This meant that several forward units lost their way, with the armoured units swinging too far to the east. In order to gain their bearings, Allied armour crews navigated by the sun and the stars as they pushed south towards the river.

Other difficulties faced by the Allies during their advance included locating the best points for crossing the river, which lead to delays. Vehicles moved up and down along the northern bank searching for the best places to cross. 'In some places fascines were thrown into position to permit the passage of tanks to the southern side.'[13] In the end, suitable sites were found and by mid-afternoon most of the armoured regiments were across the river with 2nd Canadian Armoured Brigade west of Rouvres and 4th Canadian Armoured Brigade east of Maizières. Once across they began to regroup in order to push on to their final objectives.

Back on the north side of the River Laison, Allied infantry had left their Kangaroo armoured vehicles and were moving through the valley on foot, clearing out the last vestiges of a diminishing German resistance.

The general situation for the Allies at 1800hrs was good. The armoured regiments had reorganized themselves and resumed their advance towards their objectives south of the river. On the right side of the Corps front 7th Canadian Infantry Brigade and 10th Canadian Infantry Brigade on the left, had passed through positions taken earlier in the day and by last light had reached their objectives. 'In the main, TRACTABLE had proceeded extremely satisfactorily during the first twelve hours of the operation.'[14]

The Allies had broken through strong German defensive positions and were able to continue the advance. In the Laison Valley, several prisoners were captured who told the British and Canadians that their attack had taken 'them completely by surprise. Their disorganization on finding our tanks and infantry on top of them was so complete that they could take no effective counter-action.'[15]

However, an incident occurred on the afternoon of 14 August that could have had a massive detrimental effect on the success of the operation. RAF heavy bombers, mostly Lancasters, began the second phase of the air campaign at 1400hrs with the first wave hammering German positions in Quesnay Wood. But subsequent waves of aircraft miscalculated and dropped their bombs some 8,000m to the rear in the Haut Mensil area. This resulted in a relentless bombardment on Canadian and Polish positions from 1430hrs to 1545hrs. Units hit included 1st Polish Armoured Division HQ, 2nd Canadian Army Group Royal Artillery (AGRA) HQ, 3rd Canadian Infantry Division HQ and 4th Canadian Infantry Division HQ. Casualties were light, sixteen killed and forty-seven wounded in this friendly-fire incident. However, the greatest damage was done to equipment and vehicles. There was a heavy toll in tanks and transport vehicles, and several artillery guns were hit as well. In this incident the Allies were fortunate as the losses did not delay the progress of TRACTABLE.[16]

On the evening of 14 August Allied units along the corps' front received new orders for the advance to be continued and for the capture of Falaise to be completed. Once the main roads east of Falaise were secured, 4th Canadian Armoured Division was to drive on Trun while on the left, 1st Polish Armoured Division was also to advance on Trun after crossing the River Dives.

Progress was slow but steady. Against heavy German anti-tank and mortar fire 2nd Canadian Armoured Brigade on the right with, on the left, 4th Canadian Armoured Brigade, in tight cooperation with infantry, moved forward fighting every step of the way. The main objective was to secure the high ground along the Falaise–St Pierre-sur-Dives road. The Germans, however, had other ideas and, on the reverse slope in the area of Versainville had set up a defensive line of anti-tank guns and tanks. South of Épaney the Germans also held the woods on the Canadians' left flank.

Several attacks on these positions yielded no results. On the evening of the 15th an attack by 2nd Canadian Armoured Brigade, for example, was unsuccessful. The following day the Canadians launched a two-pronged attack that after hard and heavy fighting saw them finally take their objective on the high ground of the Falaise–St Pierre-sur-Dives highway.

The Germans began retreating but kept behind small machine-gun units with anti-tank weapons to slow down the Allied advance and fight a rear-guard action. From Ussy, 2nd Canadian Infantry Division continued their advance while 6th Canadian Infantry Brigade supported by tanks from 27th Canadian Armoured Regiment entered Falaise. By the following evening, Falaise had been cleared of German defenders with the exception of a group of fanatical Germans from 12th SS Panzer Division holding on in a strongpoint that was finally destroyed on the morning of 18 August.

The capture of Falaise completed TRACTABLE. The struggle by the Canadians fighting the Germans down the Caen–Falaise road also came to an end. One by one the German defensive positions had been smashed and more than 2,000 prisoners had been taken by the Canadians. Casualties suffered by the Allies during three days of fighting in this operations amounted to more than 2,000 killed, wounded and missing. 'There now remained the task of closing the Falaise-Argentan gap and liquidating such enemy forces as would be trapped.'[17]

The Germans were almost completely enclosed save for the gap which the Allies were squeezing. The line of steel and men, by midnight on 16 August, ran along Third US Army's front from Argentan to La Ferté-Macé north-west to Second British Army's front at Flers to Conde then east to 12th British Corps front at Ouilly to Falaise. That was the border of the pocket, but the gap itself between Argentan and Falaise was being relentlessly tightened by 2nd Canadian Corps attacking from the north, 5th US Corps from the south along with another armoured division (French) advancing on Trun. German armour that had only a few days previously been pounding the American pressure in the Mortain sector without success had now retreated to the eastern end of the pocket. Indeed, German units and formations were now fleeing through the gap as fast as they could go. On 17 August Allied air reconnaissance discovered that the roads in the Trun area were filled with German units, mostly transport and tanks heading east through the gap. The units that were moving through the gap included 2nd Panzer, 2nd SS Panzer, Panzer Lehr, 26th Panzer and 116th Panzer Divisions. Still stuck in the Falaise pocket were 1st, 9th, 10th and 12th SS Panzer Divisions.

Allied armour was attacking towards Trun on the left of 2nd Canadian Corps. Indeed, the 16th of August saw the 1st Polish Armoured Division cross the Dives River and then concentrate their focus in the Jort–Courcy–Vicques area in preparation for an attack southwards. While this was happening, elements of 1st British Corps further north were advancing towards the east. For example, 51st (H) Division had secured St Pierre-sur-Dives on the river's right bank while Mezidon had been taken by 49th (WR) Infantry Division. However, no German activity had yet been seen by the British 6th Airborne Division as they moved from Troarn north towards the sea.[18] West of the village of St Sylvain, in preparation for 1st British Corps' advance on Lisieux, 7th British Armoured Division was concentrating its armour to get themselves into a position where they could lead this attack.[19]

1st Polish Armoured Division began an advance towards Trun where they would drive from Jort to Vaudeloges to Trun after receiving orders on the afternoon of 16 August to attack.[20] North-east of Falaise 4th Canadian Armoured Division held the high ground where they received orders the same day as the Polish did to attack south. This was part of the plan for closing the gap that also included 10th Canadian Infantry Brigade seizing a bridgehead across the River Ante at Damblainville while 4th Canadian Armoured Brigade had orders to advance along the Falaise–Mandeville to Trun road.[21]

Early on the morning of 17 August, 4th Canadian Armoured Division mounted their attack but ran into heavy German resistance with anti-tank guns south of Damblainville and were unable to cross the Ante River. Plans changed and the Canadians moved east, crossing the Dives River at Morteaux and then drove south. This change of plan confused the Germans to the point that by last light on the same day, the leading elements of 22nd Canadian Armoured Regiment were only 2km north of Trun.

At 1445hrs on 17 August, a message was received at First Canadian Army HQ that came from Montgomery the Commander-in-Chief of 21st Army Group:

> It is absolutely essential that both the Armoured Divisions of 2 Cdn Corps, i.e. 4 Cdn Armd Div and 1 Pol Armd Div, close the gap between the First Cdn Army and Third U.S. Army. 1 Pol Armd Div must thrust on past Trun to Chambois at all costs, and as quickly as possible.[22]

By midday on 18 August, Trun had been captured and secured by Allied troops and armour. The Poles had swung round to the east in order to get to Chambois but came up against heavy German armoured and infantry formations in the Les Champeaux area. Fighting was heavy and hard and by dusk on the 18th, 29th Canadian Armoured Recce Regiment had fought their way north of St Lambert-sur-Dives where they were held by German defenders.

An officer of this Canadian Regiment showed courage and determination on the morning of the 19th. This officer, Major David Vivian Currie had been ordered to attack the village and had under his command a total of 175 all ranks, 15 tanks and 4 self-propelled anti-tank guns. The previous evening Currie had entered the village on foot to carry out his own reconnaissance while under heavy German mortar fire. As he did, he came across two-knocked-out Allied tanks on the edge of the village and helped to evacuate the crews back to the Canadian lines. 'The attack went in without artillery support, as the guns allotted for the task were still out of range. Major Currie, in the face of intense opposition by enemy armour, artillery and infantry, personally led his forces to a point in the centre of the village, consolidating a position there and organizing his defences.'[23] However, the Canadians quickly came under intense German fire and actual counter-attacks that the Germans kept up for 36 hours. During this fighting most of his officers were either wounded or killed yet he continued to direct the resistance of his troops to the vicious German counter-attacks. None of which managed to dislodge the Canadians from their position in the centre of the village. During the very early hours of 21 August the Germans mounted what would turn out to be their last infantry attack in the village. Accurate Allied tank fire directed by the force commander smashed into the German troops, breaking up their attack. They had, by noon on 21 August, lost the village of St Lambert.

German morale by the 21st was plummeting, and the escape route via Trun-Chambois was closed to them. Major Currie's force had given the Germans a massive blow. They'd lost more than 300 killed, 500 wounded and over 2,100 prisoners taken by the Allies, 7 tanks destroyed and 2 probably destroyed, more than 12 88mm anti-tank guns smashed and 40 armoured and other vehicles destroyed. For this action Major Currie received the Victoria Cross.[24]

As far as the Poles were concerned, by the morning of 19 August they were locked in a bitter, intense battle with the German Panzer units attacking from the south, west and east in the difficult tank country south of Les Champeaux. The Germans were desperately trying to keep the narrow passage of escape open, which explains the ferocity of the fighting. Ecorches and Hordouseaux had been taken by midday. The Poles had rolled into the Coudehard–Mt Ormel area with leading elements arriving within 4km of Chambois, all the while locked in a desperate struggle with the German Panzer units. Even under the bitter fighting conditions 1st Polish Armoured Division had advanced rapidly and continuously finding themselves at times ahead of their supply units without ammunition or fuel. This meant that they would have to temporarily stop their advance, while still fighting, in order to wait for the supply units to fight their way to them.[25]

Despite the determined efforts of the Germans to smash through the Canadian lines at St Lambert, on the evening of 19 August Canadian 29th Recce Regiment was within 1km of Chambois. However, 1st Polish Armoured Division had broken through the German defences and captured Chambois at 1900hrs. They had fought continuously against some of the crack German Seventh Army Panzer divisions until they took the town and were able to join up with the Americans and the French.

At this juncture the Falaise Gap was still not completely sealed off and the next 48 hours saw feverish activity by the Allies to see that it was. While the advancing armour was racing south towards Chambois on 18 August Canadian infantry were moving into positions around Le Marais–La Chapelle to ensure no German units escaped via the Trun area. Ensuring the gap between Trun and Chambois was shut tight was top priority. Over the next 48 hours elements of 2nd Canadian Corps moved rapidly throughout the Trun area in a constant tightening up process. 'At 1100hrs on 19 Aug the Corps Commander issued orders for further moves as he emphasised that encirclement must be complete and that NO Germans were to escape.'[26]

The clearing of Falaise of all German resistance had been undertaken by 2nd Canadian Infantry Division and, once completed, 12th British Corps took over the city and the area along the line of the River Dives so that 3rd Canadian Infantry Division could build up its defences around Trun.

Recently arrived south-east of St Lambert-sur-Dives was 4th Canadian Armoured Division who were to also move into the Trun area. The remaining area was to be covered by 1st Polish Armoured Division after its link up with the Americans.

While Allied armour and infantry were doing their utmost to close the pocket and trap the Germans, Allied artillery was hammering those German units trapped inside. Indeed, so heavy was the artillery that the area between the River Dives, L'Abbaye and Bierre had become known as 'gun alley'.[27] 'For three days medium and field regiments fired continually as they switched from target to target on masses of German infantry, vehicles and tanks struggling eastwards.'[28]

The carnage and slaughter was so unendurable that large numbers of German troops surrendered to the waiting Allied infantry. However, the greatest destruction wrought upon the Germans was from the air. The RAF had the task of ensuring the German Seventh Army had virtually no armour or transport left to salvage. The destruction began on 12 August when the Allies first observed during daylight hours large formations of German movement along the roads leading east through the Falaise-Argentan area. By 21 August the escape routes had been completely cut off and the Germans were caught out in the open as 'thousands of sorties were flown by 83, 84, and 2 Groups of Second Tactical Air Force'.[29] On the two days between 18 and 19 August the German escape route inside the pocket had narrowed to the Trun–Vimount–Flers road that had become a bottleneck of armour, transport and infantry, sitting ducks for the Second Tactical Air Force. To provide the reader with an idea of just how terrible the destruction from the air was for the Germans, 83 and 84 Groups destroyed 2,311 transport vehicles and damaged another 2,641. In tanks, the numbers destroyed were more than 172 while 179 were damaged. These were the claims made by the air crew during the two days. After the battle had moved further east the Allies made a count of the burnt-out hulks lining the roads leading out of the Falaise Gap. They counted 252 tanks, self-propelled and assault guns had been destroyed. Another 3,061 transport and other vehicles had also been destroyed.[30] 'Such was the fate that befell an army deprived of its Luftwaffe at the hands of an army whose air support was effectively employed as a powerful and deadly weapon.'[31]

Inevitably, with such a concentration of both German and Allied troops in a smallish area there were bound to be incidents of Allied aircraft attacking their own troops. For example, American fighter bombers, Lightnings and Thunderbolts, attacked Canadian troops in Falaise on the night of 17 August. The next evening, 1st Polish Armoured Division suffered more than 120 casualties when they were mistakenly bombed by RAF aircraft. From 16 to 18 August First Canadian Army suffered 358 killed and wounded and 63 vehicles destroyed or damaged by Allied aircraft mistaking them for Germans.[32]

In order to free up some of their trapped troops the Germans mounted fierce counter-attacks against the Allies on 20 August through Camembert and Sarvie. 2nd SS Panzer Division had been one of the formations that managed to escape the gap and subsequently began a series of ferocious counter-attacks against 1st Polish Armoured Division who sustained heavy casualties but also managed to repel the attacks. The Germans, too, suffered heavy casualties in these attacks. So bitter was the fighting that the Allies air-dropped supplies and ammunition to the Poles to sustain them. In the south-east, 2nd SS Panzer Division hammered 4th Canadian Armoured Division troops that were sealing off the escape route.[33]

Of course, history shows us that some of the German units did manage to escape the gap but suffered heavily in the process. Most of the infantry were left behind and thousands surrendered to the Allies. During 19 to 21 August more than 12,000 German troops surrendered to First Canadian Army, becoming prisoners of war. Amongst them were some high-ranking officers which were, according to reports, Colonel Gerloch, 708th Infantry Division commander, Lieutenant General Erwin Menny, commander 84th Infantry Division and the commander of 84th Corps, Lieutenant General Elfeld.[34]

An excellent example of the destruction the Allies rained down upon the Germans during the battle of Falaise can be seen in the complete destruction of 12th SS Panzer Division (Hitler Jugend). This division was at full strength on D-Day having more than 20,000 all ranks and over 214 tanks at their disposal. As the battle of Normandy progressed their losses mounted. Throughout June they lost 1,500 men and 20 tanks. The battle of Caen cost the division even more in men and materiel. By mid-July they were down to a little more than 2,000 men and around 50 tanks. They had not been reinforced and none were coming to build up their strength. Numbers dwindled even further and by 10 August 12th SS Panzer Division was down to 500 men and 'only 16 tanks'.[35] By the end of the disaster at Falaise the division was virtually non-existent. 'The last 60 men met their fate in a fruitless attempt to force a way out of the Gap north-west of Trun.'[36]

Chapter 5

In Pursuit

With the Falaise Gap closed and the fighting in that area now over, it was time for the Allies to regroup for the next phase of the Second Battle of France. The Germans had lost the Battle of Normandy and those forces that had managed to get out of the Falaise Gap were now in full retreat towards the Seine river. The German Seventh Army was virtually wiped out and the Fifth Panzer Army severely mauled and now in full retreat against the growing Allied might constantly increasing as more and more men and materiel arrived from England. 'Much depended upon his ability within the immediate future to reorganize his shattered resources sufficiently to make a successful stand against the impending power of the Allied advance.'[1]

Before we move on to the Allied pursuit of the German Armies towards the Seine it is worth looking at the operations of 1st British Corps during the first few weeks of August 1944. During TOTALIZE and TRACTABLE the role of the British on the left flank of First Canadian Army had been a holding one. Indeed, in the north, units of 6th Airborne Division were in a static line along the wooded regions on the west side of the Dives basin between the sea and Trun. Facing east and south-east, 49th (West Riding (WR)) Infantry Division had advanced along the Caen-Mezidon railway during Operation TOTALIZE from the area of Bourguébus-Soliers to Bellen-Greville and Vimont. 51st (Highland (H)) Infantry Division, by the 16th of August, had reached St Pierre-sur-Dives after reverting to the command of 1st British Corps.[2]

1st British Corps was ordered to advance to Lisieux[3] on 16 August while the armour for this operation was to come from 7th British Armoured Division that, on 17 August, crossed the Dives River to join the battle in the Lieury–Ecots area.[4] At this time, 7th Armoured Division was ordered to attack Orbec, 51st (H) Division to capture Lisieux and 49th (WR) Infantry Division to advance on Pont L'Eveque. At this point, the Germans had begun their mass exodus to escape the Falaise Gap south of Falaise which resulted in a loosening of their hold up and down their lines.

Livarot was occupied by 7th Armoured Division on the night of 20 August. At the same time, while advancing up the St Pierre-sur-Dives–Lisieux road, 51st (H) Division captured and occupied St Julien-Le-Faucon. 49th (WR) Infantry Division was breaking down heavy German resistance and slowly moving forward in the Mezidon area. 6th Airborne Division who, on D-Day, had captured and held the area between the Canal de Caen à la Mer and the River Dives were now advancing with increasing tempo and speed towards Pont L'Eveque then onwards to Trouville.[5]

Perhaps now is a good time to look at the Allied positions in Northern France with a larger lens. General Patton's Third US Army had driven hard with virtually no German opposition while the operations in the Falaise–Trun–Argentan area continued. Patton's armour had arrived at Orleans, Chartres and Dreux by 20 August. Reconnaissance patrols had reached the River Seine at Mantes-Gassicourt and Vernon.[6]

In Brittany, Third US Army still had two infantry divisions and an armoured division undertaking operations. On the left flank of Third US Army, elements of First US Army were advancing out of Argentan eastwards while other units were in complete control of the southern side of the Falaise 'bottleneck'. First Canadian Army firmly held the bottleneck between Trun-Chambois tightly sealed while Second British Army was 'closing in from west and north to complete the final elimination of the pocket'.[7]

At this stage in the campaign the Allies now wanted to stop the retreating German forces from escaping into north-east France. To do this, the following plans were set in motion. The 12th US Army Group[8] under General Omar Bradley's command was to drive north from Mantes-Dreux-Verneuil while the right flank would follow the southern bank of the River Seine. South-west of Paris, the 12th US Army was to prepare a large enough force to capture the city when directed to do so. '21 Army Group, comprising Second British and First Canadian Armies, was to advance rapidly to the Seine.'[9]

So began the Allied pursuit of the retreating Germans that would lead to the clearing of the Channel ports and ultimately, aid in the defeat of Germany. 'Having brought disaster to the German force in N.W. France we must now complete the destruction of such of his forces as are still available to be destroyed. After knowing what has happened to their armies in N.W. France, it is unlikely that these forces will now come to us; so, we will go to them.'[10]

The first moves of the pursuit began for the Allies at first light on 21 August when 2nd Canadian Corps drove towards Vinoutiers with 9th British

Army Group Royal Artillery (AGRA) alongside. Heading north towards Livarot 4th Canadian Infantry Brigade relieved infantry elements of 7th British Armoured Division then on the right flank of 1st British Corps.[11]

By 23 August remaining Allied formations involved in the pursuit of the retreating Germans were under way and making good progress. However, limited road space meant that often these pursuing troops were restricted to single routes as the mass of forward movement continued. Had the Luftwaffe been much stronger it could have caused the Allies much difficulty in their pursuit. Most of the infantry units found themselves moving in narrow lines with brigades coming up behind and passing through them, taking over the lead as progress continued. German resistance was primarily rearguard action and it wasn't until 2nd Canadian Corps reached the line of the Seine that the Germans began to react, especially in the towns or cities.

River crossings caused immense problems for the Allies as most of the bridges had been destroyed either by Allied air power or by the Germans blowing them up as they retreated. The unsung heroes of this advance were the divisional engineers who did efficient and speedy work in either rebuilding the bridges or repairing them as well as clearing out roadblocks and keeping the roads in good order.

As they rolled on towards the Seine, in the first 24 hours of the advance, according to reports, three Canadian divisions managed to reach and cross the rivers Vie and Touques. By 25 August the Canadians had managed to cross the Risle River at Brionne, Fontaine and Valleville.[12] The Canadians made contact that evening with elements of First US Army who had rapidly pushed up the western bank of the Seine, passing through Second British Army. With the Canadians having contacted the Americans, the US troops moved south of the Louviers–Le Neubourg road.

1st British Corps, advancing along the northern half of First Canadian Army's front, ran into heavy German resistance in the initial stages but by the night of 23 August all the divisions arrived at the Touques River and along its eastern bank had set up four small bridgeheads. At Fervaques, halfway between Lisieux and Vimoutiers, the leading elements of 7th British Armoured Division had managed to cross the Touques. At the same time, brigades from 7th Armoured Division and 51st (H) Division were now in Lisieux while further north at Coquain-Villers 49th (WR) Infantry Division had also crossed the river.

Pushing the German rearguard units across the Dives River, 6th British Airborne Division reached the Touques River and fought their way across it, setting up a bridgehead while under fire at Pont L'Eveque. Along the coast at Cobourg to Deauville formations from the Airborne Division were still engaged in stiff fighting against those German forces standing firm against the relentless Allied advance. They would not hold out for long.

During the advance eastwards 6th Airborne Division played a significant role beyond what it was originally set up to do. Its role in this advance was to carry out short-term holding operations until regular ground troops could relieve them. Lightly armed and with limited transport, this division had 'protected the entire Allied left flank by holding their positions between the DIVES and the CANAL DE CAEN A LA MER against repeated counter-attacks for seventy-three days'.[13] In addition, once the advance was under way they were also ordered to keep a strong pressure on retreating units on the German's right flank along the Channel coast.

Under the command of 6th Airborne Division were the Royal Netherlands Brigade (Princess Irene) and 1st Belgian Group (Light Brigade). While these groups were numerically small they were extremely keen to get stuck in to the fight against the Germans. According to 21st Army Group policy these two groups were 'to be given operation experience in quieter sections of the line in the hope that ultimately they would return to their own countries and form nuclei around which larger national forces might be organised'.[14]

The two groups were therefore used to take over the coastal towns that had already been captured by the Allies. However, operational necessity forced the Allies to reassign the roles and as such the Royal Netherlands were employed in front line operations while the Belgians were used to clear out German resistance along the Channel coast up to the River Risle.[15]

Initially, orders for 6th Airborne Division had been to engage with the Germans once it was clear they were retreating. Once the advance was under way however, they were forced to switch to heavy offensive operations because of the intensity of the fighting and to keep up with the rapidity of the Allied advance to the Seine. 'River crossings present a greater difficulty to the Airborne Division than to formations further inland, as they had to be carried out near to the sea where the rivers were wider and deeper and frequently tidal.'[16]

For example, it took four days of hard fighting for the division to cross the Touques River and occupy Pont L'Eveque from 21 to 24 August. This was against heavy, determined German counter-attacks. The next day, the division engaged in intense fighting at Beuzeville and finally on 26 August Pont-Audemer was finally taken, the division's final objective. Afterwards

6th Airborne Division was withdrawn from 1st British Corps and placed in reserve.

While what has been mentioned here about 6th Airborne Division's exploits in Normandy may not seem that much, when the statistics are studied they are quite impressive. Their Normandy operations covered an advance of roughly 45 miles, most of which was on foot. These operations were in conjunction with 1st Special Service Brigade (British) and 4th Special Service Brigade (British) along with the Dutch and Belgian contingents. They were lightly armed and fought in several major operations as they advanced. 'The Division had literally pushed the enemy back into the Seine, liberating more than four hundred square miles of France and capturing over a thousand prisoners.'[17]

Indeed, in a message from General Crerar, commander of First Canadian Army, to the commander of 6th Airborne Division, the general stated that 'the determination and speed with which his troops have pressed on in spite of all enemy efforts to the contrary have been impressive and of greatest assistance to the Army as a whole'.[18]

In the Lisieux area, the advance by 51st (H) Division and 7th Armoured Division was temporarily stopped by intense German fire in and around the cathedral. However, this stubborn resistance was overcome by 25 August when the British divisions were able to resume their advance to the Seine. Pont-Audemer was the main axis for 1st British Corps' advance while Bernays was the main centre of activity for the French Forces of the Interior (FFI).[19]

The Risle River was reached by 49th (WR) Infantry Division and 7th Armoured Division on the evening of 25 August and north of Brionne at Pont Anthou the divisions effected a crossing of the river. The following day, at Pont Audemer, 6th Airborne Division was relieved by 49th Infantry Division where they established a bridgehead. However, 51st (H) Infantry Division was still at Saint-Georges-du-Vièvre on 26 August but the next day both divisions crossed the Risle; 49th (WR) Infantry Division at Appeville on the left and 51st (H) Infantry Division at Pont Authou on the right. In the meantime, 7th Armoured Division had reached Routot and over the next three days these Allied infantry troops were heavily involved in attacking, defeating and clearing the remaining remnants of the German Army on the west bank of the Seine.

Chapter 6

Crossing the Seine

With most of the enemy cleared from the left bank of the River Seine the Allies began preparations for crossing the river as quickly as they could. It was only from the area between Elbeuf and the sea where the Germans retained control as they tried to protect their ferry escape routes across the river.

The Americans had arrived on the outskirts of Paris which helped to initiate an uprising by the FFI inside the city that led to its liberation. Third US Army had established a bridgehead at Mantes – Gassicourt some 25 miles north-west of Paris. Third US Army then drove to Elbeuf on the left bank of the river. At the same time, the Second British Army were in Vernon on the right bank and were getting ready to push on.

Allied air attacks had wiped out every bridge across the Seine used by the Germans in an effort to halt their retreat and completely destroy what was left of their army in the west. However, the Germans managed to withdraw the bulk of their troops across the river to the north side by using upwards of sixty ferries between Elbeuf and Vieux Port.[1] However, the losses in equipment and vehicles suffered by the Germans in this action was horrendous. 'In the opinion of the Commander 1 SS Panzer Corps, Col-Gen Joseph Dietrich, the Seine and the Falaise pocket were about equal disasters from the standpoint of equipment abandoned by the Wehrmacht in its headlong flight.'[2]

At Elbeuf, the winding River Seine looped back on itself creating a long spit of land that thrust westwards from Tourville, eight miles south of Rouen. Part of the Allied plan was to create a bridgehead across this narrow strip of land then move north and north-east and advance to Tourville by setting up a bridgehead at the railway that ran north to south through the town. This was the task of 3rd Canadian Infantry Division while 4th Canadian Armoured Division was to cross the river and capture the area between Alizan–Les Bouquets. At Morrey-En-Auge 1st Polish Armoured Division remained in reserve.

10th Canadian Infantry Brigade set up a bridgehead on the north bank of the Seine on the evening of 26 August near Criquebeuf then, using rafts and storm boats, crossed the river the next morning. On 28 August the brigade continued its advance along the east bank of the river, attacking and destroying German units defending Sotteville Sous-Le-Val and Igoville across from Pont De L'Arche.

Just east of Elbeuf, 3rd Canadian Infantry Division crossed the river after 7th Canadian Infantry Brigade had carried out an assault landing in the early hours of 27 August. Tourville was reached by nightfall of the same day. On the 28th, the Brigade pushed out east from the town capturing the high ground in that area. This action meant that the entire neck of land within the river loop was now in Allied hands.[3]

The actual physical crossing of the Seine River by the Allies fell to the Army Corps and Divisional Engineers. As the Allied lines of supply and communications increased there were delays in getting the necessary equipment for the crossing up to the front. From 27 August at Criquebeuf and Elbeuf Class 5, Class 9 and Class 40 ferries were in operation ferrying Allied units across the river. At the same time, where possible, bridges were rapidly constructed by the engineers to move as many personnel and equipment to the other side of the river as they could. Indeed, by the evening of 27/28 August Class 9 Folding Boat Equipment and a No 40 Bailey Pontoon Bridge were operating out of Elbeuf and transporting traffic.[4] By the end of August the Polish Armoured Division Engineers had built a Bailey Pontoon Bridge at Criquebeuf, replacing the ferries that were established a few days before, increasing the amount of personnel and materiel that could be moved across the river. At Pont-De-L'Arche a 500ft class 40 Bailey Pontoon Bridge had been constructed by Canadian engineers and was carrying heavy vehicles to the other side of the river.

By 28 August German units were still fighting defensive actions on the left bank against 1st British Corps and 2nd Canadian Infantry Division. 4th Canadian Armoured Division and 3rd Canadian Infantry Division were ordered to cross the river with all speed to ensure those German units still fighting defensive actions did not escape and to support the British and Canadians engaging them. Elsewhere, on the right, the high ground running from Alizay to Boos was to be captured by the armoured division[5] while along the right bank of the Seine elements of 3rd Canadian Infantry Division were to advance out of Tourville northwards to Rouen.

Extending from Elbeuf north to Rouen, the Forêt De La Londe formed a narrow neck of a large loop of the Seine River. At the narrow point of this isthmus the Germans had set up defensive positions in the area of Port Du Gravier–La Chenais to ensure the evacuation of their forces from the whole of the peninsula.

> Except on the extreme German right, which was open level ground protected by fire from north of the SEINE, the isthmus consisted of heavily wooded, hilly ground with a maze of tracks approaching it through the forest. Along the Railway line running north from Port Du Gravier the enemy found good cover, high ground, good observation and excellent fields of fire. In well-prepared positions were the most determined German troops, including men from Paratroop and SS units, with orders to hold at all costs.[6]

Now the Germans waited for the Allies to come. Their strength was estimated at two battalions.

Troops from 2nd Canadian Infantry Division attacked these positions completely unaware of the German strength. Their maps were ineffective, the air photos were not available in sufficient numbers or in sufficient detail to be of much use and they had no detailed plans. The battalions from the division attacked the German positions after having been in relentless pursuit following a month of hard and difficult fighting. They were under strength and had several new reinforcements inexperienced in battle. They would soon gain that experience.

Troops from another unit, 4th Canadian Infantry Brigade, ran into heavy German resistance on the morning of 27 August as they advanced from Elbeuf north along the western shore of the Seine. They were pinned down. Attack after attack over the next three days by all of the Brigade's battalions failed to dislodge the Germans. The Allies suffered heavy casualties in these counter-attacks with twenty-three officers of the brigade killed or wounded in just one day of fighting – 29 August. That night the brigade was withdrawn to rest, refit and rearm. They were replaced by 8th Canadian Infantry Brigade which was ordered to keep the Germans contained in the Forêt De La Londe area.

The situation of the Canadians on the north side of the isthmus was little better. Le Buisson and La Vacherie were captured and occupied by elements of the Brigade on 27 August. That night, the Brigade was ordered to take up a position that would put them behind the Germans. However, this also blocked 4th Canadian Infantry Brigade's progress at Port Du Gravier.

At first light on 28 August, the Camerons of Calgary (Canada) and the South Saskatchewan Regiment attacked but were driven back by heavy German mortar and machine-gun fire. They tried again at 2130hrs but met the same result and had to withdraw. 'On the morning of the 29th the two regiments on the left, after sustaining very heavy mortaring, began to withdraw apparently as a result of a false order given by the enemy on the Canadian formation's radio frequency.'[7]

By late afternoon of the 29th the Allies realized that the Germans were withdrawing. By 30 August the Allies were still crossing the Seine. Early that morning 8th Canadian Infantry Brigade drove across the bridges at Elbeuf joining the continuing advance of 3rd Canadian Infantry Division. Coming in behind them was 5th Canadian Infantry Brigade crossing at noon with the task of relieving 7th Canadian Infantry Brigade at Tourville.

By this time the Germans had pulled out of the city of Rouen completely, which 5th Canadian Infantry Brigade entered on 31 August. The liberated population received the Canadians with open arms. Later the same day, 6th Canadian Infantry arrived in Rouen and continued onwards.[8]

Last of the formations to cross the river Seine were the two infantry divisions of 1st British Corps. The British had been involved in heavy sustained fighting at the mouth of the river against strong rearguard German units. 51st (H) Infantry Division and 49th (WR) Infantry Division arrived at the Seine on 29 August. The Highland Division stood at points along the loop south of Duclair, while the 49th waited to cross at points in the area around Forêt De Brotone below Caudebec.[9] The Highlanders conducted large patrols on 30 August that saw them cross the river and enter Duclair, now free of German occupation forces who had left some time before. The Royal Netherlands Brigade, crossing further west at Vieux Port did not encounter any German resistance as they advanced. Finally, on 31 August the rest of the Highlanders crossed the Seine at Elbeuf over the bridges heading directly for St Valery.[10] The next day, using ferries and storm boats the 49th completed its river crossing between Quillebeuf and Rouen.[11]

Chapter 7

Operation ASTONIA: Liberating Le Havre

As the Germans retreated northwards towards Belgium in the hope of making a stand at the Somme, the Allies pressed on, their advance increasing in its tempo. August 30th saw General Crerar lay out a plan for the immediate capture of the port of Dieppe. At the time, the port facilities at the town were urgently needed for the Allies to land supplies and materiel. The task of clearing Dieppe went to 2nd Canadian Corps. 1st British Corps was ordered to take the peninsula west of the town and move on to capture and hold Le Havre, another port whose facilities and resources the Allies urgently required.[1]

To capture Dieppe, it was thought that a very heavy air and naval bombardment of the German defences around the town and the port would be required and the plan was for the operation to be completed by 2 September 1944. Leading elements of 2nd Canadian Division, who were to be the first Allied units to liberate Dieppe, rolled forward to Rouen, flooding into Totes and taking that town as they advanced. They met virtually no German opposition. The defenders that had been there had either been wiped out or had packed up and left with the rest of the retreating German forces.

The combined naval, military and air operation to take the city of Dieppe was known at Operation FUSILADE. However, as the Allied advance continued it became more and more clear to the Canadians that there was no German opposition in the city. Frantically, phone calls were quickly made to the RAF and Second Tactical Air Force to stop the air attacks that would have reduced Dieppe to rubble. FUSILADE was cancelled quickly once the defensive situation became clear.

Early in the morning of 1 September elements of 8th Canadian Recce Regiment entered Dieppe. By the time darkness fell the whole of 2nd Canadian Infantry Division was in the city. The inhabitants, remembering the tragic disaster of the Dieppe Raid by the British and Canadians on

19 August 1942, greeted the liberators with joy and enthusiasm. 'Less than twenty-four hours earlier the Germans had dealt the last bitter blow of their four years' occupation of Dieppe by systematically demolishing all quays, bridges and blockhouses in the city.'[2]

2nd Canadian Infantry Division remained in the area for the next two days to rest and recuperate as well as bring on reinforcements that had only just arrived.[3] Despite the chaos and destruction the Germans had left behind in Dieppe the engineers and administrative services of First Canadian Army were in the city shortly after the liberation. Work on repairing the damage was quickly under way. 'The harbour was swept of mines and by 6 Sep the port was ready to receive its first cargoes.'[4] Indeed, ten ships arrived on the afternoon of 7 September bringing 3,000 tonnes of ammunition, petrol and supplies to support the Allied advance. The railway that before the war had run from Dieppe to Amiens and had been destroyed was now back up and running. The first train carrying 400 tonnes of fuel pulled out of the Dieppe station on 9 September bound for Brussels and the Second British Army.

By the end of August, the rapid Allied advance had made it possible for some formations to have a short rest period before continuing on. However, as events moved swiftly onwards across the entire Allied front it forced a change in 21st Army Group's thinking. With the British 7th Armoured Division now in Amiens, that was captured on 31 August, General Montgomery ordered the First Canadian Army to keep up the momentum and continue the advance to Abbeville and Pont Remy. As such, on 2 September, 4th Canadian Armoured Division reached the Somme and the following day 10th Canadian Infantry Brigade formed a bridgehead over the river in the Pont Remy area. That same afternoon, the whole of the division crossed the river using the bridgehead. North of Abbeville, 1st Polish Armoured Division had crossed the river and continued the pursuit of the retreating Germans, assuming the lead in the Allied armoured pursuit.

21st Army Group's rapid advance from the closing of the Falaise Gap is impressive. In 11 days of chasing the retreating Germans, elements of First Canadian Army had travelled 137 miles from Trun to Dieppe while the Second British Army had completed 202 gruelling miles from Amiens to Vimy. Throughout the advance the Allied front remained at roughly 50 miles wide with neither of the two armies covering any less than 10 miles in a day. This is including the days it took for bridging operations for crossing the Seine.

> The breath-taking speed with which this great advance had been completed was a measure of the staggering defeats that had been inflicted on German military power at Mortain, Caumont and Falaise, and the resultant demoralisation of the German armies in the west.[5]

Throughout the Allied advance the Germans had suffered heavy losses, some 8,036 prisoners[6] being captured by the First Canadian Army from 23 August to 1 September. According to Allied reports, the total number of prisoners taken from the opening of Operation TOTALIZE to early September was approximately 26,000, although according to reports across the entire front of 21st Army Group some 44,000 prisoners were taken with 'a number that was at least equal to the of the prisoners taken' classified as killed, wounded or missing.[7]

What these figures meant for the Germans was that from September onwards they would have to fight their withdrawal actions with roughly 100,000 troops less than what they had at the beginning of August. The Germans had lost approximately the same numbers of troops when they were fighting the Americans from Brittany to the Seine. One can see the pressing need for a German withdrawal when faced with numbers like this.

By this time, German Seventh Army had been all but decimated as can be seen in a German order dated 29 August that laid out plans for completely reorganizing what was left of that army. Five infantry divisions that had suffered terrible losses were to be sent back to Germany. These were the 276th, 277th, 326th, 363rd and 708th Infantry Divisions and the weapons they had were to be distributed among those German units that remained behind the Somme line. These units were instructed, in the 29 August order, to prepare defensive positions that were to be monitored by the Somme Corps, a special headquarters the Germans set up for preparing the defences behind the Somme.[8]

Still the Allies relentlessly pursued the Germans. On 3 September newly promoted Field Marshal Montgomery (he had been promoted to this rank two days previously), issued a communication to all his commanders laying out his intentions to destroy and decimate all German forces they came across. The orders to all the forces of his command were:

- To advance eastwards and destroy all enemy forces encountered.
- To occupy the Ruhr and get astride the communications leading from it into Germany and to the sea ports.[9]

Third US Army by this time had reached Nancy and had crossed over the Meuse at Verdun while First US Army had pushed far enough that its forward elements were in Belgium just south of Mons. On the right flank of 21st Army Group, the British had taken Arras and on the evening of 3 September units of the Guards Armoured Division entered Brussels. Antwerp was occupied the next day by 11th Armoured Division.[10]

While the Ruhr was extremely important for the Allies to enter into Germany and end the war, before they could do that the Channel ports needed to be cleared. This task was handed to the First Canadian Army. They were to destroy the German fortresses they had built in the Channel ports from the Seine to the Scheldt Estuary. While the Allies had captured Antwerp, they could not use the massive port facilities there until the Germans defending the Scheldt Estuary had been defeated.

> The situation emphasized the potential value of the smaller Channel ports, particularly Boulogne, where it was intended to establish a terminal for a cross-Channel petrol pipeline. 1 British Corps was assigned the task of investing Le Havre. 3 Cdn Inf Div was directed on Boulogne.[11]

The planning branch of 21st Army Group prepared a study in March 1944 on the operations required for capturing Rouen and Le Havre. They thought this would take place about 90 days after the Normandy landings, or D-plus-90, with the objective of taking the port of Le Havre in the same plans. However, 89 days after the landings, 1st British Corps made its preliminary plan on 3 September for an assault on the port.[12] This was to be Operation ASTONIA. 1st British Corps was made up of 51st (H) Infantry Division with 33rd Armoured Brigade under command, as well as 49th (WR) Infantry Division with 34th Tank Brigade under command. In overall command of the corps was Lieutenant-General J.T. Crocker.

All of these forces were already north of the Seine by 3 September. The day before the Highland Division had captured St Valery-En-Caux and by dusk on the 3rd, 49th (WR) Infantry Division had 'made contact with the perimeter defences of Le Havre'.[13] They had driven down the right flank of the Seine Estuary when they came face to face with the German defenders. Interestingly, on the evening of the 3rd High Command of 1st British Corps sent a demand to the German garrison to surrender the port of Le Havre. The following day they received the reply from the German commander. The answer was no.

The German commander, Colonel Eberhard Wildermuth, had every reason to feel confident for Le Havre was strongly protected with natural and man-made defences. Under interrogation, Wildermuth stated he had a hope that the assault on Le Havre by the British would not materialize and, as a result, a siege would be imposed instead.

> This hope stemmed from the fact that the Allies probably knew that the harbour had been made unserviceable, and that Le Havre as a port, had, for the time being, been destroyed. But it was a forced hope, and later Wildermuth admitted that in his heart of hearts he realised that a siege at that stage of the campaign was unlikely.[14]

The port was surrounded on three sides by water – the open sea was on the west side, the Seine Estuary was to the south and on the east was the flooded valley of the River Lezarde. For a ground assault to be made it would have to come from the north. This, however, would not be easy as the topography aided the German defenders. For example, at Octeville the high ground commanded the northern approaches to the city 'and to the north-east were two high features, Northern Plateau and Southern Plateau'.[15] Extensive minefields had been sewn throughout this high-ground area. In addition, from the Lezarde Valley at La Rive to the coast west of Octeville, the Germans had constructed strong wire defences. Even worse news for the British was a strong anti-tank ditch that ran between 'the minefields along the northern slope of the natural features'.[16] This ditch, identified in Allied aerial photos, was 20ft wide and 10ft deep.

Along the outer defensive positions to the north the Germans had built several concrete infantry strongpoints bristling with anti-tank guns and machine guns. Immediately west of the river Lezarde on the northern plateau, the British forces had identified eleven strongpoints. Inside the city, the British believed there were approximately twenty-eight artillery batteries of four guns each, almost all of which were pointed to fire out to sea. Also, in Le Havre itself were Fort Ste Addresse and Fort Sanvic that the Germans had reinforced for the defence of the city. These, '... together with many roadblocks, pillboxes, fortified houses and concrete shelters, completed the defensive system with which the enemy now faced our assault'.[17]

The British believed that the Germans had some 8,700 troops in total for the defence of the city. This figure was made up of roughly 4,000 artillery and flak personnel and 1,300 naval troops. 'If the enemy showed any sign of weakness and presented the opportunity, penetration of his main positions was to be made.'[18]

At the end of the war, while a prisoner, Colonel Wildermuth, commander of the Le Havre garrison, was interviewed by the Allies and he gave his own estimate of the ability and size of his troops. He had a staff of elderly reserve officers and he stated that he was pleased with their ability and conscientiousness. As far as infantry was concerned, he stated he had roughly 4,500 of 'varying quality'.[19]

> He considered that his best troops were a battalion of 36 Gr of 245 Inf Div. These men were well trained and knew the problems of the defence. Battle-experienced men on leave from the eastern front, hastily banded together into two battalions, had not yet shaken down into a smooth-working team.[20]

However, the commander also stated that his Protective Regiment (5 Sicherungs Regiment) was of limited fighting value as most of the men were ill or infirm in some way. Having considered the quality of his troops and the state of his defences, the garrison commander told his superior (15th Army commander) that 'the fortress could be held against an assault for 24 hours in unfavourable circumstances, or 72 hours if circumstances favoured the defence'.[21]

How then, were the British going to overcome these defences for a ground assault against the city? The main answer to that was that they would carry out the assault in stages. The first part of the plan was to 'soften up' the German defences in the city using the Royal Navy, RAF Bomber Command and artillery fire. This began on 5 September when HMS *Erebus*, a Royal Navy monitor, began counter-battery fire with her two 15in guns. She also took on counter-battery fire on 8 September but on both occasions *Erebus* was hit by shells from a shore battery and was forced to withdraw. *Erebus* was joined on 10 September by the battleship HMS *Warspite* and for six hours both ships pounded the concrete artillery batteries in the 'perimeter defences of the fortress'.[22]

The RAF also began their 'softening up' procedures on 5 September, continuing through the 6th and the 8th as well. They hammered German targets in the city and also around the defended area beyond the city. Some 4,000 tons of bombs were dropped by more than 1,000 bombers over this period. According to reports, these attacks were delivered onto the targets with extreme accuracy. Prior to the ground assault on Le Havre, the RAF dropped some 900,000 leaflets on the German defenders. A further 22,000 were fired by Allied artillery batteries. Attempts to influence the Germans holding the defensive positions in Le Havre were not just confined to leaflets. The British broadcast propaganda messages designed to reduce German morale and induce mass desertion. 'There seems little doubt that all these preliminary operations were factors which contributed in no small degree to the speed and comparative ease with which the reduction of the fortress was achieved.'[23] Wildermuth stated that the damage done by these air attacks was slight, 'but he did admit that two anti-aircraft batteries were made useless, the telephone circuit was damaged and the streets made impassable by rubble'.[24]

The ground assault on Le Havre was to take place in four different phases by two divisions. Phase 1 would see 49th (WR) Infantry Division fight their way through the German outer defences on the left flank and capture the Northern Plateau. Once done, they were to drive onto the Southern Plateau and establish a bridgehead. On the right flank, 51st (H) Division, in Phase 2, were to set up a base north of the Forêt De Montegeon. While this was happening, 49th (WR) Infantry Division was to attack and secure the whole of the Southern Plateau. Phase 3 was the destruction of all German defences around Octeville by 51st (H) Division. The completion of this phase would see the Highlanders capture the high ground on the north edge of Le Havre. Finally, from these last positions, both divisions were to relentlessly attack German defenders within the city until the fortress was secure[25] '... a programme of heavy bombing of targets for Bomber Command immediately preceding the assault was integrated with the Corps Plan.'[26]

Also available for the operation were a total of eight field artillery regiments comprising 4th AGRA (Army Group Royal Artillery) and 9th AGRA that included six medium and two heavy regiments that meant the total number of guns for supporting artillery was more than 500. Another counter-battery and counter-flak unit had also been included in the plan.

> Besides timed concentrations, the corps commander could order, and divisions could request, 'victor' targets. When one of these was ordered by the C. R. A. (Commander Royal Artillery), every gun which could reach the target, and was not otherwise engaged, would take part in the shoot. The call to fire on a 'victor' target took precedence over counter-battery or counter-flak targets.[27]

While the task of capturing Le Havre had been given to 1st British Corps the actual assault was the responsibility of the 49th and 51st Divisions. Part of the allotment of assault troops given to each of these divisions was 30th Armoured Brigade Headquarters under the command of Brigadier Duncan who was in charge of all of the units of the 79th Armoured Division used in the assault on the city. Those units were as follows:

49th Division			
	Sherman Crabs	Crocodiles	AVREs
56th Brigade	A & B Sqdns – 1 Troops C Sqdn 22 Dragoons	A Sqdn 141 RAC	222 Assault Sqdn RE less No 2 Troop 617 Assault Sqdn RE
146th Brigade	C Sqdn 22 Dragoons less Troop		No 2 Troop 222 Assault Sqdn RE
51st Division			
152nd Brigade	B Sqdn 1 Lothians & Border Yeomanry	C Squadron 141 RAC	16 Assault Sqdn RE
153rd Brigade	C Sqdn 1 Lothians & Border Yeomanry		284th Assault Sqdn RE

The plans and preparations for the attack were affected by terrible weather. The hammering rain quickly soaked the soft clay soil that for most armoured vehicles made the area a quagmire. The original 'D-Day' for the attack was set for 9 September but the unrelenting rain forced the Allied planners to push it back by 24hrs.

> The use of sand tables and cloth models of the minefield-breaching operation and the areas to be assaulted proved valuable, and particularly so to 51st (H) Inf Div, which was to assault in darkness.[28]

Sunday, 10 September dawned with sunny skies. After a period of rain, the soil had hardened enough to allow tanks to move without getting bogged down in mud. In Le Havre, the French civilians came out in droves to enjoy the sun and relatively warm air. Children played near gun positions and in the tank assembly areas but at 1700hrs that surreal atmosphere was quickly shattered as the town was treated to half an hour of accurate bombing followed by an artillery barrage. Just as this was dying down, the leading tanks rolled forward from the start line, heading for the town and contact with the German defences at 1745hrs.[29]

Earlier that morning, at 1000 hrs, 'the two great ships began the bombardment of the enemy's batteries'.[30] The fire from the 15in guns of HMS *Warspite* destroyed the shore battery that had previously scored hits on *Erebus*. 'During the next six hours the guns of the two vessels pumped 300 15in shells into the defences of Le Havre.'[31] At 1645hrs the assault began with the bombing campaign. Three German targets received 4,264 tons of bombs (HE) from 900 heavy bombers.[32] The hammering of the German forward defensive positions lasted for an hour before the bombers moved on to their next target. To the waiting British troops west of Montivilliers, formed up on the right bank of the River Lezarde, the precision of the bombing must have been an encouraging sight.

From the perspective of the German prisoners taken during Operation ASTONIA, the Allies discovered that their estimation of the effect the bombing had on the enemy was not as great as they would have liked. The prisoners told the Allies that while they were very afraid of the bombing, the German casualties were very light because of the 'excellent shelters, including those supplied for the civilian population'.[33] 'The most important result was the breakdown in communications, with prevented the German artillery commander from controlling his resources, and precluded centralised direction of the defences.'[34]

On the ground, 49th Infantry Division began its drive down the Lezarde Valley at 1745hrs and 40 minutes later the Flail tanks that had been supplied for the operation began smashing through the minefields and the wire defences. For the loss of four Flail tanks the operation by these machines and their crews ended at 1940hrs leaving a gap through which the rest of the Allied troops could move. This gap was the centre gap in the Allied three-pronged attack and it was very difficult as only one lane was opened due to the effort required to bridge the anti-tank ditch. It was planned that two lanes would be opened in the eastern gap but only one was successfully achieved as three Flail tanks were destroyed by mines only 50 yards in. 'The gapping cost altogether 29 Flails and two command tanks – most of which were disabled by mines – and six AVREs.'[35]

Here is a detailed look at the efforts of units of the 79th Armoured Division attached to the two British divisions involved in the liberation of Le Havre.

A Squadron, 22nd Dragoons, using their Flail tanks, began moving through the minefields on the Southern Plateau towards German strongpoints that were the objective of 56th Brigade. However, this initial assault was not entirely successful as only two lanes through the minefields were half completed due to heavy going and the loss of several of the Sherman Crabs (Flails) as they blew up on mines. 'In the right hand breach four were disabled in this way, the fifth Crab in the troop completed and widened the gap to 20 feet. The centre lane was cleared to 24 feet with the loss of three Crabs and the left lane with the loss of two.'[36]

Another Sherman Crab tank burst into flames when it suffered a direct hit from German artillery fire. The officers who wrote *The Story of the 79th Armoured Division* report state that if not for the determination and enthusiasm of Captain T. Barraclough of the 22nd Dragoons, the lanes would not have been completed.

With these lanes completed the infantry drove through, attacking the German strongpoints on the other side of the minefields supported by tanks from A Squadron 141st RAC and a troop of tanks from 617th Assault Squadron RE. However, they lost two Crocodile tanks even before they could get off the start line and another was destroyed in the minefield before it could get to the German defenders. Despite this, six Crocodile flamethrower tanks were able to get to the German strongpoint, which they flamed with great enthusiasm and the Germans capitulated after 11 minutes.[37]

One AVRE was hit and destroyed by a round from a German 88mm gun while another blew up in the minefield and a third became wedged between a destroyed tank and a Bren gun carrier also destroyed. Three that were left supported the Crocodiles in their attack against the German defenders resulting in the destruction of the 88mm gun position.

Due to heavy casualties, another infantry company was brought up to continue the assault on two German strongpoints (identified as 6 and 7 on the maps of the assault) and by late evening both had capitulated and more than 40 prisoners captured. However, one of the key objectives for 51st Division, Strongpoint 8, was still offering resistance. After an hour of waiting the Crocodiles and AVREs were able to attack this last objective.

A road, with minefields on either side, that crossed the anti-tank ditch and led to the German defensive positions was at the heart of the 56th Brigade's front. To deal with these minefields, two troops of Sherman Crabs from 22nd Dragoons (A and B Squadrons) began to flail through the fields situated either side of the road. After 40 minutes of flailing while under heavy German fire, a 24ft lane to the anti-tank ditch had been cleared. Now the ditch had to be crossed and so the Allies brought up an Small Box Girder (SBG) bridge which was hit and put out of action. Another was brought up and it too was hit by artillery and mortar fire 500 yards from the ditch. However, it was repaired and eventually winched into position by engineers of the Royal Engineers and was ready by 2055hrs.

On the road, a Churchill Bridgelayer ran over a mine and had its track blown apart and was unable to move. However, a path was cleared around it by 49th Divisional Royal Engineers but the road became completely blocked when an AVRE that came up to try to tow away the Bridgelayer also hit a mine and had its track blown off, making it useless. The road was finally cleared the next day.

Mines claimed five Sherman Crabs on the left side of the road as they tried to clear a lane through to the anti-tank ditch as well. Mortar fire hammered the SBG bridge while the troop commander's AVRE hit a mine also on the right side forcing the Allies to abandon the lane that had been made on that side of the road. On the left side, a second lane had been cleared to the ditch but mines claimed three Crab tanks in the first one and that lane was abandoned. The second lane was the lane completed by 1905hrs which the infantry poured through, supported by armour from 141st RAC and a troop of 617th Squadron, enabling them to take two more German strongpoints.

Strongpoints 1 and 2 were soon taken: at 2035hrs the Crocodiles flamed No. 3 which went up in smoke; but Crocodiles got off course and missed No 4 which, however, fell later, disgorging about 30 prisoners. The Crocodiles then went for strongpoints 9 and 10 and wiped them out.[38]

Under the cover of darkness elsewhere along the front an AVRE attacked and destroyed another 88mm gun position and at a range of 80 yards blew up a pillbox with its petard. Other AVREs had begun the process of hauling railway sleepers to the front to carpet gaps and ensure that the tanks could get through. Kangaroo personnel carriers were being used to move the infantry and an entire battalion managed to pass through the open lanes in the minefields in these vehicles.[39] Since this battalion's immediate objectives, German strongpoints 9 and 10, had already been taken they moved on to their next objectives.

At the same time, on the blocked road that ran south-west from Montivilliers, Royal Engineers from 49th Division RE were having difficulty trying to clear the disabled and destroyed vehicles that were stopping tanks and infantry from reaching their objectives. This was remedied when Major J.O.M. Alexander, the commander of 617th Squadron RE, managed to lead five AVREs down a steep slope while on foot so that they could clear the vehicles and other roadblocks. These vehicles managed to clear the blocks by blowing them up with explosives. In one case, a bulldozer was brought forward to fill in a crater created by these explosions only to be destroyed by running over a mine itself. However, the crater was filled and by 0700hrs the job was done.

AVREs were also being used to cross the River Fontaine, which they did twice, and were able to pull mines away using signal cable. They also filled in craters all while under fire from German artillery and machine guns. With the infantry now having reached their first objectives, the Southern Plateau was in Allied hands.

The effectiveness of this part of Operation ASTONIA can be seen through the comments of Colonel Wildermuth during his interrogation. He stated that the Allied artillery gunners kept up their fire throughout the night and that the huge dome of bright light from searchlights that lit up the fortress like moonlight helped them to see the targets.

> Command during the hours of darkness was almost impossible with means of communication, wireless and roads, hopelessly damaged. Companies thrown in for relief reached their assembly points late, and with considerable casualties. When daylight came, Wildermuth realized a counter-attack was out of the question, and he ordered his troops to take up the defence of the second position, on the east and north-east edge of the forest of Mongeon.[40]

Crocodile flamethrowing tanks, mostly Shermans and Churchills, had 'been most effective in "flaming" enemy strongpoints there into submission'.[41]

In the 51st Highland Division's sector the attack was much later due to the fact their positions during the day were overlooked by German defenders positioned west of the airfield on high ground. Therefore, at midnight the Highlanders began rolling forward for their assault on the German defences. Three columns set out with visibility at only 30 yards.

> In each case an AVRE led, followed by the Flail Troop Leader, then two AVREs with 'Snakes', and AVRE with S.B.G. and finally the remaining Crabs and AVREs. Bomb craters made direction-keeping difficult, and, although coloured lights and tape had been put out, so inaccurate was the Bofors tracer that the right hand column (with AVREs from 284 Assault Squadron RE) overshot the salient of the ditch and had to come in around the corner. The other two columns (with AVREs from 16 Assault Squadron RE) also veered to the right.[42]

Progress was slow, despite the fact that they did not encounter any minefields in their sector before they reached the anti-tank ditch. One AVRE was lost when it fell into the ditch but by 0240hrs a bridge had been successfully laid across the ditch. 1st St Lothians and Border Yeomanry managed to cross the ditch by dropping fascines. Once on the other side they began flailing to clear a way forward.

However, elsewhere things were not so positive. For example, four Crab tanks were disabled or destroyed after driving over mines in the right lane and the same thing took place in the middle lane. However, five Crabs managed to get through in the left lane only to be destroyed later after encountering another minefield that had not been flailed. Despite heavy German shelling of this left lane, the infantry managed to get through and attack their targets.

One battalion of Highlanders managed to take a bridge that was east of the Fontaine-la-Mallet church, while another attacked and captured German strongpoint 11 and the third battalion, in readiness for their assault on German positions at Mont Trottins, drove down the main road west of the Fontaine valley.

Crabs from C Squadron, the Lothians, attacked the German north-east gun position supported by three AVREs and half of C Squadron 141st Royal Armoured Corps along with infantry. The Southern German gun position was assaulted simultaneously by the other half of C Squadron 141st RAC, three more AVREs and infantry. By 1600hrs both positions had been cleared of German defenders and prisoners taken.

> By the 11 September 1944, at 1100hrs, Allied troops supported by 617 Squadron RE found themselves within 1000 yards of Le Havre suburbs. An additional 200 prisoners were taken when AVREs attacked and captured another German gun position during this action.[43]

Phase 2 began at 2359hrs on 10th September with 51st Division rolling forward. Using the right gap made previously by 49th (WR) Infantry Division, the Scots (Highlanders) moved in behind the German defences and within ten minutes their gapping teams were hard at work.

Bridging the anti-tank ditch would have to be done in darkness and the lack of cloud to reflect the searchlights made it hard going.

> As a result of the heavy going, bad visibility, and resulting difficulty in keeping direction, the gapping teams took an hour instead of the estimated thirty minutes to reach the ditch. By 0240 hrs, in all three lanes, bridges had been launched across the obstacle; two hours later one lane was complete, swept of mines, and in fit condition for vehicles to use.[44]

By noon the following day they had taken their objectives north of Le Havre. With these positions secure they were now ready to assault the German defenders west of Forêt De Montegeon. Because of the ground the Allies had taken on the 10th the armour had been able to cross the anti-tank ditch and now moved forward with the infantry.

> Bitter fighting took place in a heavily mined orchard east of the River Lezarde and the infantry were having a difficult time of it. However, this changed with the arrival of C Squadron 22nd Dragoons who, by 1030hrs, had beaten a lane through the minefield. At 1215hrs, the infantry mounted another assault on the German positions while the Crabs managed to blow 50 mines as they tore two lanes through the minefield. This allowed for the infantry to attack and for Crocodiles to be brought up to flame the German position that capitulated at 1400hrs.
>
> Earlier in the day, at 0730hrs, Sherman Crabs breached a minefield enabling the infantry to form up on Route Nationale in preparation for attacking German positions at Harfleur. The Germans held a hill that had been code named Oscar by the Allies, and at 1200hrs this position was attacked when two AVREs, and an armoured bulldozer rolled down Route B on the left side supported by infantry. 'Three roadblocks were demolished with "Wade" charges, craters filled in and a barricade at a road junction destroyed. The bulldozer dealt with a large double excavation, the AVREs assisted tanks in destroying enemy positions across the valley – and the whole force moved down to Harfleur.'[45]
>
> Using Petard fire, more AVREs on Route C managed to blow up trees and use them to fill in a ditch while under heavy artillery and mortar fire from the Germans. Despite this bombardment they, too, moved into Le Havre itself.[46]

The morning of 11 September saw 146th Brigade, of 49th (WR) Infantry Division, attacking east of the Lezarde River, four German strongpoints overlooking Harfleur that formed the right flank of the German defences. This attack began at 0530hrs with tanks and Flails supporting infantry that were, in turn, supported by one medium artillery Regiment and four field regiments. However, in the first assault, the attacking force ran into mines, which they had not expected, and the assault was only partially successful.

Even though the infantry were supported by the Crocodile flamethrower tanks, heavy fighting took place and it wasn't until 1400hrs when the final German strongpoint was taken and the German garrison there surrendered. 'By last light on 11 Sep, 146 Inf Bde troops, who had found four bridges intact, were forcing their way westward into Le Havre, the forward infantry having reached a point on the Canal Vauban north-west of the railway marshalling yards.'[47]

The same day saw the Allied attacks in the north smashing through German defences as pillbox positions felt the full weight of the flamethrowers, while also being blasted into submission by the guns of the AVRE. In the skies overhead, the RAF did their work as well, hammering the German defences all day long with bombs and rocket fire. This began with an attack by 155 bombers of Bomber Command from 0730 to 0800hrs dropping 857 tons of high explosives on the Germans. Throughout the day, rocket-firing Typhoons pounded the defences with 'their spectacular hissing projectiles'.[48]

By the time night fell, the British forward troops had reached a position at Doudenville, 1000 yards south of Octeville, Bleville and Le Heve, west of the city of La Havre. The Germans had built up a defensive line that ran north of the two forts, Sanvic and Ste Addresse. East of Fort Sanvic, 49th (WR) Infantry Division now held ground from the cemetery to the whole of the southern plateau. 146th Brigade had left Harfleur and pushed 2,000 yards along the Canal Vauban ready for the next phase.

> On the 12 September in the early morning two AVREs entered Le Havre using the left route where they cleared the way for tanks and infantry by destroying roadblocks and filling in craters. They managed to get to the docks, led by a French patrol, removed a roadblock and took more than 300 German prisoners from local barracks close by. They stayed at the docks until the infantry arrived to relieve them.
> On the Southern Plateau there was still one German position that was holding out. It had an 88mm gun that was causing havoc with the Allied armour, in particular armour from 617th Squadron. One AVRE was destroyed and all of its crew were killed. However, at 1200hrs this German position surrendered after being outflanked by another troop of AVREs and the British took 300 more prisoners.

By this point most of the German defences had been taken. Troops from 49th and 51st Divisions now began the mopping up exercises clearing the town that eventually led to the German garrison at Le Havre surrendering.[49]

Operation ASTONIA officially ended on 12 September, yet there were still German units holding out which had to be dealt with. The coastal area from Le Havre to Octeville was cleared by two brigades of 51st (H) Infantry Division. The ground from the sea to Doudenville was taken care of by 152nd (H) Infantry Brigade against very little German resistance. The responsibility for the area in the south was given to 153rd (H) Infantry Brigade, while 154th (H) Infantry Brigade attacked the defences still holding out in the high ground around Le Havre, while the last of the German strongholds at Fort Ste Addresse was attacked relentlessly by the rest of 51st (H) Infantry Division. The German garrison at the fort surrendered at 1500hrs the same day. 49th Division, meanwhile, had managed to take the southern part of the city all the way down to the docks and port facilities as well as the Canal Vauban. In this operation, they had also captured Colonel Wildermuth, who had been wounded, as well as the German artillery commander. 'Bit by bit, the last pockets of resistance in the great harbour were eliminated.'[50] 'During the morning the German garrison commander had been taken prisoner, and by late afternoon all resistance in the area had ceased.'[51]

It had taken the British just 48 hours to capture and secure the city of Le Havre and its port facilities, 98 days after the initial landings on 6 June. More than 11,300 German prisoners had been captured in this operation while the total number of Allied killed, wounded and missing was approximately 500. The key to the quick and successful victory for Operation ASTONIA was the complete isolation of the German defenders and the relentless determination, power and coordination of the Allies with which the German garrison was attacked by air, sea and land 'culminating in the concentrated and undisturbed bombardment of the defences by the Royal Artillery, the Royal Navy and above all, the Royal Air Force'.[52] 'All available arms were employed to their best advantage; the momentum of the assault was never permitted to relax; before it had time to recover the garrison was overwhelmed.'[53]

The Allied armour crews, especially those of the special armour such as Crocodiles, Flails and AVRE vehicles, were given a special tribute by Sir Donald Banks in *Flame Over Britain*:

The 79th Armoured Division under General Hobart was afforded a first large-scale opportunity to practise the armoured assault-team technique which formed part of the inspired conceptions which had led to the setting up of that novel formation. Flails, mounted in 'Crabs' to thresh a path through the minefields, 'AVREs' with their bombardment 'Petards' and miscellaneous equipment to bridge and overcome the miscellaneous anti-tank obstacles and 'Crocodiles' to bring terror to the hearts of the defenders, constituted a redoubtable trio which carried all before them.[54]

The Allied assault on Le Havre was the first time the idea of large-scale assault-team techniques had been put into practice and despite the hard going proved to be a success. This is, in large part, due to the efforts of the crews of all the specialized armoured vehicles used in the attack. The Crocodile flamethrowers, the Sherman Flail tanks and the AVREs with their petard guns. 'The lives of many infantrymen were saved (a fact much appreciated by the Corps and Divisional Commanders in letters of appreciation).' Because the entire operation had been meticulously planned the assault and capture of Le Havre had taken place over a short period of time. The same, however, could not be said for the other Channel ports.

What did the Germans think of 'Hobart's Funnies'? 'They thought it madness when they heard tanks entering the minefields and were later dismayed at the results.'[55] To them, they believed that the Crocodile flamethrowers were not British, not part of the British sense of fair play. 'One officer prisoner reported that a whole platoon, caught in the open had been burned to death. Had the guns been more stoutly manned there is no doubt that Crab, AVRE and Crocodile casualties would have been much higher.'[56] Colonel Wildermuth stated during his interrogation that 'the real effective fire came from Allied concentrated artillery which had devastating results in knocking out the guns of the fortress'.[57]

The results of the opening of the port of Le Havre for the British and Canadians were mixed. Le Havre was handed over to the Americans for their use while the British and Canadians would battle the Germans holding the approaches to the port of Antwerp along the Scheldt Estuary and on Walcheren Island. While that was taking place Boulogne would need to be cleared in order for a terminal at the port for the cross-Channel fuel pipeline, code-named Pluto, to be completed. However, a large body of artillery and armour was released to 3rd Canadian Infantry Division in order for them to attack the German defences at Boulogne. This was as a direct result of the capture of Le Havre. Also, RAF Bomber Command resources would now be available for this attack along with the artillery batteries of 51st (H) Infantry Division and 9th AGRA.[58]

On 15 September 1944, General Crerar, commanding the First Canadian Army, gave orders to 2nd Canadian Corps to capture Boulogne on 16 September or whenever the required air power was available.[59] The battle for Boulogne was now set in stone.

Chapter 8

Operation WELLHIT: Boulogne Liberated

As we have previously seen, the Allies' logistical chain was being stretched hard as they continued their advance into France and there was a pressing need for the Channel ports to be liberated, rebuilt and re-opened in order to support the war effort. The Allies were pushing deeper and deeper into German-held territory and, as they did, they realised the war was becoming one of attrition. Those armies that had the best and most efficient logistics chain would inevitably be victorious. Wars of attrition are generally won by the army that can re-supply and re-equip its fighting troops faster than the enemy can. This also means being able to re-supply with better, more advanced and lethal equipment and with fresh troops, well-trained and ready to fight. The Allies needed their supply lines shortened and the Channel ports would give them that.

Antwerp was the main port that the Allies needed to capture and open as soon as possible. However, the main problem for the Allies to use the facilities there was that the sea approaches to the port, the Scheldt Estuary and Walcheren Island, were still in the hands of the Germans and would need to be cleared completely. It would take a monumental effort of time, men and materiel for the Allies to capture the approaches to Antwerp, clear them of German defenders, and get the port facilities up and running again.

That meant that, for their immediate purposes, the Channel ports needed to be cleared of German troops and operational for the Allies.

> Would be very grateful for your opinion on the likelihood of early capture of Boulogne. It looks as if port of Antwerp may be unusable for some time as Germans are holding islands at mouth of Scheldt. Immediate opening of some port north of Dieppe essential for rapid development of my plan and I want Boulogne badly. What do you think are the chances of getting it soon?[1]

This message, dated 6 September 1944, from Montgomery to Crerar indicates how strongly the Allies needed the Channel ports open. Montgomery believed he could get to Berlin quickly if he had the ports of Dieppe, Boulogne, Dunkirk, Calais and Le Havre available to him. This would give him the ability to bring across more materiel and troops from England to enable his planned move to Berlin. At the time of writing this message, however, none of the Channel ports were in operation for the Allies.

While the Allies were preparing to attack the German defences along both sides of the Scheldt Estuary and on Walcheren Island, top priority for Montgomery was the clearing of Boulogne. From there, his next priority was to capture Dunkirk and then the whole of the Ghent area. This was to be done by First Canadian Army. General Crerar flew to Montgomery's headquarters on 9 September for a conference where, among other items, the speedy capture of the Channel ports was discussed. Also in attendance were General Dempsey and General Hodges.

Later in the day, General Crerar sent a message to all of his corps commanders directing them to 'press on as quickly and as powerfully as the very favourable military situation urgently demands'.[2] His message included the following statement:

> 2 Cdn Corps has already been directed to proceed without delay, to capture Boulogne, Dunkirk and Calais preferably in that order, but without prejudice to the earlier and easier capture of anyone of them. If no weakness in the defences of these ports is discovered, and decisively exploited, in the course of operational reconnaissance – then a deliberate attack, with full fire support, will require to be staged, in each case.[3]

At the conference in Brussels on 10 September 1944, the importance of the capture and re-opening of Antwerp rose sharply as Eisenhower advised Montgomery of his desire to open Antwerp as quickly as he could. Aside from Operation MARKET GARDEN that had very high priority, opening up the port of Antwerp now had a higher official priority than it did before, especially regarding the planning by 21st Army Group. Some reports suggest that Eisenhower's sudden requirement for Antwerp to be open as soon as possible came from the meeting of the Combined Chiefs of Staff at

Quebec where Field Marshal Alan Francis Brooke (1st Viscount Alanbrooke) outlined the desire of the Chiefs to get Eisenhower to make every effort to open up Antwerp quickly. At the conference on 12 September, with the agreement of the Combined Chiefs, Brooke drafted a telegram that he sent to Eisenhower pointing out the 'necessity for the opening up of the north-west ports, particularly Antwerp and Rotterdam before bad weather sets in'.[4]

The stage, then, was set for the capture of the Channel ports. We have already seen the capture and liberation of Le Havre by the Allies under Operation ASTONIA, we will now concentrate on Operation WELLHIT, the capture of Boulogne.

On 5 September 1944, the 3rd Canadian Infantry Division had engaged with the German defences at Boulogne and it was determined by the Allies that the town had to be taken by a direct attack with heavy armour, artillery and air support. The reason for this was that the German defences at Boulogne were too strong for them to be attacked only by infantry. However, 'Bomber Command, the armoured carriers and a great force of artillery were all committed to the attack on Le Havre; and Boulogne could not be attacked until Le Havre fell and these resources were freed. From one fortress to the other was roughly 135 miles by road.'[5]

The divisional operational order from HQ 3rd Canadian Infantry Division sent out the following day outlined the difficulty the Allies would have in attacking the German defences at Boulogne and capturing the city and, of course, the much-needed port:

> Our advance on Boulogne from the south and south-east met increased resistance during afternoon and evening 5 Sep. It is apparent that enemy intends to make a stand of some sort in Boulogne area using well-prepared defence positions, including guns of heavy size, concrete emplacements and considerable numbers of automatic weapons ... Unconfirmed reports from civilians indicate a strong garrison is defending Boulogne.[6]

High hills dominated all the approaches to Boulogne on the landward side, which had been heavily fortified by the Germans. To the east, Mont Lambert rose to more than 550ft, while in the south, the feature known as Herquelingue was nearly as high.

Boulogne and its surrounding areas were heavily defended by the Germans. Mont Lambert, in the east, dominated the hills that ringed the town. The Germans had covered them with 'concrete forts, mutually supporting, with wire and very thick minefields.'[7] Within Boulogne itself the Germans had built many defensive fortifications and shut down the harbour, by covering it with more concrete defensive positions and lots of wire.[8]

Boulogne is situated at the mouth of the River Liane that forms the harbour for the town. The city is surrounded by high geographical features of varying kinds. To the north, about a mile from the town, half-way toward Wimereux lies Fort de la Crèche that sits on a feature 229ft high. The Germans had heavily fortified the Fort that now formed a significant part of the defences of Boulogne.

> Fort de la Crèche is a dominating feature to the north of this badly blitzed port. It stands on the coast a mile outside the town, just inland from the highway. Although most of its concrete is concealed, and it is thus not very impressive, its tactical importance is apparent for it is situated on an eminence which towers over Wimereux to the north, Boulogne itself to the south and the lower ground immediately inland. Mont Lambert is apparently less of a fort, but an even more dominating feature. It is a very high hill from the top of which all of Boulogne can be seen. Treeless, and covered only with scrub and gorse, it is furrowed with trenches and dotted with pillboxes. From the point where the road to Desvres passes over the top all the other roads to the north and south are easily dominated, and one can see almost as far as Gris Nez.[9]

Before the war, the area from Boulogne to Cap Gris Nez to Calais was already a French fortified area. Since their occupation the Germans had methodically and systematically improved the coastal defences to a point where, by the time the Allies began operations against the defences in September 1944, they were mutually supporting and interlocking. They had added radar installations, underground tunnels, strong reinforced-concrete gun emplacements, dugouts, minefields and wire entanglements on top of heavy earthworks. The Germans had also prepared all the bridges in the area to be blown up if attacked and added minefields into the mix, making it slow going for an attacker. Every approach to Boulogne from the south and the south-east was covered by these defences in one form or another.[10]

The slopes of Mount Lambert and Herquelingue were very steep and had been heavily fortified by the Germans with gun positions in open emplacements, pillboxes, trenches, weapons pits while in Mont Lambert, specifically, they created a system of underground tunnels that also had gun positions that could be pulled back into the tunnels away from detection from enemy eyes. The Germans planned that in the event of an Allied attack from the sea, the commander of the fortress could pull back to Mont Lambert and use the underground facilities as his headquarters from where he could continue to direct the battle. The Herquelingue slopes were also studded with concrete gun emplacements, some covered, some in the open. This feature also included pillboxes, trenches, shelters and several guns had been set up on the southern ridge to cover the road from Boulogne to Samer.[11]

Lieutenant General Ferdinand Heim, an experienced senior officer, commanded the garrison at Boulogne that had an overall strength of 10,000 troops. 'Its quality was not especially high, the 2,000 infantry consisting of a fortress machine-gun battalion and two fortress infantry battalions, all made up of low-category men.'[12] Indeed, Heim was a professional soldier having previously served in Poland and Russia. However, according to the interrogation report on him he claimed he had been arrested after serving in Russia and then was suddenly recalled to command the fortress at Boulogne. He arrived to take over his command in August 1944 about the same time that the only experienced infantry division at the fortress, 47th Infantry Division, was withdrawn a few weeks later. To replace this division Heim received two and a half machine-gun battalions who were inadequately trained and had been depleted due to their journey from Germany, where they were under constant Allied air attack.[13]

The German garrison at Boulogne was strong in artillery but many of its guns, including its 12in guns, were unable to fire landward. Their engineer and artillery equipment and personnel were from the 64the Infantry Division. Many of the dual-purpose 88mm anti-aircraft guns were present along with nine 15cm howitzers that were capable of firing into the landward side. Other than the 88s, there were few anti-tank guns.[14] As for the morale of the garrison troops they knew the war situation and 'it was clear to them from the first that they were a lost outpost. But to a certain extent the enormous strength of the defences behind which they stood compensated for the low morale of the garrison.'[15] It must be said that between 11 and 13 September, upwards of 8,000 civilians had been evacuated from the city. This took place under German orders with the Canadians setting up control points from which they could direct the evacuees to safety. 'All day on 13th Sep the road was lined with men and women "carrying with them such meagre possessions as they could carry without transport," for the refugees were denied even the use of wheel-barrows, hand-carts and bicycles.'[16]

The operation to take Boulogne was designed to be carried out in four phases. The main assault would come from the area around Mont Lambert in the east by the 8th and 9th Infantry Brigade Groups. This assault would be supported by heavy bombardment from the air and from artillery. Once this phase was completed both brigades were to proceed to the centre of the built-area, secure it and then capture the crossing of the Liane River before the Germans had a chance to blow up the bridges. Phase Three was to be the capture of German strongpoints and defensive positions around the area of Fort de la Crèche, Outreau and Herquelingue while the final phase was the capture of the high ground at St Etienne and Nocquet on the coast.

Intelligence was key to the planning stages of Operation WELLHIT and in this instance the intelligence the Allies received was instrumental in the success of the operation. Specifically, intelligence from the French Forces of the Interior (FFI), who were well-organised and well-trained, and provided the Allies with valuable information such as; German positions, minefields, roadblocks and other defences. They were used to identify places where Allied patrols could take place, while also providing excellent information on German positions and defences that could be woven into the Allied fire plan so they could be dealt with in the assault. FFI members even provided guides for the Allied columns as they rolled into Boulogne itself during the attack.

Prior to the assault, Lieutenant General Simonds, commanding 2nd Canadian Corps, received an influential guest in the form of Major General Sir Percy Hobart, originator of 'Hobart's Funnies' and commander of the British 79th Armoured Division. Simonds wanted several of the 'Funnies' for the assault on Boulogne. These were three squadrons of Flail tanks, two squadrons of AVREs and two squadrons of Crocodile tanks. It was Simonds' hope that the German defences at Boulogne could be softened up enough that a large-scale armoured operation with these specialty vehicles might not be needed.[17]

Early in September 1944, 79th Armoured Division received HQ 31st Armoured Brigade and placed it under its command. At the same time, units of 79th Armoured Division that would be involved in the assault on Boulogne were put under the command of Brigadier G.S. Knight. These units had only just finished fighting in Le Havre and had now been directed towards the imminent Allied attack on Boulogne.

The 3rd Canadian Division that had overall responsibility for the assault had command of two brigades that would take on the brunt of the fighting. They were; 8th Canadian Brigade and 9th Canadian Brigade. Both brigades were given the following units from 79th Armoured Division.

Formation	Crabs	Crocodiles	AVREs
8th Canadian Bde	C Sqdn 1Saint-Lothians & Border Yeomanry	41st RAC less B Sqdn	81st Assault Sqdn Royal Engineers
9th Canadian Bde	A Sqdn 1Saint-Lothians & Border Yeomanry	41st RAC less B Sqdn	87th Assault Sqdn RE

According to the reports, the idea for the assault on Boulogne, originating from Lieutenant General Simonds, 2nd Canadian Corps, was quite different to the normal order of battle. In fact, it was a complete reversal of the normal way of doing things.

> The infantry were to seize and hold a penetration through the 'crust', and the exploitation a further three miles into the centre of the town was to be carried out by three columns entirely armoured. Each column was commanded by a 79th Armoured Division Lieutenant-Colonel and consisted largely of 79th Armoured Division components.[18]

While the Allies built up their artillery they kept up a steady fire on German defences in and around Boulogne. To make the German gunners believe there were many more guns ranged against them than was the case, the Canadians used a technique called 'roving troops' where artillery guns and their crews would fire from one position, move as quickly as they could to another and fire from that position.

> The 'moving troop' trick was successful in deceiving the enemy gunners, as we know from the interrogation of the German artillery commander, who admitted that he had no idea how many guns were opposing him and that his observation post had been entirely unable to plot the whereabouts of our batteries.[19]

On 13 September 1944 General Urquhart, the army commander, wrote to Montgomery concerning the capture of Boulogne:

> While the rapid fall of Le Havre has favourable potential influences, it is most important that the effect so gained should not be more than lost by an unsuccessful attack on the next objective, Boulogne. I, therefore, want Simonds to button things up properly, taking a little more time, if necessary, in order to ensure a decisive assault.[20]

An excellent example of how high-ranking officers can make a major difference in getting things done quickly and correctly can be seen on 15 September when the question of bomber support was still up in the air. The day before, a meeting was to take place with representatives from Bomber Command but these individuals did not arrive. However, the following day, General Simonds 'his own Chief of Staff and General Crerar's, and the Senior Air Staff Officer of No 84 Group, flew to Headquarters Allied Expeditionary Force at Versailles and duly "buttoned up" the question of air support at both Boulogne and Calais'.[21] Despite the presence of two Air Vice Marshals the first set of discussions were not productive. Both of the RAF men, one of them from Bomber Command, did not want to commit any more than 300 to 400 heavy bombers for each port. They wanted to supplement the heavy bombers with as many medium bombers as they could.

With a stalemate beginning to form, the corps commander put his case to three Air Chief Marshals, Leigh Mallory, Tedder and Harris when they arrived for a separate meeting. They agreed without hesitation that in order for Boulogne and Calais to be captured quickly the full measure of air support should be given to both operations. The details were quickly worked out and Operation WELLHIT was set to begin on 17 September 1944.[22]

As far as the air campaign went, after Le Havre was captured the tactical air forces of the Allies began targeting German defensive positions in and around Boulogne. Before the ground assault began, fighter-bombers, medium bombers and rocket-firing Typhoons carried out forty-nine attacks mostly targeting German gun batteries. The results of these air operations were analysed by investigators from the 21st Army Group Operational Research Section who reported that:

> Air attacks before the assault had not done significant damage to infantry defences, and broken communication cables had often been relaid; although they may have lowered enemy morale, the effect does not seem to have been marked ...[23]

These gun positions were also hit by Allied artillery although 'ammunition shortages prevented heavy counter-battery fire before the actual day of the assault'.[24] The Allies brought up 328 artillery pieces to the operation to use against the German defensive positions and especially against the fortress within Boulogne and the surrounding area.

During this operation, Canadian gunners were joined by the divisional artillery of the 51st (Highland) Division and the 9th British Army Group Royal Artillery, both of which had been rapidly moved from Le Havre as that operation wound down. All of this artillery was there to support the 3rd Canadian Division that would carry out the ground assault. All of the artillery was coordinated by the artillery commander of 3rd Division, Brigadier P.A.S. Todd.[25] Within all the artillery regiments that made up the Allied artillery force there were four heavy regiments, each with six 7.2in howitzers and 155mm guns. 'Of all our guns, these great ordnance were the best for shattering the enemy's heavy concrete positions. Two heavy anti-aircraft regiments, 2nd Cdn HAA Regt and 60th HAA Regt RA, were deployed ready to operate in the ground role. Their principal task was to burst their 28lb shells in the air over the enemy gun pits.'[26]

Further artillery support came from an unexpected source – the large guns on the 'South Foreland east of Dover'. There were four huge guns that took part in the attack on Boulogne by shelling German cross-Channel gun batteries in the area of Cape Griz Nez and Calais. The idea was to ensure these German guns did not interfere with the Boulogne assault. There were two 14in guns code-named 'Winnie' and 'Pooh' manned by the Royal Marine Siege Regiment and two 15in guns of Royal Artillery's 540th Coast Regiment. The only way the gunners could aim their huge weapons was by air observation of their shells hitting the targets. On 17 September these four heavy artillery guns repeatedly smashed German gun battery positions and a direct hit was scored on one of the German 16in cross-Channel guns located near Sangatte.[27] This was at a range of over 23 miles. Interestingly, the 15in guns fired until their barrels were worn down and their shells could no longer reach the French coast.

The air attack began on 17 September at 0825hrs when the first wave of heavy bombers, Lancasters and Halifaxes, arrived over the city.

> Suddenly huge bursts of dust and smoke plumed out on the slopes of Mont Lambert ... Over the peak of Mont Lambert appeared a tight concentration of low [artillery] air bursts, designed to keep the flak crews there below ground ... A later wave of bombers, directed on the peak of the mount was preceded by a Pathfinder which dropped a white smoke marker. The arty seemed also to lay smoke here. A swarm of planes then materialised out of the sky as before, and once again huge clouds of smoke blotted out the shape of the hill-top.[28]

Supporting the heavy bombers was a counter-flak programme where the fire originally would be predicted and then corrected by Air Observation pilots flying in their Austers over the battlefield, directing the bombing runs of the heavies.

> Above at least three planes were in the air for practically the entire day. They reported twelve known and at least eight unknown Hostile Batteries [German Artillery Sites] as being active and observed thirty-four bombards on them. They were also the source of much general information.[29]

The city of Boulogne, specifically the German defences, was hit with 3,232 tons of bombs in this one attack of the operation. The total number of aircraft included 540 Lancasters, 212 Halifaxes and 40 Mosquitoes with only two aircraft lost. The bombing for this attack was very accurate according to RAF personnel situated on the start line for the ground assault witnessing the bombing, one of whom, an RAF Group Captain, was in contact with the Master Bomber aircraft. This close cooperation meant that the Allies could be sure that the white markers laid down by pathfinder aircraft were at the right places for the bombers to hit their targets.[30]

Yet despite the amount of explosives dropped on the Germans the results were not as effective as Allied planners hoped they would be. 'British operational researchers found that only a relatively small proportion of the enemy's guns had actually been destroyed or damaged. The extensive cratering impeded armoured vehicles supporting the ground attack.'[31]

One German soldier who had been in an underground bunker while the bombardment by the Allies was taking place later told his captors that the experience was like being at the bottom of a cocktail shaker.[32] Indeed, the Allied researchers who looked into the effects of the bombardment by air and artillery on the Germans noted that the targets that had been within the limits of the bombardment had been taken much faster and with greater ease by the ground forces. 'The bombing certainly gave, as always, a fillip to the spirits of our own infantry which was no small factor in their success.'[33]

For Operation WELLHIT, provision had been made for spectators of the battle, for an audience to watch as the bombs reigned down. Accordingly, instructions were issued on 15 September once it became known that a large number of navy, military, air force personnel and the press wanted to watch the battle. As such, a stand was set up 2km east of the town of Neufchatel that was outside of the heavy bombing zone and, therefore, relatively safe. This stand provided for an excellent observation platform of Boulogne and the surrounding area. However, the instructions to staff officers, and no doubt to the rest of the spectators, concluded with the usual disclaimer that the Allied force accepted no responsibility for those attending the spectacle within the divisional area.[34]

The ground assault began at 0955hrs, the moment after the last bomb had fallen on the first target, with the 8th Infantry Brigade (Canadian), under the command of Brigadier Blackader attacking on the right flank. On the left flank, Brigadier Rockingham's 9th Infantry Brigade (Canadian) began their attack with two columns – the Stormont, Dundas and Glengarry Highlanders and the North Nova Scotia Highlanders. However, around La Tresorerie and Wimille there were heavily defended German strongpoints that the Allies believed could hinder their assault so these were dealt with as quickly as possible. The Germans had placed three 12in guns on a hill at La Tresorerie that commanded a view overlooking Boulogne and its approaches. This position was attacked at 0925hrs by the North Shore (New Brunswick) Regiment but made slight progress due to encountering minefields. In fact, the North Shore 'did not clear all its objectives until 19 September. Nevertheless, it seems to have kept the Germans busy enough to prevent them from interfering with the main attack'.[35]

> The stream at Basse Cluse was crossed by a troop from 81st Squadron who used a fascine to make the crossing at 1100hrs. Four Crabs from C Squadron 1 Saint-Lothians & Border Yeomanry were lost when they flailed a lane through a minefield after crossing the stream under an artillery barrage. They were followed by infantry who reached their first objective. With one Flail left it began to widen the lane and blew up 20 mines making it the axis for 8th Canadian Brigade.
>
> On the right, the same stream was crossed near Denacre close to a demolished bridge enabling the infantry and Crabs to cross. At 1645hrs, another troop from C Squadron, having crossed the stream, had begun flailing through the same minefield and reached its objective. However, in this case, the Flails missed a mine that a Canadian Sherman tank rolled over so the lane that had been carved through the minefield was not used.[36]

The targets for the rest of 8th Brigade were the German defences between Mont Lambert and La Tresorerie, particularly the area around Marlborough and St Martin Boulogne. The Marlborough defences were attacked by Le Régiment de la Chaudière who also captured a radar station near Rupembert intact. By the time night fell, they had taken Marlborough and were preparing to move on from there. The German defenders at St Martin Boulogne were attacked in the morning by the Queen's Own Rifles of Canada who captured the railway station at 1100hrs and by evening were within a stone's throw of the Boulogne citadel. The biggest obstacles facing the troops of 8th Brigade throughout their assault were minefields and enemy shellfire, yet despite this they made steady progress. This was largely down to the special armoured support from 79th Armoured Division. The Flails were used to breach the minefields while the AVREs 'would fling their bombs from their petards, and some of the assaulting infantry were to be carried forward to their objectives in Kangaroos'.[37]

Kangaroo personnel carriers drove the infantry to La Cocherie where, with the support of two AVREs, they dismounted and began their assault. One troop of special armour from 87th Squadron supported the infantry that were attacking German positions on Mont Lambert. 'The AVREs advanced down the main road petarding houses and defended positions and one was knocked out, complete with crew.'[38]

Finally, the Crocodile flamethrower tanks were used to attack any German infantry holding out in pillboxes or other hardened positions. Oddly enough, these vehicles surprised the German garrison at Boulogne. They had not been in direct communication with their counterparts at Le Havre and so had no idea the role these Special Armoured vehicles had played in that garrison's downfall. The Allies, on the other hand, were fully aware of the importance of these specialty vehicles had played at Le Havre and used that knowledge in their planning of the assault on Boulogne.

9th Infantry Brigade began its assault on the Mont Lambert defences the moment the last bomb fell with the tanks of 10th Armoured Regiment (The Fort Garry Horse) (Canadian) leading the way. Behind the tanks came the infantry carried by Kangaroos and half-track armoured personnel carriers. Behind those vehicles, came the AVREs of 87th Assault Squadron RE along with Flail tanks that had also been provided for the assault. The Flails were to smash a path through the minefields but German counter artillery fire was so heavy these vulnerable vehicles were unable to do their jobs effectively. The Stormont Dundas & Glengary Highlanders (SD&G (Canadian)), led the main infantry assault along the main road from La Capelle in Kangaroo tracked armoured personnel carriers, moving as fast as was possible under the cover of a huge barrage of artillery fire that had been timed in stages in order to prolong the effects of the heavy bombing and reducing the effectiveness of German opposition.

> As they swept forward, a hail of small arms projectiles ricocheted from the armoured vehicles but failed to stop them. S.D.&G. rode forward until mines made further progress impossible; then the infantry leaped from the Kangaroos, and proceeded on foot. In 45 minutes, all objectives were captured.[39]

By this time, however, the German gunners situated on commanding positions on the close hills and the slopes of Mont Lambert began their own programme of heavy artillery fire as the Allies moved forward. However, despite the heavy artillery fire from the Germans the Canadian sappers of the 18th Field Company Royal Canadian Engineers cleared a path through the minefield that proved to be vital as the assault unfolded.[40]

There was a dominating slope of ground on Mont Lambert known by both sides as the 'Mont Lambert Feature'. Both the Germans and the Allies knew that this feature was the key to the defence of the Boulogne port. Indeed, General Heim, commander of the Boulogne garrison at the fortress/citadel knew that once the Allies took this sector of land defending the port, stopping their advance would be impossible for his forces. He later complained, after being captured and during his interrogation, that he had not had enough time to complete the defences because Operation WELLHIT began and he turned his attention to that.[41]

The North Nova Scotia Highlanders got as far as the minefields in their Kangaroos and after that they began the slog up the steep slopes on foot, hampered by heavy German machine-gun fire from pillboxes that had survived the bombardment. 'These were overcome with the help of AVREs and the hard ascent continued. Towards night Crocodiles and Flails were able to come up and the area was steadily cleared. By the day's end a great part of Mont Lambert was in our hands.'[42] Nevertheless, the Canadians fought hard, fierce battles for every step they made up the slope against many pillboxes with machine guns, slowly but surely taking each of them out. Flamethrowers and the petards of the AVREs were instrumental in destroying more than twenty pillboxes. The mud and scattered minefields on these slopes made the advance for the supporting tanks of 10th Canadian Armoured Regiment difficult, but they managed to keep going.

At the end of the first phase, three assault teams from 31st British Tank Brigade were tasked to drive into Boulogne, right into the heart of the city where they were to seize three important bridges over the river Liane. These teams were made up of troops of Flails, Crocodiles and half a troop of AVREs along with one platoon of Canadian infantry provided by the Glengarrians for two of the teams while the North Shore Regiment provided infantry for the third team.

This vital thrust to the river encountered great difficulties from our own bomb-craters as well as from enemy roadblocks. Craters were from 30 to 50 feet wide and 20 deep.[43]

In the late afternoon of the same day, the special armoured columns were ordered to move forward into the town itself with the objective of capturing and holding bridges over the River Liane. Commanding 1 Saint-Lothians & Border Yeomanry was Lieutenant-Colonel C.J.Y. Dallmeyer, D.S.O., T.D. who was also in charge of Column A of this advance of specialty armour. They set off at 1520hrs but the craters and piled rubble completely stymied their advance. Eight of the tanks managed to get to the citadel in the town but by nightfall none of them had actually reached the river or the bridges. However, in the darkness, a Crab and a Crocodile were lost in some of the large craters and the advance was ordered to stop for the night.

While Column A was now bogged down Column B had made good progress up until it reached the outskirts of Boulogne on the south-easterly main road. Commanded by Lieutenant-Colonel J.K. Shepheard, D.S.O., C.R.E. of 6th Assault Regiment RE column B had come up against huge craters made by the earlier heavy bombing. Tanks fell into these craters on both sides while accurate shelling from German artillery fire added to the confusion by also creating craters in the road. Shepheard was wounded when his tank was knocked out by German shellfire. After some flailing, the column was finally back on the move again having lost four tanks. The commander of the troop from 41st RAC, Lieutenant C.D. Gregory, jumped in a French taxi and lead the entire column down the city streets towards their objective. As they drove on they encountered little in the way of German resistance but many more craters making the going slow and difficult.

However, Column B reached the bridge it was supposed to capture by 1905hrs only to find that it had been destroyed by the Germans.[44]

Many of the advancing armoured vehicles were blinded by the dust from the heavy shelling and bombing as well as from the tracks of other vehicles floundered in the craters. The engineers tried to fill the giant holes with earth that had been blown out but because it was so pulverized the tanks couldn't get enough traction to move forward.

> With these obstacles confronting them, and much heavy enemy shell fire coming down upon them, it is not surprising that neither of the two armoured columns succeeded in reaching the bridges to which they were directed. Instead, they spent the night fighting in the streets of Boulogne, where they were joined by S.D.&G. Highrs, as one column besieged the Citadel.[45]

After some difficult driving, the two Glengarry infantry assault teams along with their armoured vehicles reached the Liane River early in the morning of the 18th only to discover that the Germans had blown up the three bridges that were their original objectives. The third team found the same situation.

> Thus, at the end of the first day, a considerable wedge had been driven into the enemy's fortifications in the Highland Brigade's sector, while in the 8th's good progress had been made. At the extreme north of the position, the North Shore Regiment had a foothold in the La Tresorerie strongpoint. All along the line, however, the operation had gone more slowly than the forecast.[46]

It appears from reports that the First Canadian Army planners assumed that Boulogne would be captured within a day, the 17th, and that the same troops that were to attack the city would be able to attack Calais on the 19th. This, of course, proved to be wildly optimistic.

Some reports indicate that more pre-arranged concentration of artillery shells had been fired by Allied gun batteries than had hitherto been fired in any one operation in Europe up to that time. This concentration and communication of effort between the gunners and the infantry went on throughout the first day and well into the night, yet it did not entirely silence the enemy guns. Reports from the gunners of 9th Canadian Infantry Brigade and 13th Canadian Field Regiment indicate that two factors were instrumental in the failure of the Allied artillery to silence the German guns despite the overwhelming artillery bombardment on the first day. The first was due to the use by the Allies of a two guns to one concentration – two Allied guns to one German. The second reason was that the Germans had constructed their gun positions out of very strong concrete as they had originally been designed for coastal defence. This meant that for any of the Allied artillery fire to have any effect the German guns had to have a direct hit for them to be put out of action 'as the crews apparently had good protection from our fire'.[47]

Great progress was made by the Allies on the 18th as they pushed forward with their assault on the German defences in and around Boulogne. The fighting was hard and gruelling. The Queen's Own Regiment of Canada took their objectives in Boulogne and then pushed north towards Fort de la Creche, which they eventually managed to take. The German gun positions at La Tresorrie were finally captured by the Allies using two assaulting companies. They finally captured all three concrete gun casemates along with other fortified observations posts all situated in the fort using PIATS (Projectors Infantry Anti-Tank),[48] smoke and phosphorous bombs. Meanwhile, the Chaudiere encountered heavy fighting as they pushed on to the Colonne de la Grande Armée. In the northern outskirts of Boulogne, the Queen's Own continued their advance while the North Nova Scotians finalized their capture of Mont Lambert.

> Mont Lambert was not yet fully in our hands, and the armoured columns, although the Citadel was besieged, had failed to secure the river crossings. Marlborough and St Martin-Boulogne were largely in our hands, but the heights to the north around Napoleon's monument were still in enemy tenancy.[49]

The Allies used the heavy bombing campaign as counter-battery fire yet despite the huge number of bombs dropped on German defences this campaign was not entirely successful.

> It had been hoped that the Heavy Bombing of Targets 2,3,4 and 5, west of the river, would render hostile batteries in this area inactive. In fact, however, Air Op's spotted batteries active even during the bombing (although presumably not in the actual target areas) and C.B. [carpet bombing?] was therefore carried out in this area during the bombing.[50]

Early in the morning of the second day of the battle, 18 September, 9th Canadian Infantry Brigade along with the S.D.&G. Highlanders were in the city of Boulogne itself, fighting the remaining Germans holding out in the market square and in the old Citadel.

Meanwhile, that same morning, Column A of the Specialty Armour continued their advance at 0630hrs to the Citadel where they stopped outside the high wall. This wall had only two gates and was peppered with machine-gun posts that brought down a great deal of fire on the infantry, forcing them to stop the advance. However, things changed quickly when Sergeant W. Grant of the Lothians, commanding a Sherman tank, opened fire on several positions along the wall, destroying four German gun posts.

While this was taking place, the remainder of the column moved into the market place itself where they joined up with Lieutenant Sloan of B Column. At this point, several Germans surrendered, coming out of their defensive positions with white flags. The force now split up, with some armour and infantry advancing towards the river while the rest of the armour turned for the main gate of the Citadel. Three mines were cleared from the gate which was blown by two AVREs. 'The two AVREs left to support the company pinned by machine gun fire, petarded the main gate and demolished the rails which blocked it. At this moment white flags appeared on the battlements and the Adjutant came out with 30 men to arrange surrender.'[51]

Mont Lambert, meanwhile, was now under attack by North Nova Scotia Highlanders who were clearing out the last of the German defenders dug into the mountain slopes. The following account taken from *Vanguard, The Fort Garry Horse in the Second World War* illustrates the way in which the German positions were captured by the Allies.

> The attack began at first light, with two columns surging forward through the ground haze. The left-hand column moved in on the South-east face of the feature, and the right column went over the summit and on down to Le Chemin Vert. In each case, tanks were in the lead, followed by AVREs and then infantry. Under the protecting fire of the tanks, the engineers were able to emplace 70lb charges in and around the enemy dugouts, and the infantry, following in closely, took out the prisoners. One by one the dugouts surrendered, and the commander of the mountain's garrison gave himself up by 1100hrs.[52]

The citadel in the centre of Boulogne, situated in the 'upper town', sat on a limestone hill and was surrounded by high walls. It overlooked the port – the prize the Allies were after. On the 18th, this citadel was captured by the Glengarrians supported by AVREs. The method of capture included modern and ancient ways of warfare. While the majority of the troops used modern methods of assault one resourceful Major, J.G. Stothart, found a tunnel that lead into the interior of the citadel. A local civilian showed him the entrance to it and he ordered a platoon to move quickly through it. Churchill tanks rolled forward to the walls of the citadel and began raking the ramparts with heavy machine gun fire (Besa) while the front gate was blown up. While this was taking place Stothart and his platoon were moving rapidly through the tunnel and popped up inside the citadel in the middle of the confusion, taking the German defenders completely by surprise. White flags were soon waving and more than 200 prisoners were taken by the Canadians.

One of the bridges had been repaired by the engineers by 0430hrs on the morning of the 19th, which meant that light traffic could now cross the river. This enabled the British Highland Light Infantry (HLI) to cross the Liane River and establish a bridgehead on the other side.

> The mess created by the enemy demolition was soon cleared up and the timber carted to the site. The biggest snag was that no one could find a hammer, saw, nails, or, in fact anything except one small hand-axe. The sappers didn't have them since they were an assault team with the infantry. It was out of the question to send back for them, so being good sappers, they set to work fitting the timbers together with good healthy air. The job was finished by 0415hrs on 19 Sep and tested by carefully driving a 5-cwt over it. Before dawn the transport of the battalion (including 3-ton lorries) was across the river.[53]

Regarding the units of 79th Armoured Division attached to the Canadians for the operation, early in the morning of 18 September reinforcements had arrived in the form of a company of infantry for Column B. Column B was part of the three-column attack on the German defences in the city itself using mostly Specialty Armour, from the 79th, to support the Canadian infantry. This enabled three groups of infantry and armour to set out early in the morning to round up more Germans and take them prisoner. Near Column C's bridge objective, Lieutenant Gregory attacked German transport vehicles and shot them up with machine gun and tank fire. That same day another group of Crocodiles captured more than 200 prisoners emerging from a tunnel. C Squadron, 1st Saint-Lothians & Border Yeomanry, commanded by Major R. de. C. Vigors, fired several HE rounds on a German artillery position at Chemin Vert, destroying it.

The same day, orders came through to B Column that they were to withdraw to reserve which they did at 1700hrs. However, on the way, they lost an AVRE to German fire but the crew managed to escape.

However, the Allies, particularly the infantry, ran into difficulty on Mont Lambert and their attack had stalled. Column C, commanded by Lieutenant-Colonel H. Waddell, 141st RAC, was ordered to provide armoured support to the beleaguered infantry. This all took place on 17 September. With the arrival of C Column, a new assault on the German defenders on Mont Lambert was quickly planned out to start at 0700hrs the following morning. It began with the German positions at Herquelinque being pounded by A Squadron 1st Saint-Lothians & Border Yeomanry while the rest of the Column drove hard on the defensive positions on the steep slopes of Mont Lambert. This assault was made up of two teams each with a Crab, two Crocodiles, three AVREs, two troops of tanks and a company of infantry (Canadian). 'The Churchills go up with difficulty but the Shermans took an hour longer. There was little opposition by now, only a few stray shells from Boulogne, and the position was a "field day" for the AVREs and Crocodiles.'[54]

> Four AVREs under Captain A. Richie, RE, went up the slope to the last massive stronghold, fired their Petards and out came the Germans. Another pillbox received salvoes from six Petards and more Germans appeared. By 1100 hours Mont Lambert surrendered: General Heim, the Garrison Commander, had withdrawn to Le Portel.[55]

At 1700hrs on the 18th the German position at Le Chemin Vert also surrendered. An hour later, Column C began a slow laborious drive through the streets of Boulogne, carefully dodging the craters in the road and the rubble strewn everywhere. They were heading towards the bridge that was their main objective but at this point had no idea if it had been destroyed by the Germans. On the way to this target the armoured vehicles of Column C captured fifty prisoners, destroyed a German 105mm gun and a machine gun nest. Sergeant James, A Squadron, 1st Saint-Lothians fired a 75mm round from his Sherman tank at a house that forced fifty Germans to surrender. However, just before the bridge at the main crossroads Lieutenant K. Macksey of 141st RAC had his Churchill tank hit by shells from a German anti-tank gun, forcing it to stop. As this tank was the pilot tank for the entire column it was decided to stop the column's advance until the following morning.

The next morning, Column C arrived at its designated target, which was supposed to be a bridge but realizing that it was gone they turned their attention on the nearby sugar factory on the other side of the river where there were still several German infantry and artillery positions. This action of switching to the sugar factory now brought down heavy German fire on Column C. The day before Lieutenant Macksey had been taken prisoner by the Germans and he was now on the opposite side of the river in the sugar factory with this group of Germans. However, at 1200hrs the Germans surrendered, apparently with a good deal of encouragement from Lieutenant Macksey. Upwards of 300 Germans surrendered at this time. Macksey must have persuaded the officer in command that resistance was futile. With the capture of so many prisoners and the position no longer a threat to the Allies, Column C was ordered into reserve.[56]

By this time, Canadian infantry had managed to cross the river on armoured vehicles and tanks brought up during the night for this purpose. Sherman Crab tanks followed and attacked German positions in Outreau. West of this village a gun position was attacked by the infantry, supported by two troops of 87th Assault Squadron RE from a distance, owing to the heavy proximity of mines. Although one AVRE was hit and incapacitated, the crew managed to bail out safely.[57]

The infantry now attacked German positions at Honriville and were supported by an armoured force of two Shermans, two Crocodiles, two AVREs and a Crab (Flail). This force was under the command of Captain M. Crickmay RE who had 'commanded the advance guard of column "A" with great skill'.[58] They set out at 1545hrs on the 19th driving through a built-up area before reaching the position where the infantry attacked German blockhouses and a gun position. As with most of the other roads and tracks the armour faced, the road they were on was also full of craters, rubble and large pot holes. One of the Crocodiles almost immediately ditched in a large bomb crater while under heavy fire from the German guns. The crew of the second Crocodile managed to get their winches and cables out in an effort to free the first Crocodile but their trailer was hit and burst into flames. Each of the Crocodile flamethrowers towed a trailer full of fuel for the flamethrower weapon.

Captain Crickmay, using the Petard gun on his AVRE, fired several rounds at the German blockhouses, hitting two and destroying them. At the same time, the Crabs began to Flail the area and managed to clear 20 yards, blowing up four mines. A few minutes later Crickmay's AVRE received two direct hits and he was killed. Lieutenant P.S. Newman, 1 Saint-Lothian & Border Yeomanry, commanding the Crabs, ordered the entire force to withdraw. All of the ditched tanks were recovered during the night, except for the first AVRE, by the light from the burning trailer and most of the crews got back to the withdrawal line. These actions marked the end of the second phase of Operation WELLHIT.

North of the port, the 8th Brigade continued hammering German defences there while the stubborn German strongpoints in the south received the full force of the 9th Brigade attack. The 19th also saw the HLI break out from its bridgehead on the Liane River under heavy German fire.[59]

> 'Murderous fire came from all directions which was heavier than the battalion has yet experienced.' It had 64 casualties and four supporting Flails were knocked out. The Glengarrians took up the struggle in the afternoon with the help of tanks, AVREs and Wasps [flamethrower-armed Universal Carriers]. They seized the village of Outreau after extricating themselves from a minefield and captured many prisoners.[60]

The HLI reached their objective at 1030hrs that was just north of Le Portel where they took upwards of 500 German prisoners. Later in the mid-afternoon, the Battalion attacked German positions a kilometre north-east of Le Portel at Honriville. Joining this attack was the S.D.&G Highlanders who were to pass through the HLI bridgehead and mount an assault on German gun positions at Turbinghem along with further positions at Outreau then push east where they were to capture two sugar factories near Liane. Once through the bridgehead they began their attack at 1600hrs.

On a hill about 250ft high, situated between Outreau and the sea the Germans had placed a battery of six 88mm and four 20mm guns, a position known by the Allies as 'Buttercup'. For the Allied assault on Boulogne to succeed and for the port to be opened this position needed to be dealt with quickly. The attack on this position began on the 19th with a very heavy concentration of Allied artillery fire.

> The target had been allotted one medium concentration and four field 'stonks' ... The result was magnificent surprise. The infantry, following the fire closely, swarmed over the hill with bayonets and grenades before the last rounds had fallen. At no time were they more than 250 yards from the bursts. The nearest position was overrun and its three 88s taken intact; the troops rushed for the other three but these were blown up. The action resulted in the taking of 185 prisoners, but during it Major Stothard's only two remaining officers were wounded. It was now nearly dark and the company consolidated its position and remained on the hill all night.[61]

More than 800 bombs fell on this target and yet just one German 88mm and two 20mm guns were hit. More than 2,000 rounds were fired by the German 88mm guns before the Allies managed to silence them as they swarmed over the hill.

The next phase of Operation WELLHIT was the destruction of the German defenders on the Outreau Peninsula. This operation was handled by the North Nova Scotia Highlanders supported by the machine gun Regiment, The Cameron Highlanders of Ottawa (M.G.). The Germans were dug in on the top of a high hill at Herquelingue which the Camerons successfully destroyed on the night of 18/19 September. However, on the lower slopes of the hill some 400 German soldiers were hidden in underground passages while the Camerons remained in the casemates they'd just captured on the summit. The 20th saw the North Nova Scotias advance when suddenly they came under heavy fire from the hidden Germans. However, several Canadian tanks poured heavy fire onto these German positions and they were forced to surrender the following day.[62]

The Allies knew that the heavy bombing of these German positions had little effect and once they managed to overrun them they found the casemates connected by underground tunnels, each with diesel and electric generators providing these tunnels and casemates with heating and power. The Germans dug in here were mostly naval troops and were very comfortable. 'Perhaps because of the superior facilities of their quarters they looked cleaner and more soldierly than the usual prisoners. Their ammunition supply was in no way depleted. There was an ample stock of food, which might have lasted three months. The battery also possessed a dug-in, well equipped hospital.'[63]

Elsewhere, along the coast of the Outreau Peninsula the North Nova Scotias continued their advance, capturing the village of St Etienne, then mopped up the remaining Germans at Nocquet, Ningles and Le Portel.

> As night fell on the 19th of September 1944, Boulogne was cleared of German defenders. Yet, in the North, the Germans holding Wimille still held out against the Allied assault. Once the Crocodiles were brought up and they hit the positions with fire, the Germans at Wimille surrendered. The following day, Wimereux also fell to the Allies.
>
> The area of factories across the river which led to the docks saw heavy fighting. Bulldozers were in constant demand to push the rubble into the bomb craters enabling the armour to move much more swiftly on their targets and not ditch.[64]

While this was taking place the last of the German defences on the northern outskirts of Boulogne were under attack from the 8th Infantry Brigade. The main German strongpoints were Wimille, Fort de la Crèche and Wimereux. With their work on the Outreau Peninsula finished the North Nova Scotias attacked Wimille and ran across heavy German resistance. However, they managed to overcome the defenders and the following morning captured the village, taking many prisoners. At this point the Allies were now running into some of the best troops of the Boulogne garrison that slowed their advance.

In this area, the defences at Fort de la Crèche were probably the strongest so the Canadians decided to attack Wimereux first. They dropped smoke on the Germans at Fort de la Crèche then attacked the town. Due to the number of civilians in Wimereux the North Shore did not deploy heavy bombardment against it. The Allies used one field Regiment of artillery and some captured light German guns to support the infantry as they slowly moved into the eastern side of the town. A German machine gun position at the railway station was taken out by a battery from 3rd Anti-Tank Regiment RCA. Since the Germans had placed most of the heavy guns in Wimereux to face towards the sea, the Canadians were able to capture the town on the 22nd without suffering many casualties.

September 22nd was the sixth day of the battle for Boulogne and by early morning the only German positions left were Fort de la Crèche plus both the forts at Le Portel and a few small positions holding out in Wimereux itself. The night of the 21st and 22nd saw the Allies move up their tanks and M10 self-propelled guns very close to Fort de la Crèche and train their guns on the Fort. When dawn arrived, the defenders must have been dismayed to see the 75mm guns of the M10s pointing at them ready to fire. Five hundred men of the German garrison at Fort de la Crèche surrendered at 1045hrs. The whole of Wimereux had also been liberated, the remaining German holdouts having been mopped up and surrendered as well. That left just Le Portel that had yet to be taken.

> Le Portel, the core of the whole defence, was assaulted that afternoon. Two teams of Crabs, AVREs, and Crocodiles stood ready to reduce the Northern fort, and another team led by Lieutenant R.W. Grundy, 141 RAC, went into action against the Southern fort. Before a shot was fired, a white flag was spotted and Lieutenant Grundy came back carrying Lieutenant General Heim, the Garrison Commander, who surrendered to the 3rd Canadian Divisional Commander at 1630hrs.[65]

Brigadier Rockingham, commanding 9th Canadian Infantry Brigade, trying to avoid further bloodshed, sent an ultimatum to Lieutenant General Heim. Essentially, the ultimatum laid out the facts for Heim. It stated that the Germans had lost Boulogne, that the Allies, mostly Canadians, had taken more than 7,000 prisoners and that all of the defences in the area had been neutralized or had surrendered. Rockingham stated that the north and south forts of Le Portel were the last holdouts. These positions were now completely surrounded.

The ultimatum continued by stating that if Heim surrendered neither side would take any more casualties, however if Heim decided to keep holding out then Rockingham stated 'we will attack you with every means at our disposal, during which time we will incur some casualties but there is no way of assessing how many you will incur'.[66] He then gave the German general one hour to decide.

Ten minutes prior to the expiration of the ultimatum at 1255hrs German defenders were seen coming out of the northern fort at Le Portel, their hands up, white flags flying while walking over to the HLI positions where they surrendered. However, the southern fort, where General Heim was, remained firing intermittently at the Allied positions.

Using loudspeakers set up on scout cars, the Allies continued sending the ultimatum, telling the German defenders in the south fort that time had run out, that holding out was useless. From the fort itself the remaining Germans could see the soldiers of 9th Brigade and 10th Armoured Regiment tanks preparing for an assault on their position. But just as they were ready to attack, from the southern German strongpoint came the white flag. 'General Heim surrendered to Brigadier Rockingham at 4.30 p.m. and the last fighting ceased after the German commander sent a cease-fire order to a detachment isolated on the harbour mole, which had fought a single 88mm gun to the bitter end.'[67]

WELLHIT had taken the Allies six days to subdue and capture all of the defences in and around Boulogne, especially the harbour and the Outreau Peninsula. They took 9,535 prisoners of which more than 250 were wounded. Canadian and Allied casualties during the entire operation amounted to 634 killed, wounded and missing. 'The enemy force had been only a little smaller than that at Le Havre, and the two Canadian brigades engaged against it had lost more men than the two British divisions that took the larger city.'[68]

They were fortunate that the German defenders' will to fight was not stronger otherwise the Canadian casualties could have been much higher. Indeed, the one thing that analysts stated after the operation was that the German artillery caused most of the problems for the Allies and most of the Canadian losses. This might have been because the destruction of German artillery batteries at Boulogne was less effective than at Le Havre. There are some reasons for this. First the effort by Bomber Command was not as heavy as it had been at Le Havre. Second, there was an ammunition shortage that prevented really heavy artillery bombardment on German positions prior to the actual day the assault began. Another reason might be because the Canadians used light concentrations of artillery, two guns to one and also because the German construction of their gun batteries was exceptionally strong and would have required much heavier and longer bombardments to be destroyed. An example of this would be the gun battery south of the harbour at Honville consisting of six German 88mm guns. Allied artillery fired more than 5,700 rounds in a circle that was 300 yards in diameter but it was not enough to silence the German position and they were able to keep firing until they were physically overrun. Another factor was the Canadian Artillery Intelligence, or the lack of it. 'Our hostile battery lists before the operation contained some dummy positions, on which bombs and shells were wasted, while some actual batteries were omitted. Eight previously unknown batteries were reported in action on 17 September.'[69]

During his interrogation, General Heim gave his impressions of the battle. He

> was most impressed by the tactics of attack and the close co-operation of all arms to rout out position after position. The ability of the artillery to lay down a curtain of fire and smoke under which infantry and tanks crept until the strongpoint was reached was most effective. These timed barrages enabled the Canadians to be at their objective at the very moment the artillery fire lifted and as a result when the German came out of his bunker he was immediately faced by Canadian infantry and tanks.[70]

Interestingly, Heim had not been told about the loudspeaker work mounted by the Canadians as propaganda.

> He did know however that a number of small strongpoints had disappeared without a trace on the first day or two of the assault. He enquired of his interrogators whether they could explain these mysterious abductions and he was rather surprised to find that words, and not bullets, had caused them to surrender.[71]

There is no doubt in this author's mind that 79th Armoured Division's contribution to the assault on Boulogne and its subsequent success was substantial. The cratering from heavy bombing was one of the main reasons why it took much longer than had originally been planned for the city and port to be captured. However, the assault team technique used in the capture of Boulogne, and its employment in a variety of ways, proved to be a success, one that the Germans were unable to counter. 'Boulogne with its harbour was a valuable prize to the Allies and its capture a fine chapter in the history of the 79th Armoured Division.'[72]

However, not all reports on the liberation of Boulogne agree with the above statement. The Allies were suffering a logistical nightmare and it would take them some time to repair and open the port of Boulogne. As a result, their immediate logistical problem wasn't altogether fixed with the capture of Boulogne. The Germans had extensively damaged the harbour installations through demolition while bombing for the operation had also caused considerable damage. 'Several ships had been sunk across the harbour mouth, most of the cranes had been destroyed and the locks damaged. Consequently, the port could not be used until 12 October, and there was no immediate alleviation of the Allied supply problem.'[73]

That meant that now the Allies would have to take Calais next in the hope that its facilities could be quickly brought on line.

Chapter 9

Operation UNDERGO: Calais Liberated

Operation UNDERGO, the operation to liberate Calais, was next on the list for the Allies in terms of clearing the Channel ports. Montgomery's initial plan that the port at Antwerp be taken as soon as possible at the expense of operations against Calais and Dunkirk was later revised so that Calais and the naval guns at Cap Gris Nez were captured as quickly as possible 'lest otherwise their great guns might prevent the free use of the port of Boulogne'.[1]

3rd Canadian Infantry Division had responsibility for Calais and Cap Gris Nez along with Boulogne. On 4 and 5 September 7th Canadian Recce Regiment ran into the Calais defences as they headed up the coast away from Boulogne. Their job was to cut the escape routes in the north for the Germans, which they did. At midday on 5 September, B Squadron cut the main Boulogne–Calais road from the high ground near Marquise. At the same time, the German garrison at Calais was contained by A Squadron while the coast road from Calais to Dunkirk was cut by C Squadron, thus completing the encirclement of the German defenders at Calais.[2]

> This was predominantly a Canadian Infantry operation. However, 79th Armoured Division played an important role in helping the Canadians to capture Calais and the Cape. At the end of the Cape were two gun batteries one at Haringzelles (four 11 inch guns) and the other at Framzelles [Fraemezelle] (15 inch guns). Both of these were protected by a ring of 88mm and 75mm gun emplacements in concrete and in front of them was a belt of mines. Elsewhere on Cap Gris Nez at Onglevert was another German defensive position with two 75mm guns and several machine guns all situated in concrete emplacements. These guns faced inward, towards land rather than towards the sea as the much larger guns did.[3]

This screen around Calais set up by the Allies was a thin one and needed to be strengthened, with the defences, especially the naval gun batteries, at

Cap Gris Nez being sealed off. To do this 7th Canadian Infantry Brigade was sent from Boulogne to the high ground south-west of Calais that forms a T-shaped feature.[4] That is, the length or cross of the T runs from Mount de la Louve, 4km south-west of Calais, north to Noires Mottes,[5] parallel to the coast. The shaft of the T runs inland down to Mont Fiennes south of Calais by 12km. Supporting the infantry was a squadron of tanks from 10th Canadian Armoured Regiment, 12th Canadian Field Regiment for artillery, a battery of anti-tank guns and the necessary supporting services. Two key tasks had been assigned to 7th Canadian Recce Regiment – destroy any enemy in the areas east and west of Calais trying to get out of the ring the Allies had set up and to protect the eastern flank.

By 6 September the HQ of 7th Canadian Infantry Brigade was set up at Moyecques at 1515hrs. With this done, the Brigade began reconnaissance and patrolling operations in the surrounding country, 'which bore a striking resemblance to the rolling chalk downs of England where the battalions had trained for so long'.[6]

Allied patrolling was aggressive, as seen on the night of 9 September when the Regina Rifles occupied Wissant, a seaside resort that effectively cut off the German positions at Cap Gris Nez from Calais. Wissant was 6km east of the Cap and, to the surprise of the Rifles, they found the town full of civilians going about their daily lives with businesses and shops open. In order to thicken up the Allied forces in the area, elements from 2nd Canadian Infantry Division were tasked to move to the eastern and south-eastern approaches to Calais from 10 September. This gave the Canadian troops a bit of breathing space especially as another squadron from 7th Canadian Recce Regiment had recently deployed into the area to thicken up the assaulting forces.

With the increase in troop numbers and the aggressive patrolling and reconnaissance operations, intelligence from the locals began to pour in. The Regina Rifles reported that a German U-boat was sitting off Cap Gris Nez while Polish prisoners, freed as the Allies moved forward, told of an impending German counter-attack.

A new set of orders were given to 7th Canadian Infantry Brigade around this time. They were, essentially, to attack the Germans at Cap Gris Nez/Audresselles and drive them into the sea as well as clear them from Mont de la Louve.[7] To achieve this, a three-phase attack was planned that included support from a squadron of Flails, a squadron of AVREs and a squadron of regular tanks. 12th Canadian Field Regiment was to provide artillery firepower along with three other medium artillery regiments. From the Brigade HQ a command group was sent to Marquise arriving on the evening of 12 September. The following day, the attack began as the advancing troops moved in on Cap Gris Nez while the Germans began pounding them with as many heavy guns as they could muster. The Canadians suffered some casualties from this shelling.[8]

One of the first actions carried out by elements of 79th Armoured Division, tanks from A Squadron 1 Saint-Lothians & Border Yeomanry, was at Onglevert. This position was destroyed before the main assault began on the heavy German guns at Framezelles and Haringzelles. It began early on 13 September when tanks from A Squadron rolled up to within 5,000 yards of the German gun positions and opened fire with 75mm HE rounds. Shell after shell pounded the area, destroying the guns, hitting an ammunition dump that blew up and burned for six hours. In all, the tanks fired 550 rounds into the German stronghold and took 25 prisoners.[9]

As with the other operations, units from 79th Armoured Division had been put under the command of 31st Armoured Brigade and then allotted to each of the Canadian Brigades as follows:

Formation	Crabs	Crocodiles	AVREs
7th Brigade	C Squadron, 22nd Dragoons B Squadron, 1st Saint-Lothians & Border Yeomanry	A Squadron, 141st RAC	81st Assault Squadron RE
8th Brigade	C Squadron, 1st Saint-Lothians & Border Yeomanry	Two Troops from C Squadron, 141st RAC	One Troop 284th Assault Squadron RE
9th Brigade	B & C Squadrons, 1st Saint-Lothians & Border Yeomanry (after 16 September)	Two Troops from C Squadron, 141st RAC	284th Assault Squadron RE (after 29 September)

This operation against German defensive positions on Cap Gris Nez was designed to clear the peninsula and push the Germans into their strongpoints at the end of the peninsula so their backs were to the sea. The Allies created a ring around the Germans stretching from Ambleteuse to Mont de la Louve, north to Tardinghen on the coast. Though it was thinly held, patrolling and reconnaissance continued as aggressively as before with the intention of denying the Germans any useful ground as well as probing their defences. On 17 September 1944, when the main attack was launched against German positions at Boulogne, further assaults on the peninsula defences found that the main battery of German heavy 38cm guns were encased in very thick reinforced concrete. This included the pillboxes defending the gun positions. Some estimates suggested that the concrete was up to 20ft thick! This meant that the chances of destroying the guns would only be possible by a heavy direct hit from either bombing or artillery. It would likely need to be an infantry attack. The German defenders in these positions had high morale because of the size of their guns and the strength of their positions. Nevertheless, the commander of the Royal Winnipeg Rifles sent an ultimatum to the German commander 'to surrender or be blown into the sea, but secure behind his wire, mines and concrete, that haughty German scornfully rejected it'.[10]

With the rest of the peninsula cleared, the remaining Germans were now trapped in their strongholds at the very end of it. At this point a decision was taken by the Allied command to hold the Germans there in order to prepare as many troops as possible for the assault on Calais. To keep an eye on the Germans a squadron of 7th Canadian Recce Regiment was sent to relieve the battalion already there who then were sent to take part in the upcoming attack on the city of Calais.

Intelligence reports from a variety of reliable sources enabled the Allies to build up an excellent picture of the German fortress and defences at Calais. These defences were formidable indeed and it was clear that it would take a major effort for the city to be captured and the port put back into operation for the Allied cause. Unlike Boulogne that was surrounded by high hills that the Germans had heavily fortified, Calais' defences were based on marsh ground and water obstacles.

> A ridge running into the town west of the flooded area offered the only dry approach to the city, but this feature was commanded by the defences of the great Noires Mottes battery of four 40.6cm coastal guns, and by other strong positions at Sangatte and Vieux Coquettes.[11]

To the east and south of Calais, the low ground in that area was covered by several strong artillery and infantry positions the Germans had built on both sides of the Calais/Gravelines and Calais/St Omer roads. The city of Calais was a natural defensive strongpoint having been built by the French on a series of islands that were joined by canals and dykes making the defences 'more formidable by weapon positions whose fire could mow down anyone rash enough to try to cross the waterways'.[12]

Details of the defences in and around Calais indicated that they consisted of six principal areas, which were; Noires Mottes, Belle Vue Ridge, Vieux Coquelles, les Baraques, the city of Calais itself and the eastern and south-eastern approaches to the city. The battery of four big guns at Noires Mottes had been built in concrete casemates and were surrounded by wire and mines. Surrounding the fortress were a variety of shelters, anti-aircraft and light guns, pillboxes with machine guns along with infantry strongholds. 'The whole formed a solid bristling mass of wire, guns and mines, stretching two kilometres along the coast north-east from Escalles, with a depth inland almost as great.'[13]

Also forming a major part of the Calais defences was the ridge running east from Belle Vue, which was covered by two large railway guns, several machine-gun nests and wire. At Vieux Coquelles, along the Boulogne/Calais road, was a heavily armoured strongpoint facing the south-east that included machine-gun posts, anti-aircraft machine guns and several of the 88mm guns plus infantry and artillery positions. Behind this position was another defensive strongpoint at les Baraques, some 2km north, consisting of coastal defence guns and mines, and infantry, anti-aircraft and anti-tank positions along the roads from Calais to Ostend, and Calais to St Omer covered the south-eastern and eastern approaches.[14]

As for Calais's defences centred around the old citadel, these were made up of infantry, anti-tank guns and machine guns in pillboxes plus heavy guns in concrete casemates that had been built on the islands. This, along with the canals and dykes, made the entire Calais defences a very hard nut to crack for the Allies.

However, perhaps one of the key saving graces for the Allies was the poor calibre of the commanding officer of the Calais garrison, Lieutenant Colonel Ludwig Schroeder, as outlined in some reports. Indeed, in his Special Interrogation Report, conducted after his capture, the Allied examiners had a poor impression of him. They stated that he appeared to be a 'mediocre' and 'accidental' leader and that he was assigned to the role of garrison commander not because of any particular skills or abilities he had but because he was available at the time.[15]

The report goes on to state that during his interrogation Schroeder said he had little faith in the men under him, especially the conglomeration of fortress troops, harbour technicians, home-guards and sailors. Morale was terrible, he had no confidence in his officers and he believed his troops would likely fall for Allied propaganda as most of his troops were either foreign volunteers or *Volkdeutsche* (Germans who had lived in other countries).[16]

After several delays, a divisional order for the operation to capture Calais and the surrounding areas was issued on 22 September calling for an attack by two brigade groups. Both groups were to be supported by air bombardment, artillery bombardment and armour attacks. The task of attacking and/or capturing or destroying the garrison, including the areas of Noires Mottes, Bellevue, Coquelles and Calais, fell to 7th Canadian Infantry Brigade. For attacking and destroying the German defences in the Escalles area, that task fell to 8th Canadian Infantry Brigade. Once all the mopping up had been done in the Boulogne area, 9th Canadian Infantry Brigade was to drive to Calais to relieve the units at Cap Gris Nez where they were to either capture or completely destroy the German garrison there.

As far as the air bombardment went the German defences at Calais were to feel the same effect as those in Boulogne did: heavy smashing, battering destruction. This part of the plan was considered to be an integral part of the operation.[17] At this stage, the Allies decided to carry out an experiment. They selected five targets for the bombing campaign that lay between Sangatte and Calais. Zero Hour was to be marked when the last bomb hit the first two targets. Half an hour later the next target would be hammered for an hour with the last two getting 15 minutes of pounding every half an hour. 'What the Allies wanted to do was minimize the cratering destruction from the bombing so the bombs for target 4 were to be fused so that the target was hit by the blast effect so that the cratering could be reduced.'[18]

As far as artillery was concerned the Canadians decided to use the same guns and battery troops as they had at Boulogne. 'As soon as Boulogne was conquered, the artillery moved by two main routes to deploy where it could engage Calais.'[19] By 23 September, the guns that had been involved in Boulogne had completed the trip to Calais and were now within range to begin the heavy bombardment of the German artillery batteries; twenty-one in all, starting from Zero Hour minus 73 minutes to Zero Hour minus 35 minutes. Each of the German batteries were engaged using a concentration of fifteen guns to their one.[20] Within the fire plan there was provision for heavy anti-aircraft guns to deal with their German counterparts. Also, on hand, were Air Observation Posts in the small Auster aircraft that would fly over the battlefield and direct Allied fire onto those German batteries that were still active. Typhoon fighters firing rocket projectiles were also part of the plan as they were to direct their rockets onto German artillery batteries as well.[21]

> The comforting snorting and grinding of the armoured devices of 79 Armd Div would be heard again, for Flails, AVRE, Crocodiles and Kangaroos were all coming to Calais, as at her sister ports, to clear the minefields, flame and batter the strongpoints, and protect the infantry, according to their various natures.[22]

6th Assault Regiment RE provided a Regiment and a squadron of Flail tanks along with all of its AVREs, which, for this operation were put under the command of 3rd Canadian Infantry Division, less one squadron of Crocodiles.[23] In terms of armoured support, 8th Canadian Infantry Brigade were supported by a squadron of Shermans from 10th Canadian Armoured Regiment, a squadron of Crocodiles and a troop of Flails plus two troops of AVREs. Supporting 7th Canadian Infantry Brigade were two squadrons of Flails, one squadron of Crocodiles, all the Kangaroos and two squadrons of the AVREs.

The actual day of Zero Hour for the attack on Calais had been postponed several times because of the time it took to capture and defeat the Germans holding Boulogne. Once that operation had finally ended and the troops and materiel were available for the assault on Calais, Zero Hour was set at 1000hrs 25 September.

Prior to this, the air campaign against Calais began with RAF heavy bombers attacking the German defences in the area with incendiary and phosphorus bombs as the diarist for 7th Canadian Infantry Brigade reports:

> Air Force dropping phosphorus bombs on north-east portion of Calais. There appears to be large balls of fire shooting skyward not anti-aircraft. Heavy smoke over northern part of Calais. One fire burning at harbour entrance. Four planes have crashed.[24]

In fact, eight aircraft went down, mostly due to anti-aircraft fire from German batteries in the Escalles area. This was largely because 7th Canadian Infantry Brigade had not yet had time to set up its anti-flak programme and because the heavy bombers flew over this area as they turned out to sea to head back to England. In essence, they were sitting ducks for German anti-aircraft fire. 'This was most unfortunate for then it was too late to tee up our artillery to fire on Gerry ack-ack defences, or as we say, Pancake them. As a result, we lost eight Lancasters.'[25]

The ground assault for Operation UNDERGO[26] began on 25 September 1944 at 0815hrs with the bombardment by artillery and aircraft. The first ground units began moving forward as the last bomb fell on the first two targets at 1015hrs – 'infantry supported by Flails, Crocodiles and AVREs'.[27] 8th Canadian Infantry Brigade on the left flank crossed the start line as planned. The French Canadians of the Regiment de Chaud, left of the main body of the attacking brigade, moved quickly towards the high ground north of Escalles where, relying on the effect of the bombing and artillery shelling, they moved forward on foot on ground that no armour could manage to climb because it was too steep.

Right of the Brigade's front, the North Shore Regiment pushed their assault uphill towards the German defensive positions situated on the Brigade's right flank. Right of the North Shore Regiment, now engaged with the Germans, Sherman tanks, twenty Flail tanks, seven Crocodiles and six AVREs managed to join up with the battalion. 'The armoured vehicles made it through the enemy's wire and minefields in three lanes, which were checked and marked by Canadian sappers.'[28]

> The first objective for the Canadians of 7th Brigade was the German defensive position at Chateau Pigache. For the special armour units, operations started when B Squadron 1 Saint-Lothians & Border Yeomanry began flailing at 1130hrs. As the Crabs drew closer to their objective flailing the ground in front of them, they found no mines. However, once they did reach their objective they were met with white flags as the Germans at that position surrendered. The Lothians stayed on their objective until the Infantry arrived at 1300hrs. At that point B Squadron moved on to take part in operations elsewhere.

Left of the Lothians, the infantry began attacking German positions at Belle Vue. C Squadron, 22nd Dragoons, however, stuck at Peuplingue, were constantly under fire from artillery and machine guns. On the ridge short of the Belle Vue strongpoint, the infantry had become bogged down and called for support from the tanks. This came from the tanks of A Squadron 141st RAC who fired on the German position – a heavily fortified fort. When the fort fell and the Germans surrendered the Allies discovered many dead and wounded inside. AVREs of 81st Squadron, supported infantry in an attack on German pillboxes east of the fort, destroyed five of these pillboxes before becoming held up by yet another German pillbox. To break the stalemate, two Crocodiles rolled up and shot their flames into the pillbox and in an underground dump both of which burst into flames, the pillbox was left burning. 'Further advance was impossible as the road had a sheer drop on one side and cliff face on the other.'[29]

The German stronghold at Belle Vue was taken at 1730hrs by C Squadron 22nd Dragoons who, after flailing a lane towards the German position, found no mines. This allowed the infantry to pass through without issue and attack the strongpoint. The same took place for the German HQ at Le Grand Cour where the Crabs, Crocodiles and AVREs poured fire onto the German position. By 2000hrs the position had been cleared and prisoners taken.[30]

At Noires Mottes the Allied infantry managed to tear up the high ground without running into much in the way of German resistance, but once they reached the crest they discovered to their cost that the downward slope was covered by German 20mm and heavy machine-gun fire. Unfortunately, there was little the AVREs and Crocodile tanks could do in the way of providing support, no matter how hard they tried, as they moved over the badly cratered ground.

However, the four 16in guns at Noire Mottes proved to be a difficult task for 8th Brigade. The big guns, set in concrete. were surrounded by machine guns, AA guns, mines, wire, a naturally steep slope and the anti-tank ditch.

Crabs of 'C' Squadron, 1 Lothians & Border Yeomanry, led the way up from the re-entrant to the South. Two troops flailed a narrow lane, under fire support from the rest of the Squadron and Canadian tanks, between the craters and almost to the position itself.[31]

West of here there were fewer craters, so Captain E March led a third troop towards the German positions. In this case, the Flails blew up thirty-five mines and cleared a lane through the minefield and cut through two double wire fences enabling the infantry to move forwards, followed by other specialty armour such as Crabs, AVREs and some Crocodiles. Once through, they attacked and took the German defensive positions in the area.

Yet the rest of the area, the hill and the slope, still proved to be difficult for the Allies to take. The slope itself was constantly under fire from those landward facing guns at Cap Gris Nez and from Calais. Tank fire from the Shermans, unable to hit these big guns because they were out of range, managed to take out an 88mm gun that the Germans had put on the beach that was causing a lot of grief.[32]

As an example of just how difficult taking this position was for the Allies, Captain March had a mixed armour force before he started off down the very steep slope. On the way down his AVRE, which was leading the rest of the force, fell over the edge of a German blockhouse dug in on the side of the slope after he had gone 200 yards. Because of the heavy shelling from the guns at Cap Gris Nez, the craters on the slope were large and very numerous. One Crocodile fell into a crater and managed to get free only to have its trailer blow up on a mine. Although the trailer was gone, the tank itself was fine but wouldn't start. During the night, Lieutenant I. W. Sutherland Sherriff, 141st RAC raided a German position, stole some batteries and managed to get the Crocodile started.

> After the second Crocodile had its trailer hit four times and the third had lost four bogies from direct hits, the advance petered out. After a wet night the position surrendered to the infantry.[33]

Elsewhere, R de Chaud were in the process of clearing the Germans from their defensive positions, having taken 278 prisoners at a loss of three dead and nine wounded.[34]

Meanwhile, 7th Canadian Infantry Brigade, in position east of the 8th Brigade, crossed the start line accompanied by the Regina Rifles on the left and Royal Winnipeg Rifles on the right, each heavily supported by a variety of specialized armour. Infantry from the Regina Rifles along with the armour were quickly on their objectives at Coquelle where they subdued German defences and took several prisoners. As the Regina Rifles pushed forward they ran into much tougher German opposition but, with the support of the armour, Flails, AVREs and Crocodiles, they were on the Belle Vue strongpoint by 1545hrs. Coming to the assistance of the Reginas was the 1st Canadian Scottish Regiment who had been held in reserve and were initially directed to attack Calais. Once they'd arrived in position to help the Reginas, the Scots dismounted from their Kangaroos and joined in the assault on the German stronghold. From there they moved forward towards the coast. By nightfall, all the Allied units were directed to consolidate their positions and prepare to continue the assault the following day.

> Infantry from 8th Brigade began to move along the coast road with two Crocodiles, some Canadian armour, and a Command Churchill in tow for support on the 26th. They were greeted with 20mm fire and heavy machine gun fire from German positions forcing the Sherman tanks to withdraw when they reached Ferme Tournant. However, the infantry pushed on, supported by two Crocodiles. They managed to pass a minefield without incident and when they reached the dunes at Ferme Oyez, the Crocodiles flamed the German positions there. Captain J.L. Hall, 141st RAC, the troop leader, carried out a recce on foot for workable route to Ferme Trouille. Once he found it he ordered the Crocodiles to move forward and flamed the German positions enabling the infantry to move forward and take them out. German guns, however, shelled them throughout the day until darkness fell.[35]

Elements of 8th Brigade, on the left flank of 7th Brigade, attacked the German defences in the Escalles and Sangatte areas and managed to take out both places. Indeed, at 0900hrs on 26 September, the German commander of the Sangatte battery indicated he would surrender at noon, which he duly did. By noon, the North Shore Regiment were busy rounding up the German commander and the 280 men under his command. 'This ended all organized enemy resistance in the western end of the Calais defences.'[36]

Heavy rain hampered movement for the Allies on the evening of the 25th but by the morning of the 26th the weather had started to clear which enabled 7th Canadian Infantry Brigade to swing right towards Calais, seize the town of Sangatte completely along with a section of the Sangatte/Calais coastal road.

> With effective support from our artillery, the battalion advanced in spite of enemy shelling. Leading elements pressed eastward along the coast to a point due north of Coquelles, meeting considerable resistance. After our guns had pounded the area ahead, two companies went forward again at 1520hrs with tanks, Crocodiles and AVREs and made some progress before being slowed down by demolitions, mines and booby-traps.[37]

Progress for the infantry was slow as the only way they could move forward and take out the German defenders was by house to house fighting, clearing out each slit trench they encountered, destroying every strongpoint as well.

The Allies, in the form of 7th Canadian Infantry Brigade, made great progress during this period against the substantial German defences of Calais. In a little more than a day and a half they had managed to push the Germans back to their inner defences and had taken prisoner 28 officers and 1,525 other ranks. Gradually, the assault on Calais was to become an operation by 7th Canadian Infantry Brigade almost exclusively. At the Escalles Feature, the Germans were completely cleared by 8th Canadian Infantry Brigade who, having completed their immediate tasks, were withdrawn so that they could be used as a reserve should they be needed.[38] Throughout the day of 26 September, while these operations were taking place, the Canadians were supported by rocket-firing Typhoon fighters and heavy bombers pounding German defensive positions.

In the evening, new orders came in to HQ 7th Infantry for operations that night and the following day. These were issued by Brigadier J.S. Spragge and included directions to the Canadian Scottish Regiment to push along the sea front attacking and destroying German strongpoints along the way with the view of breaking through the German defences at northern Calais. The old Fort Nieulay, situated on the western outskirts of Calais, was to be taken by Royal Winnipeg Rifles, who, once the fort was in their hands, were to force a crossing over the canal and enter the city. The Regina Rifles were to attack in the south and enter Calais from that direction. Sadly, these operations did not make the desired progress and so a decision was taken to hammer the western approaches to Calais by heavy bombers which was hoped would soften up the defenders enough that the city could be penetrated relatively quickly. As a result of this decision, on the night of 26 September, 2nd Canadian Corps requested heavy bombers to pound the western approaches to Calais, which they did, and by early morning of the 27th the Allies were two kilometres from the outskirts of the city.[39]

> The infantry attacked German positions at Fort Lapin and Captain Hall, in his Churchill tank, (Crocodile) led the rest of the Canadian Shermans towards the area where they could give the infantry much needed fire support. The Germans, however, laid down heavy fire but the infantry managed to take the positions.[40]

On the morning of 28 September, RAF heavy bombers began hammering the German defences on the western outskirts of Calais from 0830hrs to 1105hrs. Counter flak fire from Allied gunners shelling the German anti-aircraft positions kept them from causing serious harm to the bombers. Although one was shot down most of the crew were seen to have parachuted to safety. Even while the bombing and shelling were taking place, Allied infantry units, supported by armour, continued their advance into Calais. Along the coast road troops from the Canadian Scottish fought hard towards Fort Lapin but they were held up by heavy German machine-gun fire. This fire was coming from pillboxes that had been built into the walls of the fort. The Canadians called in the RAF Typhoons that minutes later roared in low, pounding the fort and surrounding areas with rockets. Once that was over, the supporting tanks began their work hammering the pillboxes with tank fire. It was only after the Crocodile tanks moved up and flamed the German defenders that they surrendered and the Fort was taken. The Royal Winnipeg Rifles faced a similar situation where they ran into heavy resistance as they tried to take Fort Nieulay, which they managed to do. 'The flamethrowers once again were the final argument which convinced the garrison to surrender.'[41] Elsewhere, the Regina Rifles had managed to reach the factories in the southern part of Calais. For the Germans, the noose was tightening.

Operations on the following day began with more heavy bombing of German defensive positions, this time east and north of Calais. The bombing

The British Army in North-west Europe 1944–5
Churchill tanks and a bridgelayer of 34th Tank Brigade during the assault on Le Havre, 13 September 1944. (No. 5 Army Film & Photographic Unit, Sergeant Wilkes, IWM, Wikimedia Commons, Released)

The Campaign in North-west Europe 1944–5
A Churchill AVRE advances in support of an assault on the German garrison at Le Havre, 10 September 1944. (Sergeant Collins, No. 5 Army Film & Photographic Unit, IWM, Wikimedia Commons, Released)

The British Army in North-west Europe 1944–5
Churchill tank crews of 34th Tank Brigade watch the RAF bombing the defences of Le Havre, 10 September 1944. (No. 5 Army Film & Photographic Unit, Sergeant Wilkes, IWM, Wikimedia Commons, Released)

British Tanks and AFVs in North-west Europe 1944–5
Churchill tanks and infantry in action during the assault on Le Havre by Canadian 1st Corps, 10 September 1944. (No. 5 Army Film & Photographic Unit, IWM, Wikimedia Commons, Released)

British Tanks and AFVs in North-west Europe 1944–5
Churchill tanks of 7th Royal Tank Regiment form up for the assault on Le Havre by Canadian 1st Corps, 10 September 1944. (No. 5 Army Film & Photographic Unit, IWM, Wikimedia Commons, Released)

Flails in Action
A Churchill tank leads a troop of Sherman Flail tanks of the specialized British 79th Armoured Division during the assault on Boulogne, September 1944. (IWM Wikimedia Commons, Released)

German prisoners marching through Boulogne after its liberation by the Allies. (Crown copyright, Archives of Canada 136333, Wikimedia Commons, Public Domain)

Aerial View of Dunkirk
Dunkirk was one of the last German outposts to surrender. Note signs painted on the roofs of some buildings by Allied prisoners of war to show their location to Allied aircraft. (Flying Office W. Moss Royal Air Force official photographer, IWM CL 2620, Wikimedia Commons, Released)

British Tanks and AFVs in North-west Europe 1944–5
Churchill tanks of 7th Royal Tank Regiment advance during the assault on Le Havre by Canadian 1st Corps, 10 September 1944. (No. 5 Army Film & Photographic Unit, IWM BU 1193, Wikimedia Commons, Released)

British Tanks in North-west Europe 1944–5
A Churchill tank of 'B' Squadron, 107th Regiment Royal Armoured Corps, 34th Tank Brigade, Odon Valley, Normandy, 17 July 1944. (No. 5 Army Film & Photographic Unit, IWM B7639, Wikimedia Commons, Released)

The British Army in Normandy 1944
An RAF Typhoon landing at a forward airstrip, as supply lorries pass in the foreground, 26 July 1944. (No. 5 Army Film & Photographic Unit, IWM B8146, Wikimedia Commons, Released)

The British Army in North-west Europe 1944–5
British and German troops man a checkpoint at Dunkirk during a truce to allow refugees to enter British lines, 4 October 1944. (Captain E.G. Malindine, No.5 Army Film & Photographic Unit, IWM B10500, Wikimedia Commons, Released)

Bombardier C. Bailey of the 5th Duke of Wellington Regiment (600th Regt RA) sets out on a 'recce' patrol in the Dunkirk perimeter, 3 March 1945. Photo: Sergeant Hewitt, No.5 Army Film & Photographic Unit, IWM B15109, Wikimedia Commons, Released.

The British Army in the Normandy Campaign 1944
Churchill AVREs of 79th Armoured Division moving into Caen, 10 July 1944. (Sergeant Christie, No. 5 Army Film & Photographic Unit, IWM B6901, Wikimedia Commons, Released)

The British Army in the United Kingdom 1939–45 Churchill Crocodile flamethrower tank, 79th Armoured Division, 13 February 1944. Photo: Sergeant Brown, War Office Official Photographer, No. 5 Army Film & Photographic Unit, IWM H35809 Wikimedia Commons, Released.

The British Army in the United Kingdom 1939-45;
Churchill AVRE laying carpet from a bobbin, 79th Armoured Division experimental trials, 26 April 1944. (Sergeant J. Mapham, War Office official photographer, No. 5 Army Film & Photographic Unit, IWM H37860 Wikimedia Commons, Released)

The British Army in the United Kingdom 1939–45
Sherman Crab Flail tank under test, 79th Armoured Division, 27 April 1944. (Sergeant J. Mapham, War Office official photographer, No. 5 Army Film & Photographic Unit, IWM H37860 Wikimedia Commons, Released)

The tank–harbour area near Boulogne, 1944
Two Sherman tanks are pictured on a beach with the tide out. In the distance, are two more Shermans, next to an army truck. (C.A. Russell, IWM LD5562, Wikimedia Commons, Released)

Britain's Coastal Defences 1939-45
'Winnie', one of two 14in guns emplaced at St Margaret's near Dover, 10 March 1941. 'Winnie', and its sister gun 'Pooh', came from the reserve stock of guns for the 'King George V' class of battleships, and were mounted on modified naval barbettes. Named for the Prime Minister, 'Winnie' was in place by August 1940 and 'Pooh' in February 1941. Manned by Royal Marine gunners, they were mostly employed in counterbattery fire with German batteries on the French coast. (Mr Puttnam, War Office official photographer, IWM H7918, Wikimedia Commons, Released)

Royal Air Force – 2nd Tactical Air Force, 1943–5
Squadron Leader K.K. Majumdar of 268 Squadron RAF waits in the cockpit of his Hawker Typhoon FR Mark 1B for the take-off signal at Fort Rouge in France, autumn 1944. (Pilot Officer T. Lea, RAF official photographer, IWM CL 1176, Wikimedia Commons, Released)

Royal Air Force – 2nd Tactical Air Force, 1943–5
A road near Chambois, south-east of Trun, Normandy, filled with wrecked vehicles and the bodies of retreating German soldiers following an attack by Hawker Typhoons of 83 Group. (Flying Officer N.S. Clark, RAF official photographer, IWM CL910, Wikimedia Commons, Released)

Royal Air Force – 2nd Tactical Air Force, 1943–5
Airmen of No. 419 Repair and Salvage Unit, aided by an AEC mobile crane, remove a damaged Hawker Typhoon Mark IB, MN413 'I8-T', of 440 Squadron RCAF from the landing strip, following a wheels-up landing at Lantheuil, Normandy, on 1 August 1944. (Pilot Officer R.R. Broom, RAF official photographer, IWM CL652, Wikimedia Commons, Released)

Royal Air Force – 2nd Tactical Air Force, 1943–5
The aftermath of an attack by Hawker Typhoons of 121 Wing on German armoured vehicles which had massed at Roncey, south-east of Coutances, Normandy, to counter-attack American forces on 29 July 1944. The wrecked vehicles include a Panzer IV tank and two SdKfz 251 half-track armoured personnel carriers. (Flying Officer N.S. Clark, RAF official photographer, IWM CL631, Wikimedia Commons, Released)

Royal Air Force – 2nd Tactical Air Force, 1943–5
Clouds of dust are raised as a Hawker Typhoon Mark IB, MN529 'BR-N' of 184 Squadron RAF, takes to the air from Bazenville, Normandy for another sortie against German ground targets. Under its wings are rocket projectiles that caused so much havoc for the Germans. (Flying Officer A. Goodchild, RAF official photographer, IWM CL147, Wikimedia Commons, Released)

Operation UNDERGO
This photo by RAF Bomber Command shows Cap Gris Nez before Operation UNDERGO on 26 September 1944. The main guns sited here would be either captured or destroyed during this operation. (RAF Bomber Command, Wikimedia Commons, Released)

Canadian armour moves into position for an attack on German troops south of Caen, France
The vehicles shown are British Armoured Recovery Vehicle conversion of Sherman IIIs (M4A2), REME, 79th Armoured Division, summer 1944. Note large winch pulley on front glacis plate and specialized storage on hull sides. (Library and Archives Canada, ID 4233174, Wikimedia Commons, Released)

Aircraft of the RAF 1939–5 – Hawker Typhoon
Ready for another sortie over France, Hawker Typhoon 1B, MN304 'FJ-N' of 164 Squadron RAF, runs up its engines in preparation for take-off at Thorney Island, Hampshire. (Flying Officer B. Bridge, RAF official photographer, IWM CH13344, Wikimedia Commons, Released)

The British Army in North-West Europe 1944–5
Sherman and Stuart tanks of the Guards Armoured Division advance towards the German positions at Arras on 1 September 1944. This image is an example of the way the Allies advanced into France and towards the Channel ports. (Sergeant Hewitt, No. 5 Army Film & Photographic Unit, IWM BU270, Wikimedia Commons, Released)

Operation TRACTABLE
Pictured are vehicles of 3rd Canadian Division advancing on German positions at Bretteville-le-Rabet towards Falaise to cut off the German retreat, 14 August 1944. (Library and Archives of Canada ID3396206, Wikimedia Commons, Released)

went on from 0900hrs to 0955hrs and was very successful. Forward elements of Canadian Scottish reported several bunkers in the Fort Lapin area still held German troops who were putting up resistance. They were soon dealt with.

> During the night 27/28 Sep, two companies had succeeded in crossing the canal along the western perimeter of the city – near the citadel – by boat, by swimming, or even by pulling themselves across on ropes. These intrepid souls were, however, cut off by a belt of enemy fire; their radio batteries began to fail, and they found themselves without food or water. There they remained, unable to dislodge the Germans, and unable to withdraw themselves.[42]

Elsewhere, the Winnipeg Rifles had managed to reach Greviere on the Calais/Marquise road, while the Regina Rifles had fought their way into the southern outskirts, reaching the railway junction beside the canal. The Regina Rifles then began preparations to cross the canal and push into the city during the night. These preparations were completed by 1830hrs and the Rifles were poised to attack the Germans in the city when a message came from Lieutenant Colonel Schroeder, the German commander of the garrison, asking for a truce.

At Andres, a detachment of Civil Affairs from 2nd Canadian Corps received a communication from the Germans on 28 September that they were ready to surrender, or at least to consider it. A meeting was duly set up and a message was sent back to the German commander, Lieutenant Colonel Schroeder outlining the conditions for the meeting. These were: 1) that General Spry, the Canadian commander, was prepared to meet Schroeder the following morning at Pont sans Pareil at 1100hrs German time. 2) Once the Germans had received the message and agreed to it they were to stop all German fire and the Allies would then stop all fire against the Germans. 3) Schroeder was to travel to the meeting in a car bearing a white flag and everyone in that car would have their personal safety guaranteed and 4) The Germans would need to make early acknowledgement of the arrangement so that the Allies could give all units time to be aware of the meeting and to cease hostilities.

The Germans agreed, and so on 29 September at 1100hrs German time, the meeting took place. On the Allied side, General Spry and his aides met with four officers from the German side, that included Lieutenant Colonel

Schroeder. However, the original message that indicated the Germans were ready to surrender turned out to be wrong. Instead, they wanted Calais to be declared an open city claiming that the civilians were suffering from the constant attacks by the Allies as well as a shortage of water and food. At the time, there were 20,000 civilians and so a truce was agreed to take place on 30 September to end at 1200hrs. The truce would allow time for the civilians to be evacuated from Calais.

Once the meeting between the two sides was finished, General Spry issued orders that an attack on Calais was to take place once the truce ended. After a two-hour preliminary air bombardment immediately after the truce ended, the first phase of the attack was to begin at 1400hrs on 30 September. The ground assault was to begin after German defences in the city had been hammered by medium bombers, then by rocket-firing Typhoons for a two-hour period. After this, the Queen's Own Rifles of Canada (Q.O.R. of C.) were to attack the eastern bank of the perimeter canal using infantry and medium machine guns supported by various armoured vehicles such as AVREs, Crocodiles and Flail tanks. 7th Canadian Infantry Brigade were to take advantage of this attack in the east by any means necessary, while 7th Canadian Recce Regiment were to get as close to the German defences and overwhelm them as much as they could with the help of the Cameron Highlanders of Ottawa (CH of O).[43] The entire phase was to be supported by artillery guns whose effort was to add to the confusion and smoke from the incendiary bombs, by firing smoke shells and air-burst HE shells. The plan for artillery was that each of the regiments would be given a specific target area that they would sweep with artillery fire as well as search for additional targets for 55 minutes starting at 1300hrs.

The second phase was to be the main assault on the German garrison at Calais with the aim to completely destroy it. Zero hour for this attack was to be at first light on 1 October 1944. In support of this main assault would be the same level of artillery and air bombardment as with the first phase.

The divisional order for the final Allied destruction of the German garrison at Calais stated that the assaulting forces were: to engage only 'enemy weapons firing at our own troops and engage any active enemy patrols,' also to ensure that 'regrouping which would have taken place if NO armistice declared may be made as required' and that the Allies 'must NOT be first to fire before 1200 hours'.[44] 9th Canadian Infantry Brigade facing German positions on Cap Gris Nez were not affected by these instructions.

The operation to destroy the German long-range guns on Cap Gris Nez was a separate operation to the main assault on Calais.

> The value of Calais as a port for 21st Army Group was not the essential issue, but the Cap Gris Nez batteries could dominate the harbour of Boulogne and effectively render the movement of shipping in the Straits precarious.[45]

Reports written shortly after the war indicate that the German troops in this area were largely naval troops numbering approximately 1,100. However, the morale of these men was intertwined with their belief in the invincibility of the concrete casemates their guns and pillboxes had been built into. At Haringzelles there were four very large cross-Channel 38cm guns that had a range of 45,000 yards and fired seaward. The remainder of the batteries on Cap Gris Nez were located at Floringzelle. These were made up of four 28cm guns at the Grosser Kurfürst Battery, each with a 360-degree field of fire with a 45,000-yard range, three 17cm guns at the Battery Gris Nez with a 24,600-yard range situated near the lighthouse with a wide field of fire and three 15cm guns at the Battery Wissant, fixed to fire out to sea. 'All were encased in reinforced concrete and steel casemates similar in design to those at Boulogne and impervious to any but a direct hit.'[46] Supporting these guns were several 20mm AA guns, anti-tank ditches, machine guns, pillboxes, minefields and wire.

For this operation, 9th Canadian Infantry Brigade was to relieve the 7th Canadian Recce Regiment who had been facing the German garrison here since 22 September. Their task was to either destroy or capture intact the big guns on Cap Gris Nez. To do this, the North Nova Scotia Highlanders (Nth NS Highrs) and the Royal Hamilton Light Infantry of Canada (RHLI of C) were to be deployed, supported by engineers and specialty armour of AVREs, Crocodiles and Flails. On the left flank, the Nth NS Highrs were to attack the heavy gun positions at Haringzelles along with the control station at Cran aux Oeufs and either destroy them or capture them. On the right, the RHLI were to take the Floringzelle fort and its gun positions, as well as the strongpoint at the lighthouse.

According to reports, the fire plan for the heavy bombers and artillery support was comprehensive. The artillery was to pound German positions and strongpoints in the area 10 minutes before the ground assault began and end ten minutes after zero hour. From that point onwards the Allied field guns of 14th Canadian Field Regiment, were to remain on call to lay down fire on targets of opportunity identified by the advancing ground troops. The medium and heavy guns were to continue firing for an additional hour.

Also part of this attack, were the heavy Royal Artillery guns on the Dover coast. They were to fire on the German heavy guns and one battery:

> ... at St Margarets' Bay, Kent on 19 Sep engaged the gun positions at Floringzelle, firing a total of 68 rounds which damaged three of these seriously. The fourth suffered only slightly. A British officer in an air O.P. directed this fire, and when his plane was fired upon by anti-aircraft guns, turned his attention to these and had the satisfaction of silencing six of them. Eventually their worn condition forced the Dover guns to cease fire, but there is no doubt that by thus drawing the fire of the Cap Gris Nez batteries, they materially reduced our own casualties.[47]

On 28 September the bombing campaign began with the arrival of the heavy bombers over the area at 1800hrs. This went on until 1925hrs. Over the days prior to this attack the same German positions had been receiving a lot of attention from the RAF heavy bombers. For example, 26 September saw 2,808 tons of HE dropped on the region. Any German strongpoints that remained defiant were to be hammered with rockets from the rocket-firing Typhoons.[48]

The ground around Cap Gris Nez rose from sea level to a ridge 328ft high, which provided for a division on the Cap south and east of the German defences. On each battalion front was a stream on the seaward slopes. At the lighthouse, the Germans had built their defences on a 50ft high promontory. The weather in the days preceding the assault had been fairly dry but rather than make things easier it made the craters and minefields more difficult to cross than softer ground. Bridges that the Allies would need to cross were still intact at the time of the assault and one of those bridges was large enough to take tanks. The actual area of the attack that led to the gun batteries, pillboxes, machine gun posts and the fort was relatively flat and devoid of woods, providing little in the way of natural cover. However, both assaulting forces on both flanks were able to form up under the cover of woods well behind the start line. At Moscau Farm, the RHLI formed up well hidden from the Germans and the Highlanders managed to form up on a wooded slope between Andresselle and Onglevert.⁴⁹

The attack began on the morning of 29 September with clear weather and the artillery fire plan began at first light. It was already underway when the assaulting troops moved off at 0645hrs. The heavy bombing campaign was also under way by this time with more than 198 heavy bombers taking part. They dropped a total of 837 tons of HE plus 18 tons of incendiary bombs, however, the roads were so badly cratered due to the bombing that the tanks had to take to the fields or get bogged down in the craters.

> This was particularly the case on the Nth N.S. Highrs front. D Coy Nth N.S. Highrs had to make a slight detour as AVREs with fascines advanced first to bridge the anti-tank ditch. The company moved northwards to the road running west from Onglevert, where it was held up for a short time by machine-gun fire from a pillbox on the north flank. This obstacle was quickly flamed out by a Crocodile and the company was able to reach the northern-most gun.⁵⁰

North-west of this action and on the right, B Company had advanced across a bridge meeting little in the way of German resistance. However, the supporting armour, Flails and Crocodiles either got bogged down or lost their tracks after driving over mines. Despite this, the one remaining gun in this position was finally dealt with by an AVRE that managed to breach the minefields and get close enough to fire its petard shells through the slits of the gun positions and this, along with hand grenades thrown in by the infantry on foot, persuaded the German troops still standing to surrender. C Company had followed the same route as D Company, and now attacked the control tower at Cran aux Oeufs against minimal German opposition. However, to achieve this, two minefields had to be breached and one by one the Flail tanks were taken out until that last one managed to get the entire company onto its objective safely. For the Highlanders, the entire operation lasted until 1030hrs when they were able to form up and concentrate their forces in the Ambleteuse area.⁵¹

At Floringzelle, the attack by the RHLI was going well. They too ran into little opposition from the Germans. A Company tore across country but were slowed by mines and obstacles that seemed to be their only real trouble.

Despite this, they were able to quickly clear out all the German defences northwards up to Le Chatelet. Following an inter-battalion boundary west to Audinghen, B Company attacked Franzelle and quickly mopped up German defences there, with the troops in all the gun positions quickly surrendering. The first part of the RHLI advance was finished by 1000hrs and what was left of the German defenders moved into the strongpoint at the lighthouse where they dug in. This momentarily halted the Allied plan until 1500hrs when the Canadians attacked the Germans at the lighthouse. By the time night fell a report from B Company stated that this area was now clear of the German defenders.

> The whole action on Gris Nez lasted but a few hours, and our casualties were very light, - three officers and 39 men, of whom five were killed. We took as prisoners 26 officers and over 1,500 other ranks, all of whom declared that they did not know what was happening.[52]

With the guns at Cap Gris Nez now silenced, the Allies could use the port at Boulogne safely without the worry of shelling from German guns. This operation meant that Allied shipping could now safely use the Strait of Dover and as soon as the approaches to Antwerp were clear, would be able to use that port as well.

The 29th saw the Specialty Armour in action again when the German position at Haringzelles was attacked. Here, two fascine crossings were made by AVREs of 28th Assault Squadron RE over the River du Noirde. This action paved the way for the Crabs of C Squadron 1st Saint-Lothians to get across the river and Flail two lanes through the minefield leading to the position. While this was taking place, other Crabs used their guns in the fire support role and once the lanes had been cleared a troop of Crocodiles began moving down both of them. Two Crocodiles were lost in the left lane but a third managed to get through and it flamed the German position. 'Although flame could not be poured into the gun turrets, crews came out as soon as they realized that the minefield was breached and their expectation of life poor.'[53]

In the right lane, the Crocodiles flamed German anti-tank positions, convincing them to surrender. They then poured HE rounds into the fort at Cran-aux-Oeufs. Crabs led the infantry down the hill towards the Germans but all the Crabs except one got bogged down along the way. More Crabs and

Shermans tried another way to get to the fort, but they were all disabled by mines, or hit with German shellfire. Yet, the infantry was able to put their attack in and take the fort.

At 0645hrs, the Allies attacked German defensive positions at Framezelle with Captain E.C. Pattenden RE leading a troop of AVREs along the Tardinghen/Onglevert road. To get to the gun positions they were attacking meant that the troop had to cross two streams and climb the slope that was mined and heavily cratered. The going was slow and difficult. Three AVREs were bogged down while the remaining three managed to get them out. A decision was taken to slowly wind through the mines and push through the double fences. Pattenden lead the way and when his AVRE was in range he opened fire. 'The AVRE behind him broke its track but two more AVREs under Lieutenant D.K.R. Lawson RE made a second path and deployed to the right to cope with pillboxes. These surrendered but Lieutenant Lawson was wounded.'[54]

Captain Pattenden managed to get to No 4 gun and place charges around it but before he could finish the Germans surrendered. Immediately afterwards, the Germans of No 1 gun also came out, white flag flying.

By this time, there was one German position near the lighthouse that was still active. The Crabs, Shermans and some self-propelled guns (likely M7 Priests) poured fire down onto this position for more than an hour and a half. This was followed by an artillery barrage that enabled the infantry to move up to the Germans on the right side. Once the barrage ended the infantry attacked. At the same time, three AVREs and two troops of Crabs entered Framezelle village and virtually destroyed it, forcing the German defenders there to surrender.

At the lighthouse, the Germans hoisted the white flag and Lieutenant A.G.S. Wilson 141st RAC picked his way gingerly through the minefield, collected the deputy German commander and brought him back to the Allied lines where he surrendered what was left of his force to the Allies.[55]

Now, only Calais still held out. The truce had caused considerable confusion as the civilians were evacuated using both Allied and German transport. Interestingly, the German drivers, once out of the confines of the fort and the city, immediately requested to be taken prisoner by the Canadians. After a brief delay permission was granted. One of the drivers was the personal chauffer of Lieutenant Colonel Schroeder, who sent several requests asking for the return of this individual. The Canadians ignored them. The Canadian Scottish tried to get food to some of their comrades stranded in isolated positions near the canal during the night of 29 September and managed to do so while under fire. The truce at this point was still in place.

The following morning Canadian civil affairs officers met with three German officers at Pont sans Pareil to discuss surrender. The Germans wanted to surrender that afternoon at 1400hrs, but the Canadians stated that hostile operations would began once the truce ended at 1200hrs. Essentially, they were told they should surrender immediately if they wished to avoid more bloodshed.[56]

When the air campaign resumed just after 1200hrs, once the truce was over, it appeared that the Germans had misunderstood the Canadians. Indeed, when a German officer finally was able to make contact with the commander of CH of O, he accused the Canadians of 'a breach of faith, for it seemed that Lieutenant Colonel Schroeder had, in fact, ordered his men to lay down their arms'.[57]

As the pre-planned artillery bombardment began, the commander of CH of O, Lieutenant Colonel Klaehn was desperately trying to get into Calais to accept the German surrender. This he managed to do once the artillery programme stopped. At 1600hrs, elements of 7th Canadian Infantry Brigade entered the city from the west where they ran into hundreds of Germans ready to surrender. Finally, the German garrison commander drove to the Allied lines, flying a white flag from his car and surrendered to the Canadians. 'The battle for Calais was over; the rest of the operation was merely a question of clearing roads, rebuilding bridges, and collecting the few harassed German stragglers.'[58]

The fort east of Les Barraques still had to be taken and this was done on the 30th when the Crocodiles attacked it. The fort had water on three sides of it making it difficult for the attack to take place. However, fire from the Sherman 17-pounders and flames from the Crocodiles did the job and the Germans surrendered. 'It also discouraged another fort and some huts over a mile away, who put out white flags with eager rapidity.'[59]

Operation UNDERGO was now finished. The Channel ports were largely clear, with the exception of Dunkirk. Both General Crerar and General Spry sent messages of congratulations and thanks to the unit commanders on 1 October 1944.

Judging from the strange constructions found there, in addition to the countless rocket sites, it was as well that the invasion had been no later. Many a delay had been imposed by the RAF whose bombing of the sites had been magnificent, as anyone who visited them will admit; but given another year of freedom to develop and to build, there is no saying how near the Germans might have come to their avowed aim of 'blasting our cities one by one.'[60]

While it was predominantly a Canadian infantry operation to capture Calais, it is clear that without the special armour of 79th Armoured Division, clearing the French coast of Germans would have been a much more costly operation in terms of casualties, materiel and time.

Chapter 10

The Siege of Dunkirk Begins

In late 1944 Dunkirk was destined to be the last port in northern France to be liberated from German occupation. The Allies had originally planned for it to be on the list of those ports to be captured and put into use as quickly as possible to help build up the Allied war effort in Western Europe. However, as the Allies began pushing out of Normandy to pursue the retreating German armies back towards Germany, the need for the massive port facilities at Antwerp became more and more urgent. The decision was taken that the German garrison within Dunkirk would be contained with a strong perimeter.

This is illustrated in the communications between Field Marshal Montgomery, C-in-C 21st Army Group, and General Crerar, Commander First Canadian Army, that were sent on 13 September when Montgomery indicated Dunkirk should have parity with Boulogne and Calais in terms of its importance.

> The things that are important now are:
>
> - Capture of Boulogne and Dunkirk and Calais
> - The setting in motion of operations designed to enable us to use the port of Antwerp.[1]

However, later that same day Montgomery changed his mind with another communication to Crerar:

> Early use of Antwerp so urgent that I am prepared to give up operations against Calais and Dunkirk.[2]

He made his final decision the following day as to the fate of Dunkirk.

Dunkirk will be left to be dealt with later; for the present it will be merely masked.³

This order from Montgomery was interpreted by General Crerar to all his corps commanders in the following directive:

No deliberate assault on Dunkirk will be attempted; this port will however, be closely contained (4.S.S Bde is being transferred to 2 Cdn Corps for this purpose) and the garrison will be influenced to surrender by frequent bombardment from the air and the ground and by propaganda leaflets.⁴

Therefore, by 27 September, the overall policy of the Allies in regards to Dunkirk was that the Canadian army would continue its operations to clear and capture the ports of Boulogne and Calais while Dunkirk would be under siege and dealt with later.

The German garrison holding out at Dunkirk was a mixed bag of troops from many different units and even from all three services, army, navy and air force. The Allied estimation in terms of numbers of men for the garrison was around 12,000 troops supported by 170 guns, mortars and machine guns. The German army element of the garrison included units from the 226th Infantry Division, who had been detached from 67th Infantry Corps for the express purpose of defending the town.

At first, the Allies believed that General Lieutenant von Kluge, the army commander in charge of the 226th Infantry Division, was in overall command of the garrison. However, 'conflicting evidence suggested that a senior naval officer, Vice-Admiral Frisius, commanded the Dunkirk stronghold'.⁵ This was despite the evidence that suggested an army general had been brought to the port on 6 September with a convoy of supplies.⁶

Further information on the commander of the garrison came to light after a German major had been captured and taken prisoner by the Allies during a skirmish. He told his captors that he knew that an unknown colonel had taken over the command of Dunkirk when a little later a division arrived in the beleaguered town and, as the commander of the division was a senior officer he decided he should be the commandant. However, according to the captured German major, the colonel did not give up his command and the divisional commander then left Dunkirk, leaving his division behind in the town.

Later, as the siege wore on, more German prisoners were captured and from them the Allies learned that not only were there German personnel from 226th Infantry Division in the town but there were also elements of 49th Infantry Division (Wehrmacht) there as well.

Because the Siege of Dunkirk lasted until the end of the war various Allied units took part in the operations to contain the German garrison there. What follows is a detailed look at the events and actions of 2nd Canadian Infantry Division during its time on the siege lines at Dunkirk.

2nd Canadian Infantry Division

In early September 1944, 2nd Canadian Infantry Division was ordered to move from where it had been resting and refitting near Dieppe towards Dunkirk. They were to pass through the 3rd Canadian Infantry Division sector 'on the axis Ostende – Blankenberghe, with the purpose of clearing the coastal strip, between Dunkirk and the Dutch frontier'.[7]

With these orders received the Division began preparing for its departure and finally left the Dieppe area on 6 September, stopping 10 miles west of St Omer, in the Forêt de Tourneham sector.

At this point in time the German garrisons at Boulogne and Calais were still holding out and 3rd Canadian Division had been tasked with destroying these garrisons and liberating the cities. The liberation would give the Allies the thing they wanted most, usable ports on the French coast. Thus, the investment of Dunkirk was assigned to 2nd Canadian Infantry Division on 5 September during a conference in Dieppe.[8]

The structure of the Division's forces for its operations against Dunkirk were: 5th Canadian Infantry Brigade would concentrate south-west of Dunkirk in the Forêt d'Eperlecques while 6th Canadian Infantry Brigade was to capture three towns between Dunkirk and Ostend, along the coast: Gurnes, La Panne and Nieuport. 4th Canadian Infantry Brigade was to remain in reserve in the Forêt de Tournehem area. Yet, for these preparations, no actual attack on the German garrison at Dunkirk had been scheduled at this time.

Seven miles south of Bourbourgville, 5th Canadian Infantry Brigade arrived at its assembly area in the Forêt d'Eperlecques on 5 September. German activity and defences had been spotted by 8th Canadian Recce

Regiment at Gravelines and Bourbourgville. They also reported that some bridges had been destroyed by the Germans.

> The three battalions were debussed and directed to attempt to seize crossings and bridge sites on the road to Bourbourgville. R.H.C. [Royal Highland Regiment of Canada], in the lead, secured the first bridge site, and R. de Mais passed through to secure another near Bourbourgville.[9]

On 7 September, the RHC (also known as Highlanders)[10] during the day concentrated near St Folquin but by midnight they had moved to positions north of the Bourbourg Canal. The town of Bourbourgville offered the German defenders good cover and excellent line of sight. The market square covered all the approaches to the town. Indeed, the main road was covered by two 88mm guns located in the centre of the town itself. Despite this, by nightfall on 8 September, the Canadians had managed to clear the town of German defenders but suffered several casualties in the process, including three killed.[11] While this was taking place, the area around Loon-Plage was occupied by the Calgary Highlanders. They had received information that R. de Mais was still in Bourbourgville and so moved towards them to join up. Unfortunately, the information was wrong as that French Canadian Regiment had moved on.

> The Calgary Highlanders was then ordered to attack the railway station which lay to the north of the town. Progress was slow and costly, and because of the flooded fields the column was forced to remain exposed on the open road, enduring some heavy shelling. Nevertheless, after further difficulties and delays, which arose from faulty intelligence, the Highlanders managed to establish themselves around the station, and prepared to move forward the following morning to Loon-Plage.[12]

According to the report about the activities of the Division during early September and their part in the opening stages of the siege. The evening of 7 September 1944, saw the RHC pass through the area occupied by the R. des Mais on their way to the town of Berques. However, the road that would have been the direct route ensuring they passed through Coppenaxfort was closed by the sappers because the bridge across the Bourbourg Canal had been destroyed. The battalion was ordered to move towards their concentration area three miles west of Bruques by way of Looborghe through Grande Mille-Brugghe.

5th Canadian Infantry Brigade arrived at their staging ground three miles north-west of Tourneham near the town of Louches in steady, driving rain, having left Dieppe early in the morning 6 September. Now, at 0300hrs, orders came through that were different from the original orders received on 5 September. These new orders tasked the brigade with attacking and taking Dunkirk. As preparations began for this operation, the Camerons of Canada prepared to attack German defences at Gravelines. However, on the 7th plans changed again and this time the attack on Gravelines was to be carried out by 5th Canadian Infantry Brigade while 6th Canadian Infantry Brigade retained its original objectives of attacking and liberating the three coastal towns mentioned earlier.

The morning of the 8th saw 5th Canadian Infantry Brigade begin their north-easterly push towards their objective. As the Regiment passed south of Berques they encountered brief heavy shelling from the Germans and no other opposition. Les Fusiliers Mont Royale marched on Furnes while troops of the South Saskatchewan Regiment (S.Sask R) continued their drive to Nieuport. Moving in tracked vehicles,[13] the Camerons rolled into their designated positions west of Nieuport ready to attack the German defenders there.

Much of the ground around Dunkirk was low-lying, which meant that the Germans were able to flood large sections of land making the movement of troops and equipment difficult. It meant that the Allies had to stick to the built-up roads that sat above the flooded land, and this meant patrolling was also difficult, because they were out in the open. 'Kept thus to high ground and roads, the Canadian forces suffered from shell fire, which the Germans were able to bring down with more effect than ordinarily.'[14]

Overall operations against Dunkirk had finally been fixed by 8 September when 5th Brigade was ordered to contain the German garrison, not to attack it. The Allies believed that there were upwards of 10,000 mostly German troops in the garrison. Although the author of the report does not specifically suggest that the reason for containing the garrison is because it would have been too costly for the Allies to directly attack it, we can reasonably assume this is the case. The brigade was to seal off all the roads and routes leading into and out of the city from the west and the south-west. With this done, the most immediate concern became the outposts the German had set up in a wide perimeter around Dunkirk. Towns and villages that had German defensive outposts in them included Loon-Plage, Mardyck, Spycker and Berques 'with many section posts and gun positions scattered between these points'.[15] It was essential that these outposts be destroyed.

For the Calgary Highlanders to get to Loon-Plage, they mounted a series of small raids on German positions along the way, early on the morning of 8 September. Halfway to their objective, they came across a collection of houses at Les Planches. Here they began engaging the Germans with each company fighting their way forward towards Loon-Plage leap-frogging each other, all the time coming up against more and more determined resistance from the Germans. 'There was heavy fighting on the outskirts of Loon-Plage and is was apparent that the assault was going to be costly.'[16]

D Company managed to reach within half a mile of the centre of the town after mounting a flank attack on the left side. However, they were stopped by heavy German machine-gun and mortar fire. Under this heavy fire that also included artillery fire as well, the Highlanders decided the best course of action was to withdraw all three companies, each only made up of thirty men. The R de Mais were on their way to reinforce the Highlanders but it was decided to pull back before reinforcements could arrive due to the fact that the men in all three companies had not eaten or slept for two days. 'Enemy infiltration caused some concern during the night 8/9 Sep, but the following morning the defenders withdrew, and Loon-Plage was entered without difficulty.'[17]

Due to the extensive flooding of the fields in the area the Allies were forced to use the roads in order for them to advance. These roads stood 8ft above the surrounding ground and were under constant observation by the Germans. Yet, they were the only means of movement. In order to capture Coppenaxfort C Company from RHC and C Squadron from 8th Canadian Recce Regiment had to advance up the road under constant fire from German outposts.

> For the next week Calgary Highlanders remained in contact with the enemy using Loon-Plage as a base for extensive patrolling and a series of thrusts towards Mardyck, three miles to the north-east. The position was finally taken on 17 Sep, and its capture marked the end of 5 Cdn Inf Bde's operation against the Dunkirk defences.[18]

Coppenaxfort was a German strongpoint and had to be silenced. The town itself lay at the point where the Bourbourg Canal curved round in a north-easterly direction towards Dunkirk. On 8 September the Germans still held this strongpoint and were holding up the advance of RHC to Grand Mille Brugghe. To deal with the German position at Coppenaxfort C Company and elements of 8th Canadian Recce Regiment were given the task. According to the reports, this task of overcoming the Germans at Coppenaxfort was a difficult one. The raised road amongst the flooded fields and farms all around it was the only way forward for the Canadians. However, for 5,000 yards the road ran parallel to the Bourbourg Canal in a straight line with only a few trees able to provide some form of cover. The two companies advanced down the road towards their objective under heavy German fire. However, as the fire intensified the Canadians were forced to find what cover they could 500 yards short of their objective after the leading armoured car was hit and destroyed. Under the cover of night, the company moved to a nearby farm that had some rising ground where they were able to dig in until the arrival of dawn. Early morning, the break of day on 9 September, the Canadians decided to resume their attack and pushed ahead. Once they arrived in the village of Coppenaxfort, they found it was deserted. The Germans had gone.[19]

The Black Watch (Royal Highland Regiment of Canada), occupied Grand Mille Brugghe on the 10th after pushing up the Canal de la Hte Colme road under heavy German mortar and artillery fire. The Black Watch stayed in Grand Mille Brugghe until 13 September, tasked with attacking and destroying any German resistance in the immediate area. A mile to the north-west was the village of Spycker that the Black Watch took on the 12th. Almost immediately, the Germans counter-attacked with mortar and artillery fire. For two days both Spycker and Grand Mille Brugghe were under intense attack from the Germans who had, by this time, turned some of their coastal guns inland to bring to bear on the advancing Allies. The German fire was too much, and on the night of 13/14 September, the Black Watch were forced to withdraw from Spycker and ended up back at Bourbourgville unable to hold Grand Mille Brugghe as well. The R de Mais, who had engaged the Germans in the Soex-Hooge Weld-Steene area[20] covered the withdrawal of the RHC back to Bourbourgville. After this action, little activity took place on the 5th Canadian Infantry Brigade front until they were relieved by 4th (British) Special Service Brigade on 17 September.

The activities of 6th Canadian Infantry Brigade proved to be much more successful than the 5th's. Troops of the 6th managed to reach Funres, Nieuport and La Panne, their objectives, with the help of the Belgian Resistance who had attacked German positions in Nieuport and cleared them from that city by 1600hrs on 8 September.[21]

The following is an indication of just how much the Belgian White Brigade helped the Canadians in liberating territories around Dunkirk occupied by the Germans.

> At 0100hrs, a representative from the White Bde showed up at BHQ and reported that the town had been cleaned by 1600hrs 8 Sep 44 and warned Major G.B. Buchanan that some of the roads were mined. He then produced a detailed plan of the enemy's defences and mined areas. He stated the enemy strength was approx, 400 on the west of the river and 200 to 300 on the east of the river, they belonged to an arty bty which had been stationed in that area for the past three and a half years and had been reinforced by odds and ends who had retreated from areas of Dieppe and along the Seine, consisting of all arms of Service.[22]

The area between Nieuport and La Panne was a stretch of eight miles and in this area were several heavily fortified German defensive positions and strongpoints. The 6th Canadian Infantry Brigade plan was, on 9 September, to sweep through this area and clear it of German troops. Operations began at 0300hrs on the 9th when the German positions along the coastal road to La Panne Bains were attacked and cleared by the Camerons of Canada,[23] who by 1200hrs, had entered La Panne proper. Once again, intelligence from local civilians as to the location of German machine-gun posts, mines and coastal guns was invaluable in the success of the operation.[24]

On the 10th the Camerons began to move westward from La Panne but ran into and engaged a high concentration of German troops, forcing them to take shelter, which they did, inside a captured section of the German West Wall defences. 'The shelter afforded by the deserted casemates was particularly welcome, as the enemy was now bringing fire to bear from a heavy coastal gun and from AA guns.'[25] As the Camerons were taking shelter the Fusiliers Mont-Royal were moving inland from Furnes towards Adinkerke, attacking German positions in the area from Oostduinkirke to Dunkirk as they advanced. The main task at this point in the overall operations was to put as much pressure on the German defenders as possible. But the German resistance was considerable and the going was slow for the Camerons and the Fusiliers Mont-Royal over the following two days.

The third battalion of 6th Canadian Infantry Brigade, the South Saskatchewan Regiment, also experienced slow going, having encountered heavy German defensive positions in the coastal areas north-west and north of Nieuport. Their main task was to clear out the Germans in the area from Nieuport–Oostduinkirke to the sea. This, however, was no easy task as the beaches, and especially the sand dunes, were littered with mines and German machine-gun posts. Indeed, the Germans held a fort in strength one mile west of Nieuport Baines that would prove difficult to take. Plans to attack this strongpoint were made and the first attack on the morning of 10 September by A and C Companies failed.

> The enemy was found to be well dug in, in reinforced pillboxes with connecting tunnels. During the day an ultimatum for surrender was sent to the garrison commander, who rejected it in a curt written reply in German – 'There is no question of it', and in determined but broken English, 'It is indisgustable'.[26]

Later that evening A Company attacked again and this time they were successful in reaching and taking their first objective. However, there was no question of an artillery barrage to soften up the German garrison due to lack of ammunition owing to lengthy supply lines.

In the early hours of 10 September at 0400hrs, B Company entered the fray on the right flank attacking German rifle and machine-gun strongpoints but after two hours of little progress they were pulled back from the line. It was felt that the reason why this attack had not succeeded was down to inexperience and lack of drive on the part of the new junior officers and men. As the light of the new day dawned a decision was taken to send the same officers and men back to the positions they'd held the night before. In support, light anti-tank guns were brought forward but because of the sand dunes and soft ground they were virtually useless. At 1800hrs Typhoons roared in, firing their rockets and 20mm cannon, but they missed the main target.

On 12 September orders came into HQ 2nd Canadian Infantry Division for them to complete the investment of Dunkirk and to clear the German 'pocket remaining at Nieuport Bains'.[27] The following morning, the S. Sask R. made another attempt to get to the fort that was strongly held by the Germans. This they did after the Brigade commander arrived to give them a pep talk. In order to increase the pressure on the German garrison, C Company was brought up to the line from Nieuport. Another demand for surrender to the Germans was made later that evening but this time with a difference. This time, the Germans were told of the surrender of the Le Havre garrison and also given proof that the Westende strongpoint three miles up the coast had also surrendered. The proof was in the form of the German commander's pay book that was handed to the Allies when he surrendered the garrison at Westende to the Essex Scot. 'Concessions were granted relative to evacuation of wounded, protection of prisoners and the transportation of officers' baggage. The capitulation was completed on the morning of the 13th, and S.Sask R. moved forward during the day to join the rest of 6 Cdn Inf Bde in the area east of Bray-Dunes.'[28]

The Camerons were not having much success in their attempts to take the village of Bray-Dunes. On 12 September they had received orders to attack and take the village and then move on to Bray-Dunes Plage further down the road. To do this, a plan was created for a two-pronged attack using the sand dunes and the coast road. A third phase of the operation was planned that would see elements of the Camerons infiltrate the village and attack the German defenders in the hope that it would enable the rest of the company to fight through the village and clear it of German troops. Early on 13 September, the Camerons began their assault but they failed to dislodge the Germans and the attack petered out. Later in the day they launched a second attack that also met with little success. At this point, the Germans held the main road east of the village. Despite this, D Company of the Camerons had been able to capture a roadblock where they claimed to have killed 150 Germans.[29]

The order to take the village came through to the Camerons once again and this time they were to take it by first light, then attack the German defences on the high ground to the north and to take Bray-Dunes Plage. Yet again, however, their attack was unsuccessful and the village still remained in German hands by the evening of 14 September. Air attacks were tried as rocket-firing Typhoons were called upon during the day to pound the defences, which they did, and reports indicate that these attacks helped to lower German morale. However, air/ground coordination was found to be wanting during this operation.[30]

Bray-Dunes did not hold out for long, however. By late evening on 13 September, the S. Sask. R arrived to reinforce the assault by the Camerons and attack German positions north-east of Bray-Dunes. The attack went in on the night of the 14th, a silent attack under the cover of darkness and this time met with success. 'By 0500hrs 15 Sep the objective was consolidated.'[31]

With the S.Sask R. having taken their objective, that meant that the Camerons could enter the village of Bray-Dunes and finally clear it of the Germans. While this was happening, the S. Sask R. assaulted German positions along the coast and in the village of Bray-Dunes Plage the clearing of this area was completed by 1200hrs on 15 September.[32]

Elsewhere, on the same day, the Fusiliers Mont Royal attacked Ghyvelde, a German stronghold they had attacked on 13 September but failed to capture. The reason for this was poor fire support and lack of intelligence. However, the attack on the 15th was successful because they had mounted two days of reconnaissance after the first failed attempt and this time planned enough artillery fire to support the attack. The Fusiliers suffered only 12 casualties in total in this operation but captured more than 119 prisoners.[33] 'The capture of Ghyvelde, Bray-Dunes and Bray-Dunes Plage marked the western limit of 6 Cdn Inf Bde's attempt to reach Dunkirk and ended the brigade's operations in that area.'[34]

Orders arrived at 2nd Canadian Infantry Division Headquarters on 15 September early in the morning that the Division was to relieve 53rd (W) Infantry Division in Antwerp. Despite these orders, patrols continued for the next two days and the Germans were relatively inactive in the Divisional area. It appears, however, that the Germans were shoring up their defences and the perimeter around Dunkirk itself.

> Before the hand-over to the relieving force – 4 Special Service Brigade – on 18 Sep, Brigadier Gauvreau conducted a study of the operations in which the battalions had recently been engaged. The lessons brought out may well give an indication of the causes of the brigade's failure to have achieved its objectives as had been expected.[35]

This study, by Brigadier Gauvreau, had three lecturers, each one looking at a different aspect of the operations. The first part of the study was about the night attack which was run by Major G.B. Buchanan of S. Sask R. The next part of the study was on the aspect of village clearing with Lieutenant Colonel R Thompson of Camerons of Canada as the lecturer. The final aspect was on the employment of artillery and air support by Lieutenant Colonel S.H. Dobell. The key lessons that came out of this study can be summarized as:

1. Each operation required accurate and useful information and intelligence.
2. Operational plans should be simple and supported by heavy fire power, the most that can be brought to bear on the enemy.
3. Two ingredients for the success of any operation are determination and aggressiveness.
4. Each soldier needs to carry their own food and water when they are involved in infiltration operations.
5. Working and reliable radio and wireless communications and the requirement to carry spares

4th Canadian Infantry Brigade Operations

4th Canadian Infantry Brigade was also involved in the siege of Dunkirk, though mostly at the extreme end of the German defences in the Ostende area. The Brigade passed through St Omer on 9 September following Essex Scot. They bypassed Berques and pushed on to Furnes then from there on to Ostende then the final four miles to Ghistelles.[36] Ostende was occupied by Essex Scot without any resistance from the Germans who had withdrawn before they arrived. Once the Allies had taken the city and began to examine the German defences of the city itself and the surrounding areas, they realized just how lucky they had been, as they were so formidable that taking and holding the city would have been an extremely costly affair.[37]

The organization of the Brigade in late 1944 was as follows: 1st Battalion The Royal Regiment of Canada (R Regt of C), 1st Battalion the Royal Hamilton Light Infantry (RHLI), 1st Battalion The Essex Scottish (Essex Scot) Regiment and 4th Infantry Brigade Ground Defence Platoon (Lorne Scots).[38] Regarding the areas within Ostende that these battalions moved into, RHLI took up positions in the northern part of the city at the port and began the process of clearing the area, submarine pens, seaplane base, docks and canal crossing of German defenders. Once this had been achieved they then advanced eastwards to Clemskerke and De Haan. At the same time, R Regt of C, who by this time had reached Ghistelles, received orders to move out and contact elements of 4th Canadian Armoured Division currently fighting the Germans around Bruges. According to the reports, once the Regiment joined up with the armoured division they were then to begin clearing out the coastal villages from the Bruges Canal as far as Uytkerke. This they did with little or no resistance from the Germans.

Reconnaissance patrols from the R Regt of C were sent out to the Bruges/Zeebrugge Canal on the 10th of September where it was found that the Germans were dug in on the eastern side of the Canal but not on the western side. In fact, the western side was clear of Germans. 'The battalion therefore remained west of the canal, containing the enemy and preventing the withdrawal of his units from Bruges along the roads in that sector.'[39] However, the following day orders came through for the Regiment to advance to Bruges to join up with the armoured division who were preparing to attack that city. Moving as quickly as they could, the Regiment pushed through Stalhille and, arriving at St. Andre, the Royals then set up their positions on either side of the main road to the west of the city. The plan for this attack on Bruges was for the escape routes to the east and north-east to be cut, trapping the Germans.[40]

With the majority of Ostend now in Allied hands and a large area east of the city having been cleared and occupied by the Canadians, RHLI was now ordered to take part in the attack on Bruges. On 11 September RHLI units began pushing through Oudebrugge to Jabbeke then onto positions south of Bruges to assist in the assault.

> But to the immense satisfaction of both the assaulting troops and the civilian population a set-piece attack proved to be unnecessary. Early in the morning of 12 Sep it was found that the enemy had withdrawn, sparing the old city – though not its bridges – and elements of 18 Cdn Armd C. Regt (12th Manitoba Dragoons), closely followed by elements of 4 Cdn Inf Bde, entered unopposed, to be received with no uncertain fervour by the wildly rejoicing population.[41]

For the Essex Scot things were more difficult than they had been for the other two battalions of 4th Canadian Infantry Brigade. The reason for this is that they were ordered to take a German strongpoint situated between Westende and Lombartzyde on the sand dunes. This strongpoint had a commanding view of the surrounding country and had been built on concrete dugouts and emplacements that had been disguised as sand dunes. It consisted of several anti-aircraft, anti-tank guns and four French naval guns. Facing this strongpoint was Essex Scot with mortars, Bofors, 17-pounders and anti-tank guns. After two days of continuous fire from both sides, the Germans retreated to positions where they were surrounded on three sides by water with their backs to the sea. One advantage that Essex Scot had was information. Local civilians who had worked on building the German gun emplacements of this strongpoint gave the Canadians detailed information about its construction and defences. The Germans used their naval guns to little effect as they were firing them at point blank range.[42]

In order to break the stalemate and prevent a long drawn out siege of this German strongpoint, the Canadians ramped up their overall fire with increased intensity and ferocity on 12 September. As they did, the return fire from the Germans began to wane and at 1245hrs, the German commander of the strongpoint surrendered. Thus, a long drawn-out battle of attrition was avoided which would have been bloody and costly for both sides. The following statement from the Essex Scot commander illustrates just how prepared the Germans were:

> Before the Commander came out the place began to swarm with Germans who flocked out of the main entrance. By now the local population was gathering in numbers. The commander came out and I accepted his unconditional surrender. While one company was dealing with the prisoners the others moved into the positions to search the area. Everything was of course underground and the battalion disappeared into the catacombs. The booty was absolutely terrific. From what I saw of the ammunition stock and food he could have held out for weeks. The quarters all underground was the most luxurious and filled with civilian furnishings of all kinds most of it taken from the villagers ... The prisoners totalled 316 including 9 officers and 16 wounded.[43]

At this point, German defences of Dunkirk now centred on the town of Berques some five miles south-east of Dunkirk itself. 4th Canadian Infantry Brigade was ordered to Berques and arrived in the vicinity of the town on 13 September. It was strongly held by the Germans and would prove a hard nut to crack. The Germans had flooded the area south-east of the town and had set up defensive positions on the north bank of the Canal de la Colme as well as along the Furnes–Berques Canal. Both these canals ran through Berques itself. The plan for the Allied attack on the town was for a bridgehead over the Berque–Furnes Canal to be established by R Regt of C. who sent two companies to positions west of Warhem in order to cross the canal, work in behind the town and then assault the German positions at night. Elements of RHLI were to attack 'close in'.[44]

While the Royals (R Regt of C) successfully crossed the canal and took more than twenty-five prisoners, the RHLI attack failed. It was supposed to begin at 0430hrs on 15 September but quickly got bogged down in extensive minefields around the town. While they were trying to clear the minefields, they came under heavy German fire from mortars, machine guns and artillery batteries. To make matters worse, the Germans set fire to a large petrol dump that stopped the RHLI from reaching their start positions and from achieving any form of surprise due to the light from the fire.[45]

At the same time, the Royals were now meeting increasing resistance from the German defenders the result of this was that the Canadians did not commit Essex Scot to the battle. Perhaps, seeing that the attack on Berques was petering out, this might have been the reason for the attack to be called off on 15 September. Orders arrived that morning that 4th Canadian Infantry Brigade was to move to the Antwerp area. However, Berques was captured and occupied on 16 September when elements of 8th Canadian Recce Regiment entered the town at 1100hrs, only to find that the Germans had gone.[46]

By the evening of 16 September, the relief of 2nd Canadian Infantry Division began. The unit relieving the Canadians was the British 4th Special Service Brigade (4 Commando). The following day 107th Heavy Anti-Aircraft Brigade (British, part of The Royal Artillery) arrived to support the siege. Afraid that the Germans might try to evacuate the garrison in the fortress at Dunkirk by sea, the Allies decided that a heavy bombardment was in order. An ultimatum was sent to the German garrison commander addressed to 'The Commander in Chief of the Dunkerque garrison, General Lieutenant von Kluge or his representative'.[47] This ultimatum demanded the Germans surrender unconditionally or face the consequences. Those consequences turned out to be that all available artillery guns, including those of the anti-aircraft brigade each fired five rounds into the German defensive positions and the fortress itself. The Germans responded in kind with a flurry of artillery fire directed at the Allies. When this died down the Allies received a written refusal from the Germans signed von Kluge, confirming what the Allies had previously thought, that General Lieutenant von Kluge was in charge of the German garrison.[48] This, however, was later found to be incorrect as it was established that the Dunkirk garrison commander was, in fact, Vice-Admiral Frisius.

As 5th Canadian Infantry Brigade (under command of 2nd Canadian Infantry Division) was destined for Antwerp at 0600hrs on 18 September, their relief began very early. Also, being relieved at the same time was 6th Canadian Infantry Brigade. This operation was carried out with as little sound as possible as per the directive of General Crerar to General Simonds:

> Outward move 2 Cdn Inf Div and assumption of containing role Dunkirk by 4 SS Bde should be so conducted that enemy obtains no definite indications of less offensive intentions against that locality.[49]

Although the length of time that 4th Special Service Brigade carried out the siege role was short they were not inactive. The commandos attacked the German defensive perimeter as often as possible, firing mortars and PIAT rounds as mortars, making the German defenders' 'lives utterly miserable'.[50]

> But the Special Service troopers were needed elsewhere for a task which better suited their peculiar abilities – the proposed assault on the island of Walcheren, at the mouth of the Scheldt.[51]

The commander of 4 Special Service Brigade, Brigadier Leicester, was briefed on 23 September by General Simonds for the Walcheren operation. He was told that his brigade would be relieved by 154th Brigade of 51st (H) Infantry Division on 26 September. This, Simonds said, would give 4th Special Service Brigade time to practice for the Walcheren landings.

On 30 September 2nd Canadian Heavy Anti-Aircraft (HAA) Regiment Royal Canadian Artillery arrived at the siege of Dunkirk. They were there to support the infantry Regiment which, by that time, was the 154th Brigade of 51st (H) Infantry Division. An entry in the war diary of 11th Canadian HAA Battery sets out the organization of the Allied forces besieging the German garrison.

The set up here is broadly this: one brigade of the 51st (H) Infantry Division is containing the Port of Dunkerque with a thin line. 107 AA Bde is the artillery formation in support. There is also a field Regiment, an anti-tank troop, and a battery of searchlights. The brigadier of 107 AA is the C.R.A. Our job is harassing day and night.'[52]

From the diaries and reports of 2nd HAA Regiment we can get an idea of what conditions were like for the Allied troops carrying out the siege. Firstly, all the Allied artillery regiments had the German defensive positions plotted on a firing map. This meant they carried out predicted fire every day on selected targets and on those positions that popped up as targets of opportunity. The Germans had flooded the low country surrounding Dunkirk, which for the Allied besiegers, made conditions awful. 'If there should be a lot of rain, living conditions will be almost unbearable – as there is no high ground and drainage is impossible. Of course the rain did come and it turned the Allied positions into quagmires of mud.[53] The rain flooded the gun pits forcing the troops to bail them out every morning as in some cases the level of the water had reached the gun platforms.'[54] The following quote provides us with an idea of how long the gunners would endure the misery of the foul weather. 'Perhaps it was as well that the gunners did not know then that their beloved 3.7s would be pointing their long barrels at the stronghold until February 1945.'[55]

2nd Canadian HAA was an anti-aircraft unit but in the case of the siege of Dunkirk they were using their 3.7in guns in the ground artillery role, in support of the infantry. As such, they spent their days bailing out their flooded gun positions and firing hundreds of rounds into the German defences. This Regiment was a highly technical one for its time. The radar equipment that formed part of the gun sites was employed in a different role to that it was originally designed for. There were two radar stations, AA No 3 Mk IIs, that the Allies used for tracking weather balloons in order for the gunners to get a more detailed idea of what sort of weather they were dealing with. 'The information so obtained was incorporated in meteor telegrams that were required for working out the corrections to be applied to the guns in predicted shooting.'[56]

However, on 3 October, for a short period of time, the guns fell silent as both sides began negotiating a temporary ceasefire so that the civilian population could be safely evacuated. A short truce was agreed that began at 1800hrs on the 3rd and ended at 0600hrs on the 6th.[57]

The truce had two main terms. The first was as follows:

> 36 hours from 0600 hours 4 Oct to 1800 hours 5 Oct for the movement of civilians with an extension of 12 hours both ends to permit the German commander to clear and repair the road to be used for the evacuation, and to blow it up and lay mines again when the civilian move was completed.

The second was:

> Cessation of all hostilities from 1800 hours 3 Oct to 0600 hours 6 Oct, during which time there would be no change in military dispositions and no hostile acts. A guarantee was given that there would be no air reconnaissance and air or naval activity within a specified perimeter of Dunkerque.[58]

Here then, is a brief description of the evacuation that makes interesting reading. Even in the depths of all-out war humans can still carry out acts of kindness and compassion. The evacuation went according to plan. It began on schedule at 0600hrs on 4 October in heavy rain that made progress slow going until the afternoon. However, throughout the following day, heavy movement occurred and both sides agreed to an extension of four hours which was 'to compensate for an equivalent interruption caused by the temporary breakdown of a bridge. In all, the evacuation managed to get 17,500 people out of Dunkirk leaving only 500 civilians remaining. These individuals were supposed to be working for the Germans. In addition, 150 stretcher cases were included in the evacuees along with the entire hospital staff and all the ambulances.'[59]

> A great many farmers came out with their wagons and livestock, and most evacuees had a considerable amount of luggage.
>
> A total of 218 assorted lorries were finally mobilized, of which a certain number were Civil Affairs lorries kept in reserve for use at moments of congestion. About 8,000 refugees were moved by train in the direction of Lille, the remainder being dispersed locally.

There were no untoward incidents. One old man died from natural causes, and two babies were born during the proceedings.

A rapid security check was made at the control post, and this was supplemented by FFI checks on the trains and the lorries.

All arrangements proved ample, even at moments of greatest influx, when the only change necessary was an increase in the great number of lorries loaded simultaneously.[60]

In the early days of October 1944, the siege was still underway and by the 6th the Czech Independent Armoured Brigade Group arrived to take over from the 154th (H) Infantry Brigade. The relief of the Highlanders lasted until 9 October when the Czechs were fully operational. Major General A. Liska commanded this new armoured brigade group that hand under command 'two armoured regiments, an armoured reconnaissance squadron, a motor battalion, a field artillery Regiment, an anti-tank battery, and engineers, signals and necessary service troops'.[61]

The day after the Czechs arrived they received an Operation Instruction from HQ First Canadian Army essentially ordering them to closely contain the German garrison holding out at the fortress at Dunkirk and in the surrounding areas, with the aim of getting them to surrender. The way they were to do this was by carrying out active patrols, regular and heavy artillery bombardment, by preventing the Germans resupplying or sending reinforcements to the garrison fortress and also by carrying out psychological warfare against the Germans. However, the instruction did not allow the Czechs to directly assault the fortress.

As we have seen, one part of the order to the Czechs was to stop the Germans from resupplying and reinforcing their positions at Dunkirk. This included by making it difficult for the Germans to make supply drops by air, which would mostly take place at night. 2nd Canadian HAA Regiment, under General Liska's command, were given two roles. The first was using their anti-aircraft guns in the ground artillery role and the second was for what they were originally intended, anti-aircraft fire.

> A reception committee of Bofors guns was made ready to provide a hot welcome for any enemy aircraft which tried to make a low-level approach. Both light and heavy guns were ordered to be prepared

to engage any aircraft which might be picked out by the beams of searchlights, which were kept in readiness.[62]

With the Bofors gunners now in charge of the AA role they first opened fire on German targets on 26 October and shot down three aircraft that came over Dunkirk in a single night. These were mail aircraft and after these losses the Germans rarely sent any more aircraft over to drop supplies for the troops at Dunkirk.

Of course, the Germans were not idle during this time. Less than a day after the Czechs had been in action the Germans struck with an offensive operation on 9 October comprising approximately sixty men. In the area of Loon-Plage they broke out of their perimeter, stole a tank[63] and set two others on fire before returning behind their perimeter to relative safety. The Allied response came the next day, the 10th, from 7th Royal Tanks and elements of the FFI supported by artillery fire. This counter-attack managed to take back what ground the Germans had taken the day before.[64]

On the evening of 19 October, the Germans attacked again, this time 3km east of Loon-Plage with more than 300 men. This group was called 'Stossgruppe' and it appeared to the Allies that the German objective was to destroy the Allied defence post in this sector. Two German companies attacked with a third held in reserve. The attackers were equipped with machine guns, rifles, grenades, incendiary bombs and mines supported by one horse-drawn anti-tank gun for artillery support.[65] With the alarm raised the Allied gunners received calls for artillery support from 7th Royal Tank Regiment at Loon-Plage and by the end of the night they had fired more than 2,000 rounds.

> Total sum up, one officer missing, two O.R.s killed. 8 O.R.s missing, 8 O.Rs wounded. This is quite sizable, considering the post strength to be approximately twenty. FFI – 2 killed, 17 missing.[66]

Such a loss by the Allies to the Germans could not go unpunished and 7th Royal Tank Regiment planned a counterblow on 24 October supported by artillery along with units from FFI, for the sole purpose of destroying as many German positions as they could and to gain as much local intelligence as possible. However, they did not plan on occupying their objectives but instead they would withdraw back to their original start point. The operation was called Operation WADDLE and was set for 1400hrs.

It began with 2nd Canadian HAA forward observation officers moving forward with two assaulting tank squadrons. Of those squadrons one tank troop (7th Royal Tank Regiment), attacked German positions near Grand Smythe and shelled it from 200 yards away causing much damage without drawing return German fire. The supporting French contingent entered Petite Predembourg and discovered the Germans had left it empty. In Grande Predembourg, a farm was destroyed by fire to ensure that the Germans could not move in and reoccupy it. The entire raid took two and a half hours and the assaulting Allied troops were back behind their lines at 1630hrs.[67]

To General Liska, the success of Operation WADDLE offered him an opportunity to mount another assault. This was to be launched on Czechoslovakian Independence Day, 28 October 1944. The main attack was to take place at 0900hrs with a diversion attack taking place at 0630hrs. Prior to the attack the Czechs were holding the eastern flank of the defensive perimeter which was divided between 2nd Czech Armoured Regiment on the left, while on the right was 1st Czech Motor Battalion. The main thrust of the attack was for the tanks to move on limited objectives while the Motor Battalion was to create the diversionary attack earlier, drawing out the German defenders. This was to be supported by 125th Light Anti-Aircraft Regiment in the infantry role, carrying out heavy offensive operations in the south in order to cause the Germans as much confusion and discomfort as possible. At the same time, 2nd Canadian HAA Regiment was to harass them with one battery of artillery fire. During the operation an Air Observation Post was set up to direct further artillery fire on the Germans. The cost to the Czechs was two dead and fifteen wounded. A regimental situation report stated:

> Right flank - heavy opposition delayed in reaching objective. Centre and let flanks went quite well - all objectives reached. PW collected on this sector - 4 officers and 200 O.Rs. 2 Arms Regt casualties so far disabled by crew. One half-track and one scout car received direct hits from shell fire. One O.P. officer had bullet through trousers.[68]

As far as the Allies were concerned, Operation WADDLE was a great success as it forced the Germans to fight and expend what limited resources they had in terms of ammunition and manpower.

Over the next few days, the Czechs mounted two more raids on the German defenders, the first on 3 November and the second two days later. The first saw tanks from 7th Royal Tank Regiment attack a farm where they killed three Germans while the rest of the Germans holding the farm abandoned it. They left behind their arms and all their equipment.[69]

The second operation on 5 November was much larger but also a costly one for both sides. It was a reconnaissance in force carried out by 2nd Czech Armoured Regiment, 'with additional troops, including one motor company and two platoons of tank men temporarily turned infantry'.[70]

At 2nd Canadian HAA HQ a report was received at 1635hrs that indicated just how costly this operation was: 'Own troops now back but three or four tanks left in sunken road. Efforts being made to recover these now. Our casualties upwards of 60, enemy casualties 160 prisoners and a lot reported killed. Enemy infantry are trying to get forward again.'[71] The results of the heavy casualties on both sides meant that a temporary truce was set up from 1200hrs to 1900hrs the following day so that the dead could be buried and the wounded brought back to the lines of both sides.

As the winter began to draw in it became clear that the siege was becoming a stalemate. The Germans were unable to break out of their fortress in force and the Allies were unable to break the stalemate with the forces available to them at the time. 'Both sides can exploit one another's weaknesses – as it is shown by the enemy's night raids in the western sector and C.I.A.B.G.'s surprisingly successful Independence Day celebration in the east.'[72] However, the balance was in favour of the Allies who were 'better equipped and supplied both morally and physically'.[73]

Mud was one of the main problems facing the Allied gunners as they carried out the siege and tried to keep up a daily schedule of regular fire. October rains swept the area causing havoc. 'Gun pits caved in and guns slipped back when fired; an out-of-door command post was impossible; vehicles bogged down any time they left the main road; and wagon-lines and gun positions were soon mires of impassible mud.'[74]

Despite the flooding of gun pits and the mire, the Allies fared much better than the Germans did in terms of their standard of living while at Dunkirk. For example, the Allied gunners' initial deployment to Dunkirk was in fields.

Command posts for the artillery had been set up in fields under the cover of canvas while gunners made their quarters in holes in the ground that were covered over by groundsheets or tarpaulins. However, most of the command posts were in nearby buildings and the men were billeted wherever possible. But the gun sites remained in the open, subjected to inclement weather. The following excerpt from the History of 2nd Canadian HAA paints a detailed picture of what it was like for the Allies.

> Near St. Omer, however, the Germans had thoughtfully left an airfield full of small huts, and scattered all over the coast line and country-side were deserted German sites and houses, full of furniture and furnishings. By the end of our stay at Dunkirk, each troop position was a village in miniature; the men had huts of their own, varying according to individual taste from a one-man bungalow to a massive structure complete with attic and capable of housing more than a dozen.[75]

As the siege continued, the First Canadian Army, with all of its units, had pushed into Holland and Germany extending the command structure to such an extent that 21st Army Group took under its command 1st Czech Independent Armoured Brigade. This directly freed up First Canadian Army from the responsibility of the siege.

January 1945 saw heavy snow, high winds, frozen ground and frosty air. Another artillery Regiment, a motor transport company, a tank battalion and a company of engineers had reinforced the Czechs during the siege. Interestingly, the men of these new units had come from the German army. They were Czech nationals who had been forcibly enlisted by the Germans during their occupation of Czechoslovakia and were taken prisoner by the Allies during the battles in Normandy.[76]

In April 1945, the Allies discovered just how bad things were for the Germans in the beleaguered fortress. It was during an exchange of prisoners during this month, when the real picture came out.

> Food was poor, and the allowance for prisoners was miserable, unless they were willing to do such work as collecting vegetables and sugar beet. For the wounded and sick, life was pitiful – Medical care was bad, and in the hospitals, there is a deficiency of medical

stores, causing the death of several Allied as well as of a considerable number of German soldiers. The atmosphere in hospital is disagreeable because of the deficiencies in drugs and bandages.[77]

The same Intelligence Summary the above quote is from went on to state that discipline inside the beleaguered fortress was harsh indeed. Often the death sentence was carried out in order to keep prisoners and soldiers alike in line. Of the 12,000 men inside the garrison, the Germans were only able to field roughly 8,000 capable of fighting; 3,000 were unfit for duty because of medical problems or complications while the remaining 1,000, made up of Austrians and Poles, were not trusted by the Germans to have guns.

Finally, on 4 May 1945 a signal from Headquarters 21st Army Group was received stating:

> All offensive operations will cease from receipt of this signal. Orders will be given to all troops to cease fire at 0800 hours tomorrow, Saturday 5 May. Full terms of local German surrender arranged to-day for 21 Army Group front to follow. Emphasize these provisions apply solely to 21 Army Group front are, for the moment, exclusive of Dunkirk.[78]

Two days later on 7 May, Major General Liska accepted the surrender of the German garrison at Dunkirk. He then ordered his troops to march into the town and occupy it. The French ports along the Channel coast were now free of the German occupiers.

> The three great fortified harbours, Le Havre, Boulogne and Calais had fallen by storm, in spite of their great guns, their garrisons, and the Fuhrer's orders. In trying to hold these ports, the Germans had lost 30,000 troops, in addition to the 12,000 bottled up in Dunkirk.[79]

Chapter 11

The Siege of Dunkirk: 1st Czech Independent Armoured Brigade Group

For this chapter, most of the information comes from a report entitled *Outline of the Activities of the 1st Czech Independent Armoured Brigade Group at Dunkirk, 1944-1945*. At the time of writing that report, its author Brigadier H.C. Bleacker, commanding 22nd Liaison HQ believed that morality, courage and versatility typified the work of the Czechs during the long siege that lasted up to the German surrender in May 1945. Outlining the events and operations of the brigade, the report is an excellent tribute to the officers and men involved in the siege. This is seen in the way in which the mobile unit, an armoured brigade, was able to effectively adapt to static conditions in depressing terrain that was flat and wet, in squalor, for more than seven months yet remain capable of maintaining vigorous and ruthless operations against the German defenders up to their surrender at Dunkirk.

Made up largely of troops who had escaped from France, the brigade was converted into an armoured one on 1 September 1943. Almost a year later, in August 1944, after delays in equipping and training the formation, the brigade was ordered into France. At this point, it had not had a full exercise using its armoured vehicles – Cromwell tanks which, at the time of their deployment, were not up to full strength. However, for the brigade to complete its full training programme, once in France it was concentrated in the Falaise area. But once again, the brigade exercise didn't take place due to the mines and wireless silence that had been imposed before they were deployed to Dunkirk. Despite this, the Brigade arrived in the Dunkirk area on 7 October and two days later officially took over from British 154th Infantry Brigade at 0700hrs.

As we have seen, the German troops at Dunkirk numbered upwards of 16,000[1] along with 17,000 civilians who were later evacuated from the town. The Germans held a perimeter that formed a semi-circle around the town that was 21 miles long and contained several heavily defended strongpoints.

The 7th Royal Tank Regiment, 107th AA Brigade, 150th Field Regiment (artillery) and the 191st Field Regiment (also artillery), were all under the command of the Czech Independent Armoured Brigade Group for the siege of Dunkirk. Part of the land in the eastern and southern parts of the perimeter had been flooded by bad weather. The Germans had built their defences behind the flooded areas which meant the Allies had to set up nightly boat patrols that were mostly carried out by Engineers. This was a difficult task, 'due to the many obstacles in the nature of barns, houses, trees etc, met in the water which in places was 15 feet deep'.[2]

It quickly became apparent to the Czech commander (General Alois Liska)[3] that for them to contain the German garrison, an infantry task, they would have to dismount the tank crews from their two armoured regiments and the crews from their motor companies. 'The dispositions were made with 7 R.Tanks occupying the Western end of the line and the Czechoslovakia Motor Bn in the Eastern end, each with an Armoured Regiment as their next door neighbour.'[4] It was felt by the Brigade Headquarters that these two points were the most likely places the Germans would try to break free of the siege and try to escape back to Germany.

The brigade itself was trained and equipped the same way as British units, 'comprising a powerful mechanised all-arms force'.[5] The brigade consisted of an HQ with Sherman OP and Cromwell IV tanks. The Sherman OP tanks were forward observation vehicles. However, the brigade's hammer was its three armoured regiments. Major S. Rezabek commanded the 1st Armoured Regiment while the 2nd was commanded by Lieutenant Colonel F. Seda. Each of these comprised 'an RHQ of Cromwell VII tanks and a troop of Sherman Firefly VC tanks armed with the formidable 17pdr gun. Forward observers were carried in Cromwell IV OP tanks.'[6]

> The siege role ill-suited the Czechs, who had insufficient manpower for the task and lacked the specialist engineering vehicles necessary to reduce the inland defences.
>
> The successful, but costly, captures of Le Havre, Dieppe, Boulogne and Calais had given the Allies caution. Dunkirk as a prize was not required at the cost of significant casualties. The mobile formation had to content itself with maintaining an impenetrable cordon around the city, prohibited by the French authorities from mounting any prolonged bombardment of the historic centre.[7]

Each of the three regiments (initially only two), had a single armoured recce troop equipped with the Stuart VI light tank.[8] They also had 'three squadrons ("A", "B", and "C"), with Cromwell IV and VII tanks, plus Cromwell VIII 95mm close support tanks in the SHQ'.[9]

The brigade also had its own motor battalion organized in the same way British motor units were at the time, using 'M5 halftracks and Universal Carriers, the battalion including its own recce element in M3A1 White scout cars, plus 20mm Polsten AA guns and attached 6pdr anti-tank guns, 3" Mortars and Vickers Medium Machine Guns'.[10] This motor battalion was commanded by Lieutenant Colonel J. Chvalkovsky.[11]

Major V. Velimsky commanded the Brigade HQ's own armoured reconnaissance squadron that was equipped with Cromwell tanks, Humber scout cars and Stuart light tanks. As more manpower became available to the Czechs this unit was formed into the 3rd Armoured Regiment in the winter of 1944/45.[12]

On the brigade's first night on the siege line, the Germans attacked out of Dunkirk in a south-west direction, surprising the reconnaissance squadron in that sector of the line. The German force managed to overwhelm the squadron with superior numbers but within the following 48 hours their positions had been retaken and the Germans pushed back. For the entire time the Czechs were besieging Dunkirk this was the only real success the Germans had against them, even though it was temporary. From that point onwards, the Allies made significant progress.

British and Canadian heavy AA units made up of 3.7in anti-aircraft guns supported the Czechs in the siege, deploying their guns in the direct role and also supported by the 125th Light AA Regiment's 40mm Bofors guns.[13]

In addition to this, as we shall see later in greater detail, 7th Royal Tank Regiment also provided support to the Brigade with its heavy Churchill infantry tanks. There was, however, a shortage of infantry which the Allies went some way to solving by creating two battalions of 'Free French infantry formed from the local FFI (Forces Francaises d'Interieur) under Lieut. Col Lehagre, equipped and armed by the British'.[14]

Thus equipped, and despite the static nature of their operations, the brigade did have some opportunity of reverting to their main mobile armoured role. For example, on 28 October the 2nd Armoured Regiment, together with a motor company, mounted a daylight attack against the Germans, achieving complete surprise, destroying a full German battalion while suffering very few casualties.[15]

> A lightning riposte against the exposed German infantry saw over 40 casualties inflicted on the defenders at a cost of only two casualties to the CIABG. This operation drew significant praise for the manner of its execution from higher levels, including Field Marshal Montgomery.[16]

The brigade took an aggressive patrolling policy against the Germans mounting attacks wherever they could along the line. On 5 November, RAF Typhoons roared in at low level, shooting up German positions with 20mm cannon fire just prior to another armoured ground assault on the same positions. However, this attack did not achieve the same results as the one on 28 October did but the Germans did suffer heavy losses in killed, wounded and prisoners taken.

> The enemy had also been busy distributing mines and tank obstacles in the intervening week, and movement was very restricted and only possible after much clearance. 7 R Tanks, who at all times displayed the greatest keenness to come to grips with the enemy continued to make minor attacks frequently and the first six weeks were very active.[17]

The siege then settled into a quiet period that was extremely beneficial for the Czechs as it gave them a chance to increase their manpower. The new troops came from those Czech nationals who had been liberated as the Allies pushed through France as well as those troops who were forced to be part of the German Army and were also liberated by the advancing Allies. Because of this, the Brigade was able to add another armoured Regiment, another motor company and a field Regiment of artillery thus bringing it up to full strength. To achieve this, the Brigade set up an armoured training school for the new recruits at Hazebruck, using the reconnaissance squadron's techniques and record as best practice. Thus, on 15 December, the expansion programme began with the opening of the school and by 18 February individual training was complete.[18]

According to the report by Brigadier Bleacker, the motor company and the field Regiment were 'trained on the spot'. However, it is unclear if this means they were trained while taking part in the siege and in contact with the Germans. We can assume that this is what the author of this report means.

> In addition, some invaluable assistance was forthcoming from M.G.A.T. which enabled the Armoured Regiment and the Motor Companies to be ready, with reinforcements, from operation engagement early in May. This feat of training whilst actively engaged with the enemy was magnificent and was a great credit to the tirelessness of the officers involved in the training and to the keenness of the personnel concerned.[19]

The Brigade settled into a wet, cold winter where contact with the Germans was limited to patrolling. Life in the low lying flooded areas became monotonous for the besiegers and to avoid the monotony from having a detrimental effect on morale there were numerous breaks, some humorous and some tragic.

As far as the tragic incidents occurred they were mostly to do with Allied aircraft being shot down over Dunkirk. It appeared that some of the Allied air forces did not realize that Dunkirk was still being held by the Germans. According to the report, this situation happened several times 'despite the fact that strenuous efforts by our artillery to prevent the enemy from manning AA positions were made each time an allied plane appeared in the vicinity of Dunkerque'.[20]

In some cases, these aircraft that were shot down and the crews that bailed out ended up landing in the neutral ground between the Germans and the Allies. This usually resulted in hard, fierce fighting in order to get to the air crews. Fortunately, most of the time the Czechs were successful in grabbing the Allied personnel from under the noses of the Germans and getting them back to safety. However, during one rescue operation of five American aircrew who had managed to parachute out of their stricken aircraft, four of them ran in the wrong direction 'despite a barrage of tracer ammunition over their heads to stop them'.[21] In another incident RAF personnel, heading for home on leave in a Douglas Dakota twin-engined aircraft, were shot down.

After some very quick work on the part of the Czechs all occupants were recovered including the pilot who had been wounded, but the Czechs suffered some slight casualties in the battle. Needless to say, the personnel going on leave were not at all pleased at the course chosen by their pilot and navigator.[22]

The monotony was also broken by the number of visitors to the Allied HQ and its units during the siege of Dunkirk. 'The only complaint was that the Liaison HQ never had any whisky or gin after the first few days of the month. The average number of visitors for each meal except breakfast, was two; all of whom were welcome especially those who knew of our thin ration of alcohol and in some cases helped to maintain it temporarily.'[23]

These events were largely taking place at Brigade Headquarters back of the line and not on the line where the tank and motor battalion crews, used to a mobile existence, faced long periods of inactivity in what was, essentially, a static role. At Headquarters then, for those very special guests Guards of Honour would be set up while the Czech commander and officers from the Liaison HQ would lay on official lunches and dinners for their distinguished visitors. The monotony of the siege during the winter of 1944 went quickly according to the Headquarters report because of these incidents, whereas it is likely for those on the line it was much more tedious.

Other events took place that relieved the boredom. Many units were shuffled around, some sent out and others brought in. 17th AGRA relieved 107th AA Brigade, for example, during this time which reduced the number of artillery guns in support of the operation. Brigadier Bleacker, in his report, suggests that the brigade's artillery was always outnumbered compared to the number of guns the Germans had. 'They had some alarmingly accurate railway guns of 280mm calibre and some of the coast defences had been turned around so that 155mm bursts were not infrequent.'[24]

Also, during this time, some of the 7th Royal Tank Regiment's tanks had been converted to Crocodile tanks – fitted with a flamethrower with a petrol bowser pulled behind – and these were taken out of Dunkerque Force.[25]

In exchange for losing these tanks, the brigade received a French security battalion that had just been formed and lacked the knowledge and training of their weapons. Eventually, Dunkerque Force received full support in terms of training and the weapon situation was rectified. 'But nothing could remedy the fact that the French were not trained, and that their officers had no knowledge of weapons, field craft or any of the basic essentials of an Infantryman.'[26]

As the Allied effort to cross the Rhine got underway, the besiegers at Dunkirk were ordered to attack the Germans, specifically their AA positions. The orders also included the troops on the siege line trying to jam German wireless communications as much as possible as well as ensuring that any friendly aircraft flying over the Dunkirk area did not receive the attention of the German AA gunners.

As Allied airborne troops were in the area, a fire plan was laid on to last for 75 minutes which would see the Allied artillery guns on the line pounding German positions, forcing them to keep down. This enabled the airborne troops in their gliders to move through the area on their way to their landing zones. Also involved in this, in addition to every artillery and AA guns available, the Brigade commander also used as many tanks as possible.

Later, German officers who had been captured once the siege of Dunkirk was over and they had surrendered, indicated that the operation outlined above had been absolutely devastating for them. They had been taken by surprise. Again, Bleacker confirms the success of this operation by stating that 'only some 30 or 40 of our gliders were seen well to the South, and it would appear that these were not sighted by the enemy, and no news of their passing was wirelessed to Germany'.[27]

Winter of 1945 and the siege was still under way. In the early days of April, several German prisoners, officers and other ranks, who had been captured behind Allied lines provided invaluable information on pending German attacks. Indeed, these prisoners informed the Allies that the Germans were planning a large scale attack in the western sector of the line as well as in the south-west. This spurred Brigade HQ to ensure all arrangements were made to counter this attack. 'One of the officer prisoners gave us complete information of the direction and method of attack, which was immediately passed by Liaison Officers to each of the units involved.'[28]

This proved to be invaluable for the Allies, but the French units involved in these preparations had misunderstood the information they received. As a result, their defensive preparations to push back the pending German attack were not in line with those of the rest of the Brigade.

> A Liaison Officer who had been sent out by them [French] was rather surprised when he found the factory in which he was

operating his wireless taken from the rear without a shot being fired, despite the fact that he had been informed that the direction of attack would be precisely where it actually came from.[29]

The loss of the factory caused the French troops on both flanks to withdraw, leaving a Regiment of the Royal Artillery with its right flank exposed to the Germans and the left flank of a Czech anti-tank battery also exposed. The following day, two French battalions attacked the German units holding the factory but were unable to retake it. Bleacker puts this down to lack of training on the part of the French. Let's not forget that the French battalions had been formed quickly with little or no training for the task they were supposed to be carrying out. Nor had they been trained on the weapons they were to use. Over the following week the Germans would send out raids from the factory to attack the French positions.

At this stage both sides called for a cessation of hostilities in order to exchange prisoners. This was arranged before another aerial bombardment of the German defences in Dunkirk was to take place. This account is detailed in Bleacker's report:

> At great personal risk to themselves, a British and Czechoslovak officer went into Dunkerque with a flag of truce, carefully avoiding mines, and made complete arrangements. The number of prisoners had increased considerably, as prior to the April attacks there had been only 7 Czks and 21 French, apart from the Canadian and British prisoners taken before the Czechoslovak Brigade arrived at Dunkerque. They now amounted to 24 Czechs (including 8 wounded) and 115 French. The exchange was duly carried out, in fact we gave the Germans a few extra for good measure.[30]

Once the exchange was complete the bombing by Allied medium bombers began. More than sixty Mitchell twin-engined medium bombers arrived overhead and with great precision managed to blast German defences in the forward areas. The Allies believed that the Germans would move out of their positions once they realized that the bombing effort was serious and because of this reasoning it was proposed that medium bombers and fighter bombers should attack the outside German defensive positions so there was nowhere that they could shelter. However, the Germans realized early on that the bombing campaign was going to be long and arduous for them so most of the garrison moved into underground shelters and stayed in them for three days. However, the French did not want the complete destruction of Dunkirk as there were still some elderly citizens, amounting to roughly 665 people, still in the city who had not been evacuated for various reasons. For the Brigade HQ, this attitude from the French was a little strange as 'there was not a whole building in Dunkerque after the bombardment to which it had been subjected for seven months'.[31]

Since the arrival of the Czech Brigade morale had been high but now as the war was drawing to a close and as the Allies were about to liberate Czechoslovakia it began to fall. This could have been because 'all efforts to release the Brigade for service in its own country were unavailing'.[32]

> Morale did suffer as it became apparent that the Brigade was not to be permitted to join the US forces which were heading toward the Czechoslovakian homeland. Only a token force of 150 men was permitted to accompany the U.S. Troops heading toward their eventual meeting with advancing Soviet forces.[33]

Since the war was drawing to a close, with more and more countries being liberated by the Allied Armies a decision was taken by HQ to increase artillery and tank ammunition to force the Germans in Dunkirk to capitulate. They began a three-day bombardment that was uninterrupted, operating both night and day. 'From subsequent information the bombardment certainly had a most desirable effect on the Germans. The burial parties were very active and when the capitulation came, the hospitals contained 287 seriously wounded. Also, there was not a single HQ or billet that had not suffered. In fact, the whole of Dunkerque was a shambles.'[34]

Such a success was this bombardment that on the third day, a ceremony was conducted where the high command gave out decorations to British and Czech personnel. British officers and all ranks from the anti-aircraft brigade received their decorations for a job well done and 'a most creditable performance.' Prior to being posted to the siege they had been on home service. According to the author of the report, they had outlasted the Germans every time and never wavered in their duty, 'producing some very fine individual acts of heroism'.[35]

Not long after this ceremony took place a message was received that the Germans wanted to surrender. On 8 May, two officers, one British and one Czech, entered Dunkirk and met with the German commander to ask for an immediate surrender. After some negotiation surrender terms were agreed and the Germans were instructed to cease all action, give up their weapons while the commander was told to immediately report to GOC Dunkerque Force.

> The following morning a short ceremony was conducted in Dunkerque by 10 Czechoslovak Officers and 2 British Officers in hoisting the Czechoslovak National Emblem and the Union Jack, and the same afternoon, Comd. Dunkerque Force and Commander of the British Liaison HQ in separate Austers, flew over the city to see that the flags were still at the masthead.[36]

The next day the Czech brigade began the process of withdrawing from Dunkirk to travel the 680 miles back to their homeland. The commitment of Dunkirk was handed over by the Brigade to a mixture of French battalions, L of C battalions and 17th AGRA. The Brigade made the journey home in 'most excellent order, which closed, in triumph a great episode carried out with high morale, excellent spirits and fortitude, under most trying, depressing and forlorn conditions'.[37]

Chapter 12

The Siege of Dunkirk: 7th Royal Tank Regiment War Diary

Throughout this book we have looked at a variety of Allied units that were involved in the Siege of Dunkirk. The Canadians, the British and the Czechs primarily, with different types of units taking up the task, from infantry to armour. What follows here is a diary showing the tasks carried out by members of the 7th Royal Tank Regiment in the last four months of 1944.

What is remarkable about the events detailed here is that this was an armoured unit that very quickly was able to adapt to a static form of ground warfare, employing small hit and run tactics carried out mostly on foot under the cover of darkness. It illustrates how the Regiment was able to use its tanks as artillery rather than for deep penetration assaults on German lines. It also provides the reader with a vision of just how large this operation was and how much materiel and personnel were involved in ensuring the Germans at Dunkirk remained contained until the end of the war.

September 1944

Throughout the day on 1 September, 7th Royal Tank Regiment was primarily concerned with maintenance of its vehicles that included painting the vehicles with new Brigade signs, according to the diarist.

However, at 1900hrs, orders were received that the brigade was to move to a new location north of Gace, some 47 miles away. The actual area was north of Le Sap where they were supposed to move to. The move took place the following day and by 2315hrs they arrived in their new destination. 'Owing to fairly long run for Churchill Tanks yesterday (47 miles) quite a number of heavy maintenance jobs had to be done.'[1]

September 3rd saw the brigade working feverishly on maintenance jobs in preparation for another move. Orders for the next move came the following morning at 1030hrs that stated the brigade had to be in the area north of Louviers by 7 September. The diarist noted that at 1610hrs they were ordered to move to Bernay and by 1900hrs the tanks were under way. They arrived in the harbour area of Bernay 30 minutes past midnight, having driven 29 miles to get there.

Three hours later, on 5 September, more orders arrived for the brigade to move yet again. The diarist provides the details: 'Received orders for a move to area North of Seine. Route – Brionne – Pont de L'Arche. Arrived into Harbour Area Croix-Mane – about 2 miles NWest of Croix Mare – Journey 64 miles. This makes 140 Miles in 4 days.'[2] By 2200hrs the tanks had all arrived in the harbour area but they still had to get to their concentration area. Throughout the night, maintenance was carried out by the engineers and mechanics and at 1430hrs on 6 September the tanks left Croix Mare and arrived at their concentration area near Goderville at 1930hrs. They drove from Yvetot to Bolbec to Goderville. Here, according to the diarist for the brigade diary, the outline plan for the attack on Le Havre was received at Brigade Headquarters.

The following morning the outline plan was delivered to the squadron commanders who then paired up with their infantry counterparts (battalion commanders) in 56th Infantry Brigade in order to carry out initial recces of the area. The attack on Le Havre at this point was scheduled for 9 September 1944, two days away.

Heavy rain arrived on the 8th falling continuously throughout the day. The weather forced the date for the attack to be moved to the 10th, Sunday. Members of 7th Royal Tanks spent the day carrying out recces of the routes they would use to get to their Forming Up Places (FUPs) and start lines for the attack. Conferences were held between the AVREs, Flails and infantry commanders discussing the upcoming attack.

Terrible weather continued well into 9 September that caused the tanks to have to wait until 1930hrs before leaving for their 'Lying Up Positions'. The going was difficult due to the mud and the steep inclines. Two routes were used with A and B Squadrons using Route C, as well as the Regimental Headquarters, while Route A was used by C Squadron. By 2300hrs the only group that managed to get to their designated area was C Squadron. The others had not been able to reach their own areas and were ordered to stop all movement by 2300hrs so that the Germans would not hear the noise of their vehicles.

The weather cleared on the 10th enabling A and B Squadrons, along with the RHQ, to advance to their laying up positions, which they reached at

0645hrs. Tank and gun maintenance was then carried out while they waited for the Go order to take part in the attack on German positions in and around Le Havre.

The diarist provides a summary of events for the attack:

1. As we know the code name for the attack on Le Havre was Operation ASTONIA that saw 49th and 51st Infantry Divisions carry out the main thrust of the attack with 7th Royal Tanks in support of 56th Infantry Brigade.
2. Within the plan, 56th Infantry Brigade was tasked with breaking through German lines south-west of Montvilliers and taking the Plateaux nearby as Phase 1 of the operation. The plan before the attack was for the assault during Phase 1 to be carried out across a 2nd Battalion Front with specialist armour vehicles in support. 'C Sqn 7 R Tks, 1 Sqn Flails, ½ Sqn Flame throwers and a Tp of AVREs.'[3] Also, in support of the Gloucester Regiment was B Squadron of 7th Royal Tanks and other specialist armour as outlined previously. 'The Essex and A Sqn 7 R Tks were to come through the 2 leading Bns to take 2 Posts on the Plateau and get a footing on the next plateau to the South.'[4]
3. Phase 1 began with accurate bombing of German positions on the plateau for an hour then at 1830hrs the tanks and armour began moving. Supported by B & C Squadrons 7th Royal Tanks the Flails began clearing paths through the minefields. Two lanes, both right and left of the front, had been created through the minefields by 1900hrs. As we have seen earlier in the book there was a German anti-tank gun on the right lane that caused problems for the vehicles.
4. 'Flails were hit and destroyed. C Sqn 7 R Tks then started to pass through the lanes and in doing so lost 4 tanks on mines. This was due to the fact that the lanes were not properly cleared and there were other mines not shown on the overlay maps, and therefore not flailed.'[5] This action was on the right lane while on the left, B Squadron had no problems passing through the minefield. Behind the Flails and tanks came the infantry and other supporting units moving rapidly on both flanks and by 1915hrs the first German strongpoints had been captured and or destroyed.

5. On the right flank, Allied units suffered very heavy German shell fire that caused the Infantry and Tank crews to take casualties. Despite this, all German positions on this flank were taken by 2130hrs. German opposition on the left flank was slight and the operations there went according to plan. Just before dark The Essex and A Squadron had reached their objectives and passed through them taking more German positions as they went. This completed the capture of the plateau. That night, A Squadron 7th Royal Tanks stayed with The Essex while B Squadron was able to drive back to the lines and refuel and rearm. Because of the congestion through the minefields, C Squadron was unable to get back and so stayed the night on the plateau.

On the 11th the squadrons were on the move again. This time B Squadron moved back onto the plateau after refuelling and rearming and joined up with the Gloucester Infantry Regiment. By 0700hrs all of them were ready to move forward to their next objectives.

147th Brigade was ordered to advance on their objectives in the Forêt de Montegeon area, so at 0900hrs they passed through 56th Infantry Brigade's area in company with elements of The Leicestershire Regiment. However, this force had no armour supporting them as the tanks had been unable to get up to them in time so a request was made to 7th Royal Tanks for help. As a result, half of A Squadron was ordered to provide support. This group of vehicles moved forward with the Leicestershire Regiment. Fierce fighting took place for three hours with the tanks pressing home their strength and firepower enabling the infantry to take their objective. Once done, the tanks returned so they could be replenished by Stuart tanks that carried up supplies, fuel and ammunition to them. Around 1500hrs, an assault across the river south of the plateau was carried out by the Gloucestershire Regiment supported by tanks of B Squadron. The Germans opened fire with two 75mm anti-tank guns as the assault took place but both guns were quickly knocked out by the tanks and the Allies took many German prisoners in this operation. By nightfall, both A and B Squadrons were in the town of Montegeon, where they remained for the rest of the night in company with the infantry.

On 12 September, two squadrons from 7th Royal Tanks began moving towards the sea. These were B Squadron supporting the Gloucestershire

Regiment and A Squadron supporting the South Wales Borderers (SWB), who were part of the 49th (West Riding) Division at that time. Both Squadrons were heading west along the coast when they came up against a heavily fortified German strongpoint (fort) with more than 400 personnel inside. This fort was defended by an anti-tank gun that gave the advancing troops a bit of trouble, but after enduring 10 minutes of 75mm fire from the tanks the strongpoint fell and the Germans surrendered. The minefield around the fort was then quickly cleared and the force continued its advance. 'A Squadron had to deal with 3 A/TK Guns but otherwise met with little opposition. The operation mainly consisted of blasting Pillboxes and collecting prisoners.'[6]

The main German HQ at Le Havre was the objective and a troop from B Squadron raced ahead of the main force at 1100hrs with support from the infantry and entered the German garrison. Here the troop of tanks took more than 400 German prisoners of war. This number also included the garrison commander and his staff. The German commander surrendered the Le Havre garrison to the Officer Commanding 7th Royal Tanks (Lieutenant Colonel Veals)[7] on this day.

Operations to clean up Le Havre ended at 1500hrs that day for 7th Royal Tanks as they could find no additional Germans to take prisoner. From here, both A&B Squadrons began to concentrate in the Montevilliers area overnight before returning to their start line. C Squadron had moved to the rear for refurbishment and refuelling and now that Le Havre had been taken they remained there.

The following day the entire Regiment moved back to their original concentration area and began a programme of tank and gun maintenance that lasted from 13 through to 28 September. This was interspersed with more individual/personal training and gunnery practice for the tank crews.

Orders came in, yet again, on 28 September when the Regiment was told to move to an area south of Dunkirk at 0700hrs on the 29th. The first stage of this move was to see the tanks and other vehicles arrive in an area just south of Abbeville. This was done by travelling through Belmesnil–Longueville–Torcy–Enverman–Fresnoy–Blangy, finally arriving four miles south of Abbeville from Blangy. On 30 September, the Battalion continued the drive to Forest Montiers some three miles away just south-east of Rue. In all they had moved 50 miles.[8]

October 1944

On 1 October 1944, the 7th Royal Tank Battalion moved yet again, this time from Montreuil to Samar, having left the harbour at 1120hrs and arriving at Samar at 1600hrs, a distance of 30 miles.[9]

Later that evening, at 2100hrs, the Commander of 7th Royal Tanks (Lieutenant Colonel Rea Leakey) was informed of a change of command structure. The battalion was now under the overall command of 2nd Canadian Army, and under direct command of Czechoslovak Independent Armoured Brigade Group with the specific task of investing Dunkirk.

According to the diarist, the following day the tanks began concentrating at St Omer, via Desues and Lumbre at 0900hrs. By 1500hrs the tanks had arrived at their concentration point where they were ordered to relieve 154th Infantry Brigade who, at that time, were besieging the German garrison at Dunkirk. By 1800hrs this action had begun.

On 3 October, Commander Leakey attended a conference at 2nd Canadian Army HQ at Ghent where he met with Major General Liska commanding the Czech Brigade. While he was involved with that, the tanks carried out routine maintenance tasks on their vehicles and managed to get hold of a rough plan for the siege of Dunkirk.

As the tank maintenance continued throughout the following day, the positions occupied by elements of 154th Brigade were visited by Leakey in order to get an idea of what the siege entailed.

The 5th saw 7th Royal Tanks receive their first set of orders from General Liska's HQ instructing them that the western sector of Dunkirk was to be the area of responsibility for the Regiment. The handover between 154th Infantry Brigade and 7th Royal Tanks was to take place over the night of the 7th/8th. In addition, the Czech Reconnaissance Squadron was to come under command of the Regiment. The forward positions of this western sector were in the Cassel area, according to the diarist.

More reconnaissance patrols were carried out on the 6th and that evening, the troop leaders went forward to 7th Battalion Black Watch HQ to 'obtain firsthand information about the ground and the best method of holding the ground by night'.[10] The following morning the tanks of the Regiment began moving from Cassell towards the Loon-Plage area with the main body of tanks arriving around 1430hrs. As darkness fell that night, the tanks then moved up to their forward positions. Both A and B Squadrons moved forward while C Squadron remained in the Loon-Plage area in reserve.

> By 0230hrs all the area had been taken over from 7th Black Watch. Czech Recce Sqn taking up their Posn in area 173798. It was made very obvious to the Sqn Ldrs that the only way the ground could be held especially at night was by having the tops dismounted and adopting Inf tactics entirely, with a few tanks to help hold the ground during the day.[11]

The night of 7 October and into the following morning was relatively quiet. Only intermittent shelling and the pop of flares fired in the forward areas disturbed the peace. At this point, 7th Royal Tanks was made up of 47 officers and 643 other ranks.

The 8th was a relatively quiet day with only harassing fire taking place across the front throughout the day. But by late evening the activity began. At 2359hrs the Allies experienced heavy German shelling on their positions, specifically on A Squadron's front which was a precursor to a German attack in strength on one of the squadron's most forward posts. The squadron had to then 'pull in this outpost' according to the diarist, while the heavy German shelling continued. As the Germans pushed towards the main positions of A Squadron they were met with a hail of gunfire and were forced to withdraw. Things began to quieten down along A Squadron's front by 0230hrs but the Czech Recce Squadron's front was attacked with heavy machine gun and mortar fire shortly afterwards. The forward outpost of their right flank came under sustained fire as a large German patrol tried to take this position at 0300hrs, reaching within 200 yards of it when they were finally pushed back after the Czechs brought up a thirty-man reinforcement patrol. Yet while all of this was going on, the B Squadron front was quiet throughout the night. However, they did keep up normal patrol activity well into the morning.

The regimental diarist states that, on the 9th, the Germans began shelling Allied headquarters in the Loon-Plage area which was subject to several heavy bombardments. The Germans were active again at 1810hrs when they were spotted by the Czech Recce Squadron moving towards a key observation post on the right flank. The Germans moved along the canal bank with a force that was estimated to be 200 strong. This activity was accompanied by heavy and strong artillery and mortar fire on the Czech positions. This force attacked the Czech positions as well as the right hand post of 7th Royal Tanks. Both Allied positions were vacated and were immediately occupied by the Germans. This took place around 0130hrs.

The next morning at 0700hrs the Allies attacked the positions, a group of farm buildings, that had been taken by the Germans the night before. The diarist details the events:

> A Sqn ... as Infantry, with crews from the Recce TP and a number of FFI attacked and seized this enemy posn, the attack was made over ground which had natural obstacles and Wire. P of W captured were 27 OR's and 1 Offr. The enemy also suffered several dead and wounded. Our Casualties were 1 dead and 5 wounded. During the day enemy shelling increased and Loon-Plage again attracted a number of his shells.[12]

That night, the Czech tank Regiment less one squadron arrived to relieve the Czech recce squadron. After the day's activities the night was relatively quiet, the silence punctuated by the sound of intermittent artillery fire.

The morning of the 11th, things were still quiet except for normal artillery fire. However, this changed in the afternoon, when, at 1630hrs rocket-firing Typhoons arrived and swarmed down on German positions in a group of factory buildings in a 'concentrated and effective' attack. As the Typhoons roared away back to their base, tanks from the 1st Czech Tank Regiment drove quickly into the factory area, occupying it and mopping up any German defenders who had not withdrawn or been killed or wounded in the Typhoon attack. Once the factory area was secure the tanks then moved forward, attacking German positions. They occupied a series of farm buildings, buildings around a railway crossing and other buildings close by. As darkness fell after a successful day's activities C Squadron arrived to relieve A Squadron.

Early in the morning of the 12th at 0115hrs, the Germans attacked a forward position in C Squadron's area who reported they were under attack from heavy mortar fire. A force of about eighty men followed up this fire and tried to attack the squadron's position. Thankfully, C Squadron personnel at this post put down a strong, stubborn, defensive fire to such a degree that the Germans were forced to withdraw. Both sides suffered casualties in this action, according to the diarist.

Later in the morning, at 1045hrs, tanks of B and C Squadrons began heavy firing of their HE rounds into German forward positions with excellent results, causing the Germans to suffer heavy casualties. However, activity for the day was not over. The diarist states that around 2150hrs the Germans again tried to break through into B Squadron's positions but they were unsuccessful and the attack was broken up by heavy Allied machine-gun fire.

The 13th was, according to the regimental diarist, a relatively quiet day. However, the German positions at Grande-Synthe had been laying down harassing fire onto the Allied positions and so air support was called for. This arrived at 1600hrs with eight Spitfires rolling down onto the target and strafing it with cannon and machine gun fire. Some of the Spitfires carried bombs that were dropped to great effect on the German positions. Heavy rain came during the night and no further activity took place.

The 14th saw more German activity in the area around 7th Royal Tank's lines as detailed by the regimental diarist:

> 2 deserters came in A Sqn's Lines. Both were Poles. The enemy became very audacious and endeavoured to form up, presumably for an attack on A Sqn's fwd Posn at 172817. This was dispersed and broken-up by Arty and Tank Gun Fire. Patrolling on the enemy's part was quite active during the night particularly in the Northern sector area of Mardyck. Movement was heard along the coast and it is believed that efforts are being made to contact collaborators behind our lines.[13]

That night, just before midnight, 2350hrs, the Germans began firing rounds from their Nebelwerfers (rocket launchers) directly onto A Squadron's forward post and fortunately, no casualties were sustained in this attack. The rest of the night reverted back to the normal artillery fire from the Germans.

The following day was quiet compared with activities that had taken place in previous days. Both and A and B Squadrons were still in their respective forward positions with C Squadron in reserve in the Loon-Plage area. The Germans laid down intermittent artillery and mortar fire on the Allied forward positions while Allied patrolling continued throughout the night.

On the 16th the Allied units detected movement around the German forward observation posts and the heavy AA battery poured fire onto those positions with good results according to the diarist. That day C Squadron relieved B Squadron, which was then sent into reserve in the Loon-Plage area. The diary entry for this day states that the usual patrol activity took place during the night with only a smattering of artillery fire.

The 17th was also a relatively quiet day for the Regiment. The tanks of the Regimental Headquarters fired their main guns at German positions in the afternoon. These were HE rounds and, while the Germans tried to answer the fire with mortar fire, the tanks were too far away and suffered no casualties. That night, the Germans sent a twelve-man patrol into the C Squadron area but they were spotted when they set off a trip flare. Immediately, C Squadron personnel in the forward positions opened fire on the German patrol to such an extent that they were forced to withdraw.

Luck was on the side of the Allies the following day when the Czechs discovered an abandoned German 80mm gun on the coast and hauled it back into the Allied lines. They also discovered with the gun 200 rounds of ammunition which was also brought back to Allied lines where the gun was prepared for service against its previous owners. In addition to the gun, an 8cm mortar was found in good condition. The Germans were active that night although the diarist does not provide the details of their activity.

Increased activity took place on 19 October as the Germans began pouring heavy artillery and mortar fire on positions in A Squadron's sector from 0945hrs to 1115hrs. After this took place there was a lull in the German fire plan and the rest of the day was normal up until 1815hrs when the Germans once again began a heavy bombardment of artillery fire on A Squadron's forward positions. Another lull in the firing took place until 2211hrs when another intense barrage took place. This time the artillery barrage was accompanied by heavy mortar fire. Before the Allies could get themselves organized two of A Squadron's forward positions had fallen to the Germans. Intelligence from a deserter estimated the German attacking force to number around 300 men. The diarist continues the account:

> The dark night was made full use of by the enemy. The attack must have been carefully planned and the participants well briefed for the main attack was made from our left rear while a diversionary party of 50 strong attacked forward at the same time. After that attack patrols from our other posts were sent out and they discovered that the enemy had withdrawn after demobilizing the defences.[14]

The above attack and subsequent action began at 2335hrs. The result was that one Allied officer was missing, two other ranks (ORs) were killed, ten wounded and eight were missing.

The following day the Allies decided not to try to take back what the Germans had taken the day before. This day was quiet and the Regiment spent the day reorganizing their positions. The night was also very quiet in contrast to the activity of the day before.

October 21st saw the front revert back to the normal harassing artillery fire from both sides. The Allies heard several aircraft over Dunkirk once darkness had fallen but there was little other activity.

Dawn the following day revealed to the observation posts in B Squadron's sector that several containers lay strewn over the ground between the Allied and German lines. It was presumed, according to the diarist, that these were from the aircraft that had been heard the night before over Dunkirk. At 1500hrs B Squadron sent several men out to pick up the containers while being covered by the 1st Czech Armoured Regiment, laying down fire on the right side. These troops managed to collect the containers and bring them back into Allied lines. Once the containers were opened they found Panzerschreck hollow charge projectiles, mail and news bulletins. The Germans did nothing to stop the Allies from collecting these containers. However, they did mount patrols during the night. Perhaps they had no idea that the Allies had managed to grab the containers and pull them back to their side?

At 0900hrs on the 23rd, a conference was called by the Regimental HQ concerning a proposed attack on German positions at Ferme Devez, Grande-Predembourg and Petit-Predembourg slated to begin 1400hrs the following day. The diarist then goes on to state that Allied daily consumption of artillery ammunition was reduced to twenty rounds per gun, per day. Although no reason is given for this reduction. The diary also states that the Germans reduced their artillery fire as well so perhaps this reduction was to match the German reduction? More German air activity over the Dunkirk area took place that night likely to drop more supplies.

The morning of the 24th saw silence fall across the front. However, at 1400hrs the Allied attack on Ferme Devez, Grande-Predembourg, Petit-Predembourg and Grande-Synthe began. 'The result of this attack proved conclusively that the above positions were German battle outposts and were lightly manned. Each position was severely mauled by tank gunfire and the FFI led by 7 R Tks Officers demolished as much as they could these forward positions. Tanks and FFI then withdrew, leaving some tanks forward in positions of observation.'[15]

That night, German air activity took place again. Fortunately, there were only two wounded men on the Allied side from the attacks earlier in the day.

The next day was quiet, only interrupted by occasional artillery fire on both sides. The night as well was quiet.

The 26th saw a little bit more activity. C Squadron forward positions found four containers that had been dropped by air the night before containing newspapers, mail and Bazookas (Panzerschreck) for the German garrison at Dunkirk. That night the Luftwaffe came over again in an attempt to drop more supplies. One German aircraft was shot down by the 3rd LAA Battery who had previously moved into the area. Activity at night time also took place with patrols mounted on both sides.

The following day A Squadron relieved C Squadron who moved into the Loon-Plage area. Normal patrol activity took place that night as it had the night before.

Activity on the 28th increased as sorties were carried out on Ferme Devez, Grande Predembourg and Grande-Synthe areas by A and B Squadrons. The idea for these sorties was, according to the diarist, to divert German attention away from an attack going in on the east side of Dunkirk by 2nd Armoured Regiment and the Czech motor battalion. The tank sorties attracted heavy German artillery fire while the attack on East Dunkirk did not. This attack was extremely successful even though one tank was lost when it rolled over a mine. The Allies captured 16 officers and 352 other ranks. The Germans also suffered casualties of almost 200 dead or seriously wounded that were left on the battlefield. The Allies suffered five wounded in these attacks. German patrols were active for the rest of the night.

The 29th was a very quiet day according to the diarist, with only spasmodic shelling. Both sides mounted considerable patrol activity through the night.

The next day, the Allies began by reorganizing their positions. The Germans, however, remained quiet. At 1700hrs A Squadron mounted another patrol employing French troops from the Mardyck area to Grande-Predembourg, while Allied harassing artillery fire continued throughout the day as normal.

The reorganizing continued on the 31st with C Squadron relieving B Squadron who moved into reserve status in the Loon-Plage area.

November 1944

The personnel of 7th Royal Tank Regiment were busy on 1 November 1944. At 0310hrs, the Germans attacked an Allied forward post in the Mardyck area with a fighting patrol that caused some alarm. However, using heavy machine gun fire Allied units were able to fight the Germans off and 7th Royal Tank suffered just one casualty. Artillery fire from both sides that day was extremely heavy. At 1800hrs the same day, the Germans attacked the Allied posts in the Mardyck area again. One other rank soldier was wounded during this attack. But the Germans withdrew and the rest of the night was quiet.

The following day, 7th Royal Tank HQ began a reorganizing process. A Squadron held several buildings and a track junction at the forward area. The Squadron HQ moved up to Ferme Greenson putting them forward of C Squadron. 'During the night a flying bomb was reported to have been launched by the enemy from the Dunkirk area, and fired out to sea appx due NW. Enemy patrols were active in A Sqn area.'[16]

On 3 November, the tanks from A & C Squadrons were in action against the German defences in the Predembourg, Ferme Devez and Grande-Synthe vicinities. They knew that the Germans had occupied several buildings in these sectors and so the tanks moved forward, firing repeatedly at their targets with their 75mm guns. The Germans responded by laying down direct fire (DF) onto the tanks and this included fire from their 155mm artillery guns. The tanks, having carried out their duties, withdrew back to their normal positions. The diarist does not mention if any were hit or not.

At 1615hrs the Germans ordered twenty men to move down the main road from the direction of their positions around Grande-Synthe. They did not get far, as Allied machine guns opened up on them, driving the Germans back to their lines. As darkness fell so too did the quiet, although 'the enemy anticipated some action on our part for throughout the night parachute flares were being used along the whole front'. Two Allied soldiers were wounded that night.

The next day, early in the morning at 0410hrs, the Germans began pounding 7th Royal Tank positions with artillery fire but this petered out as dawn arrived. In terms of artillery, both sides kept up harassing fire throughout the day.

> At night enemy patrolling was reduced. This was probably due to the very bright moon. This curtailed our own patrol activities also. A number of explosions were heard from the centre of the

Dunkirk area. Patrol of 3 FFI failed to return. Strength of the unit 45 Officers and 643 Other Ranks.[17]

November 5th saw the Germans using Panzerschreck/Bazookas against a Sherman tank as it rolled up the Predembourg road from Mardyck. Seven rounds were fired at the tank by the Germans but only one hit and this glanced off the turret, blowing off the welded track plate. 'They were obviously using the Bazookas dropped by planes the previous night. The enemy is unskilled in the use of these weapons, due, no doubt to lack of ammunition for training purposes.'[18]

That night, the Germans launched several flares across the entire front. The diarist for 7th Royal Tank states that a German patrol was heard moving in a northwards direction near C Squadron positions. To counter this patrol, C Squadron HQ sent out a patrol as well. The result was a 'Sharp Skirmish'. According to the diary the Squadron did not suffer any casualties.

The following day, 6 November, Squadron patrols found a German lying on the ground. He had been shot the night before during the clash between the two patrols. German artillery fire increased as the night went on. By 0745hrs on the 7th, German artillery fire was concentrated on the Mardyck area and C Squadron HQ. Several buildings were hit causing severe damage. Fortunately, no casualties were suffered during the bombardment.

The same day, a French patrol moving along the dunes ran into a German minefield and one of the French soldiers was killed when he stepped on a mine. Squadron patrols captured six German mortars and plenty of ammunition on the beaches when they overran a German position. The mortars were divided up so that B Squadron on the left had two of them, another two were given to C Squadron on the right and 'the last two were kept in mobile reserve'.[19] The ammunition was divided out accordingly.

During the night of the 7th, the Allied patrols suffered a setback. On the right of C Squadron, a position that was manned by both the French and the Czechs from the 1st Czech Regiment, received a pounding from German artillery. As the bombardment died away German infantry attacked and overran the post capturing all its occupants. The Germans, with their new prisoners, withdrew back to their lines.

Dawn on 8 November saw A Squadron relieve C Squadron who moved back to Loon-Plage. This was also the area that 7th Royal Tank's Regimental HQ was situated in. In Bourbourg, A Echelon had set up its positions while in Cassel B Echelon had done the same. A Squadron patrol with the CO leading managed to get through to Ferme Augte in the afternoon of the same day. They suffered no casualties and returned intact although the Germans had peppered them with rifle and machine-gun fire. As night fell, the front went quiet.

However, that peacefulness erupted in chaos the following morning when rocket-firing Typhoons roared overhead, hammering German heavy gun positions with rockets in the Dunkirk area. At 1500hrs, B Squadron suffered an attack by a German patrol trying to infiltrate into their positions. However, they were quickly spotted and shot up with machine-gun and rifle fire. Throughout the day, the Germans laid down heavy artillery fire on squadron positions in the Loon-Plage sector, killing four French soldiers and wounding two. Throughout the night, Allied gunners answered the earlier German fire by hammering German positions.

On 10 November the day was relatively quiet in terms of patrols. Only the Allied artillery fire kept up its fire programme as did the Germans on them. The Forward Observation Officer that had been supporting the Heavy Anti-Aircraft Regiment was permanently assigned to the Regiment on this day. 'During the day he remains in Fwd O.P's. At night he stations himself at this R.H.Q. which enables him to shoot on call for both of the fwd Sqns. This also enables us to use the Czech Fd Arty Regt when the situation demands for close targets.'[20]

At 1930hrs, the Forward Squadron reported seeing a projectile that looked like a flying bomb launched from a site in the Dunkirk area behind the German lines. It was heading in the general direction of England. That night both the Allies and the Germans mounted patrols in the Dunkirk region along the forward lines. One Allied soldier was killed although the diarist does not indicate his nationality.

Early the following morning at 0700hrs, B Squadron rolled into the Mardyck sector to relieve C Squadron who then went into reserve. The rest of the day saw the usual harassing artillery fire on both sides. A Squadron remained in the Grande-Synthe area where, in the afternoon of the 13th, they attacked some German observation posts, shooting them up successfully with tank fire.

Later on the 13th, Allied Dakota twin-engined transport aircraft was shot down by German AA fire while flying over Dunkirk on the way to England. It crash-landed on the beach inside German-held territory.

The following day the Germans were active across the whole siege line or front. Allied artillery continued to hammer German positions while that night, the evening of the 14th, a patrol from A Squadron ran into a German patrol and a short, sharp battle ensued with both patrols withdrawing quickly.

The 15th was another day where the gun batteries on both sides exchanged heavy artillery fire. Normal night time patrols continued.

The next day saw more activity. B Squadron relieved A Squadron who had been in the Pont a'Roseaux area while A Squadron moved to the Loon-Plage area. C Squadron moved into the Mardyck positions which were promptly shelled by German gunners. Fortunately, the Squadron suffered no casualties. Allied gunners laid down counterbattery fire on the German gun positions but the diarist does not state if this fire had any effect.

However, as the night wore on the tempo of German patrolling operations was increased and several patrols tried to infiltrate into the Allied positions at Mardyck and Pont a'Roseaux. Squadron tanks held these patrols at bay with their machine-gun fire and fire from their main guns. Sadly, one French soldier was lost on this day and one soldier from 7th Royal Tank due to German artillery fire.

The 17th saw C Squadron patrol the Predembourg area where they came across German defenders, attacked them and cleared them from the area, according to the diarist. This took place at 1530hrs. 'Enemy arty fire was slow in coming into operation and it was not until our tanks were withdrawing to Mardyck that his arty fire came down. This was heavy calibre shells from the Dunkirk area. No tanks were damaged or casualties suffered.'[21]

Later, at 1730hrs, the Germans attacked the Allied positions at Pont a'Roseaux. The Squadron's positions in the Mardyck area were heavily shelled until 2355hrs. However, 15 minutes prior to the overall ending of the German shelling their artillery fire lifted in the Loon-Plage area and in the rear of the Mardyck sector. Around forty German troops, under the cover of night, moved slowly up the Predembourg–Mardyck road but were spotted by the Squadron's tanks which opened fire on the Germans, forcing them to move back.

Activity throughout the night took place across the front. Mardyck village was attacked by another force of Germans but this time intense fire from the French (FFI) positions and from one of the Squadron's tanks drove them away. Not too long afterwards another German force attacked from the

North but again the tanks of the Squadron held them at bay. 'It is considered that this force was the main one and was in considerable strength.'[22]

A battle between both sides ensued and lasted only 30 minutes when the Germans began to move West presumably to outflank the Allied positions.

> One tank moved west to area 150836 and was able to disperse the enemy. Whilst this tank was away the remaining two tanks were heavily shelled and phosphorus bombs were used against them. The enemy attacked immediately after the shelling and got to within 20 yds of the tanks. Again, they were driven off.[23]

Once again, at 0330hrs, the diarist writes that the Germans tried to take the positions where the tanks were but were held at bay in an action lasting 40 minutes. Yet, even after these failures, the Germans once more launched an attack against this northern Allied post at 0500hrs and were, once again, unsuccessful.

An hour later, 0600hrs on the morning of the 18th, all was quiet but an Allied artillery bombardment began by a Battery of 2nd Canadian HAA Regt, and the Czech Field Artillery Regt. According to the diarist, the Germans returned fire with more than 400 rounds of differing types of ammunition.

The rest of the day saw normal harassing artillery fire on both sides and the Allied gunners carried out pre-planned gun programmes on existing German targets. That night, the Allied units in the eastern part of the Mardyck area easily drove off German patrols.

On the 19th the Regiment saw the departure of Major Howard Jones who had been posted to take over command of the 11th Royal Tank Regiment. Activity this day was light and only took place during the day. The night was a quiet one.

However, in the early morning hours of the 20th, the Germans began to lay mines along the surface of the Dunkirk/Loon-Plage road. As dawn was creeping over the horizon, at 0530hrs, tanks began moving down the road but fortunately for them these mines had been discovered and disabled beforehand. 'As the tanks withdrew at first light in order to rest the tank crews, had these not been discovered in time, the first one on its way back would have been blown up.'[24] Around the same time a reconnaissance group from 147th Regiment Royal Armoured Corps (RAC) arrived tasked to relieve B Squadron who were currently in the Pont a'Roseaux area.

The situation at 0700hrs on 20 November 1944 was that in the Mardyck sector, A Squadron relieved C Squadron, who then moved into the Loon-Plage area. Also this day, the Allies mined both forward positions in these two sectors with anti-personnel mines. Around this time the new second in command, Major L.C. Rumsey, arrived.

The following day things were pretty quiet across the whole front, but two Czech personnel were killed and one was wounded by Teller mines laid by the Germans on the Regiment's front. 'It is believed that they were endeavouring to neutralize a Tellermine fitted with the new 43 fuze.'[25] That night, the Regiment sent out more patrols into the forward areas but they did not encounter any German patrols.

On the 22nd, the Regiment's observations posts picked up a lot of German movement in the Mardyck area which was answered by a lengthy concentration of artillery fire on German positions. The artillery activity on both sides continued throughout the night. One soldier was wounded at this time.

Dawn on the 22nd, and A Squadron from 147th RAC, relieved B Squadron 7th Royal Tanks which left the locations of the units as A Squadron of 7th Royal Tanks in the Mardyck area, B Squadron had moved into positions in the Loon-Plage sector while C Squadron held positions in Gravelines. In addition to this, A Squadron 147th RAC remained holding positions in the Pont a'Roseaux area.

Throughout the following day the Germans kept up a spasmodic programme of artillery shelling on these armoured positions. Allied counter-harassing fire continued. Other than that, the day was quiet for both sides. However, the same was not true of the 24th, when A Squadron HQ ordered the clearing of tracks within their vicinity as well as laying S mines on their northern flank. The diarist writes, 'During the night some enemy planes were heard flying low over the centre of Dunkirk which no doubt dropped supplies'.[26]

In the morning of 25 November, two squadrons of Typhoon fighter bombers roared in low and fast over the German positions, strafing them with their 20mm cannon and dropping bombs on their positions in the 7th Royal Tank sector. This was supported by a heavy artillery barrage that followed a pre-planned fire programme from HQ Royal Artillery. The diarist indicates that the nights had been bright due to clear weather that reduced patrol activity on both sides.

A lot of activity took place on the 26th, starting at 0500hrs, when 'what at first seemed to be a flying bomb overhead proved to be a Mustang aircraft which crashed in this area. Both observer and pilot landed safely and enjoyed a good breakfast in our Mess. It was interesting to note that neither of them were aware that Dunkirk was NOT in our hands.'[27]

At 0710hrs a vapour trail was observed shooting up into the sky at a very high altitude accompanied by the sound of rolling and rumbling thunder according the diarist, coming from the Dunkirk area. This was likely a V2 rocket heading for London or Antwerp. On one of the patrols an Allied soldier was killed and another wounded when they passed over mines laid by their own side. Another patrol was sent out to recover the body and were heavily engaged by German machine-gun and mortar fire. Fortunately, they were able to recover the dead soldier and bring him back to the relative safety of their lines with no further casualties.

Throughout the day, Allied gunners kept up the shelling of German positions in the Dunkirk area. That night, the Germans switched on several floodlights and lit flares as a number of planes flew over the Dunkirk area. The diarist suggests this illumination was probably to light the drop zone for the aircraft.

Dawn on the 27th saw B Squadron relieved by A Squadron who moved into the Mardyck area. C Squadron relieved A Squadron 147th RAC who then began their move back to the 34th Tank Brigade sector in Holland. Again, Allied gunners kept up their harassing artillery fire on German positions, pounding any movement seen across their lines. That night, the weather turned cold and cloudy giving the Germans the cover to begin active patrolling. 'A fighting patrol of about 30 men tried to infiltrate through the Mardyck position. Machine Gun fire from the fwd tanks and DF from the Czech Arty which was hastily brought down caused them to break up and withdraw.'[28]

At 0520hrs on 28 November, a patrol sent out by B Squadron ran into a German patrol close to the coast resulting in a quick battle that forced the Germans to withdrew in haste. The rest of the day was uneventful and at night patrols were active across the front.

However, something different took place on the following day that the diarist describes as a psychological warfare programme. 'It began at 0930hrs with light and medium bombers attacking German main defensive positions. This was followed by several Squadrons of Spitfires strafing the enemy area in general. Own arty increased their concentration and kept this up throughout the day. This culminated in leaflets being dropped in the enemy lines along with Safe Conduct passes, and broadcasts from special vehicles asking the enemy to surrender. One Spitfire was shot down during this attack.'[29] After all this activity during the day, the night itself was quiet.

The final day of November 1944, was relatively quiet for the troops of 7th Royal Tank Regiment however, the same programme from the day before took place on the eastern sector of the siege line. That evening, at 2000hrs, C Squadron took charge of two German deserters who had decided they'd had enough and surrendered in the Pont a'Roseaux area. Normal patrols took place during the night.

December 1944

As dawn broke on 1 December, A Squadron relieved B Squadron who had been patrolling and probing German defences in the forward areas. The night had been quiet and the day itself was also without incident.

The following day patrolling continued as did the artillery fire directed by the observation posts attached to A Squadron who were controlling the artillery fire worked out in the RAC gun programme. 'During the night about 16 enemy aircraft were over Dunkirk and many containers are believed to have been dropped.'[30]

The following day, 3 December, the battalion's diarist recorded that it was a normal day. In the Pont a'Roseaux area, B Squadron relieved C Squadron while Allied harassing artillery fire continued. During the night, the Germans returned fire with heavy artillery shells that slammed into the Loon-Plage/Bourbourg Road without any disruption or damage. However, just after midnight, one of B Squadron's patrol engaged a German patrol that escalated into a fire fight causing the Germans to withdraw. Two Germans were wounded but the Regiment suffered no casualties.

December 4th was a busy day for the Regiment. In the morning, Allied artillery fire continued to pound German positions but the Germans did not return fire. In the afternoon, a French patrol (FFI) from the Mardyck sector attacked a German outpost at Grande-Predembourg at 1500hrs. The Germans waited until the French patrol was within 50 yards of their position and then opened fire on them. The French patrol 'made a dash into the place and succeeded in killing one German and capturing another'.[31]

> During the night enemy planes were again over Dunkirk. 1 Deserter gave himself up to B Sqn in the area of the factory at

> 174815. Another deserter from the Dunkirk Garrison presented himself to B Sqn. Own arty fire increased during the day. Some enemy arty fired at our fwd areas.[32]

On the night of the 4th/5th a large German patrol attacked the forward squadron in the Mardyck area however, the diarist tells us that this patrol was 'driven off' by machine-gun fire and tank fire. 'Several OPs reported rockets being fired from the Dunkirk area, no explosion was heard from the source of the firing. OPs were unable to establish size of these rockets.'[33]

Allied artillery continued its harassing fire on the following day but this time the Germans responded with mortar and artillery fire. The Allies had captured a German Nebelwerfer rocket launcher (28/32cm) with shells. They then turned this weapon back onto the Germans firing twelve rounds onto the German defensive position in the Grande-Synthe area. 'The enemy were quick in retaliation and fired about 16 rounds of mortar. Although they fell in the vicinity of the Nebelwerfer no damage was done either to the weapon or the personnel firing it.'[34] That night the Luftwaffe was active again as they dropped supplies to the beleaguered German garrison at Dunkirk. One He 111 bomber was shot down by Allied Bofors guns.

The next morning, 7 December, the Germans began shelling Allied lines but the fire, that lasted all day from their 150mm and 88mm guns, was spasmodic, according to the diarist.

> At 1500 hrs RHQ Tanks fired at Grande-Predembourg. Shooting was good. Enemy quickly replied with about 15 88mm HE shells without causing any damage or casualties. Own patrols were active during the night. Enemy patrols were confirmed to be in the Pont a'Roseaux sector where clashes with our own patrols took place.[35]

On the 8th, the Germans laid more mines in the Regiment's northern forward areas. While in the rear sector the Allies continued to clear mines that had already been laid by the Germans sometime before. This same day, the diarist tells us, one of the Regiment's patrols found two dead Germans in the Pont a'Roseaux sector where there had been a strong firefight the night before. As the night approached, the Germans began shelling Allied positions in the Mardyck sector.

The following day saw the arrival of a detachment of French Marines, whose task was to protect the coastal flank in the Mardyck area. The French spent the entire day organizing themselves and setting up their HQ, while the clearance of mines by elements of 7th Royal Tank continued in the rear areas.

The same day, the Germans shelled the Loon-Plage area with their 150mm guns. Indeed, their artillery fire on the Allied siege line continued throughout the day, answered by an increase in Allied harassing fire on them. Regimental patrols continued throughout the night and loud, heavy, explosions were heard coming from the Dunkirk area.

In view of the arrival of the French Marine detachment, the 10th saw the Regiment begin to reorganize its positions. A shelter position was created with an outpost on the dunes. The French took up this position and immediately were fired on by two Spandau machine-gun posts that killed one of the Marines. These German posts were then pounded by Allied artillery fire. That night, more heavy and violent explosions could be heard coming from Dunkirk. It is the diarist's view that this was most likely from demolitions although there is no indication as to what was these demolitions could have been.

December 11th saw the Germans concentrating their machine-gun and mortar fire on regimental and infantry positions in the Mardyck area. 'This was promptly answered by our tanks and an hour later French Marines supported by fire from a troop of tanks cleaned up the area.'[36] The Allies laid more mines from the dunes to their Southern positions. The rest of the night was quiet.

At 0700hrs on 12 December, B Squadron rolled into the Mardyck sector to relieve C Squadron. Later in the morning, tanks from both A and B squadrons fired on German positions in the vicinities of Grande-Predembourg and Fame Devez. The infantry also fired 28/32cm rockets at the same German defences at Grande-Predembourg. These were shot from Allied positions in the Mardyck area. The rockets pounded several German machine-gun posts and pillboxes north of Ferme Devez. The Germans did try to counter-fire but according to the diarist it was a poor showing. However, in the late afternoon, the Germans began increasing their patrol activity inevitably bringing them into contact with the 7th Royal Tank patrols.

The 13th was a quiet day for the squadron. Commander Royal Artillery's gun programme continued with artillery harassing fire on German positions near Dunkirk. 'Own patrols active during the night. French Marines contacted enemy patrol in Sq 1484, and opened fire on them. An effort to cut them off on their return journey was unsuccessful.'[37]

The Germans didn't start firing their artillery until 2005hrs on the 14th, according to the regimental diarist. However, throughout the day, the Allies heard considerable 'noise and movement of H.D. [heavy duty] vehicles in the Grande-Synthe area. This was soundly "stonked" by supporting arty. Nothing more was heard.'[38]

Dawn on 15 December saw A Squadron relieved by elements of C Squadron in the Pont a'Roseaux area. As the German activity was quiet on this day, the tanks of A Squadron began a firing exercise on a range built on the dunes. In the afternoon, Mitchell bombers came over and pounded the German defences at Fort Mardyck at 1445hrs. German artillery fire rained down on Allied positions at Loon-Plage at the same time as the bombing took place. This was heavy 155mm fire. Fortunately, there were no casualties. That night, the squadron carried out local patrols.

With the exception of German artillery fire on Allied positions at Loon-Plage, on the 16th the day was quiet. Royal Artillery gunners continued their harassing fire of German positions throughout the night while the Germans mounted patrols under the cover of darkness.

The following day saw more activity. It began with Royal Artillery gunners keeping up the harassing fire on the Germans. It then continued with Canadian forward observation officers (FOOs) bringing artillery fire to bear on movement they had observed in the German lines.

> Enemy 150mm guns again fired at Loon-Plage during the afternoon. These guns are fired from the large Font-Ouvnage Quest and are in emplacements. Fire from own guns have no effect on them whatsoever. During the night a patrol of about 30 men were observed advancing from Grande-Synthe area. This was effectively broken up by the F.O.O. of the Czech Fd Regt. Each fwd Sqn has a representative from the Czech Fd Regt who stays with the Sqn night and day. Both are on a direct line to their guns. The

Sqn Ldr can therefore ask for fire, and get the rounds bursting on the ground in a matter of minutes.[39]

During the night of the 17th members of A Squadron heard heavy explosions come from the Dunkirk area. The diarist does not elaborate on what they were.

The 18th was another day of artillery fire and patrols. Visibility was good as Royal Artillery gunners based their shoots on their predicted gun programme. The good visibility also enabled the FOOs to bring down fire on German occupied positions within the Dunkirk area. The captured German Nebelwerfer was used again in the afternoon, this time by the Czech Bde representative who fired twelve rounds on the German defences at Grande-Predembourg and on some occupied buildings in the same area. These were fired from an excellent position of cover in the Mardyck area that had direct communication line with the observation posts. The personnel in these posts were able to provide correction information to ensure that the rounds hit their targets. The rockets have a range of about 1800 yards. Other than this activity, the night was a quiet one.

The morning of the 19th saw widespread ground mist that made artillery fire by observation impossible. As a result, the Allied gunners reverted to the planned gun programme but because of the mist they were unable to see where their rounds landed in the German area. The mist was very likely the reason why the night was uneventful.

However, despite the thick ground mist, 20 December was a much more active day. In the morning, A Squadron sent out a patrol towards Grande-Predembourg and just as they were closing on the German lines, the mist suddenly cleared revealing the patrol to the enemy gunners. The Germans opened up on them with heavy machine-gun fire. 'The officer from A Sqn who was leading the patrol was wounded. The remainder of the patrol managed to get back to our own lines along with the officer. Own patrols were out during the night. No enemy patrols contacted.'[40]

The following day the entire area was covered in ground mist making any kind of offensive activity difficult. B Squadron moved into the Pont a'Roseaux sector where they relieved C Squadron. In the Clipon area, the Czech Field Regiment sited three captured 155mm guns which were given to a company of French gunners and infantry from the 110th Battalion which was under the command of the Czech Field Regiment. The task of the French, according to the diarist, was twofold: first to intercept any German patrols moving along the beaches and second to give protection to the 155mm guns. During the night, Squadron B mounted several patrols that engaged in small firefights with the Germans in the Mardyck and Pont a'Roseaux areas.

The French also engaged the Germans, in this case a small patrol of three men who quickly returned to their lines when the French opened fire on them.

On the 22nd visibility was still pour preventing any observed fire by the FOOs; instead the Allied gunners had to revert to the programmed artillery fire. The Germans, however, did not reply with their own guns. At 2310hrs that same day, one of the squadron's patrols observed ten Germans move into a house. Immediately, using their wireless sets, they contacted the Czech field artillery who opened fire with their big guns accurately hammering the house. From that point until 0455hrs no further German activity was observed. At this time, French Marines ran across another German patrol, exchanging small-arms fire with them. The Germans withdrew safely back to their lines.

Visibility the following day was still bad and very little activity took place. The FOOs were only able to fire on forward German positions that could be seen in the swirling mist. However, during the night the members of the squadron heard a lot of German activity in the Grande-Synthe area which was immediately pounded by artillery fire from the Czech Field Artillery Brigade. The following day, the diarist states that 'Apart from daily gun programme the whole front was quiet.'[41]

Christmas Day saw high morale and the diarist states that everyone enjoyed 'a Christmas fare of chicken, Christmas pudding, and mince pies. Beer, cigarettes and cigars also added to their enjoyment. Night quiet.'[42]

The following day the temperature dropped dramatically to several degrees below zero, causing the flooded areas to become covered with ice. Tank activity was negligible but the Nebelwerfer was fired in the afternoon at German defensive positions in the Grande-Predembourg area. This was viewed by the Czech high command. As darkness fell, the squadron sent out several patrols but had no contact with the Germans. Later in the evening a single German aircraft roared overhead, firing its machine guns at Allied positions at Mardyck. The attack was over very quickly.

A Squadron was, at this point, in the Pont a'Roseaux sector where, on 27 December, they were relieved by B Squadron. However, the diarist tells us that there was no German activity in this sector on that day. Visibility was bad which meant that Allied artillery fire from the Czech Field Regiment and 2nd Canadian AA Regiment was programmed only. This was a fire plan that had been pre-programmed based on intelligence from reconnaissance patrols and from aerial photographs rather than on actual observation of the Germans by the FOOs.

On the 28th the weather was still bad and visibility was poor and Allied fire was down to harassing fire only. No German activity was observed on this day.

However, the following day the weather cleared enabling the FOOs to provide proper coordinates from observing the German positions to the Allied gunners. The Germans did not return the artillery fire.

Rain and fog arrived the next day, 30 December, reducing visibility to 500 yards. This meant that Allied gunners could not rely on the information from the FOOs for accurate artillery fire and had to fall back on the pre-programmed shoots. Despite this, the Squadron sent out several patrols during the night, but they did not encounter any German patrols and the night was otherwise quiet.

On the last day of December 1944, the Squadron's tanks rumbled forward and began firing on German positions at Grande-Synthe and Grande-Predembourg. This time the Germans did react, firing several 88mm HE rounds at the Allied positions.

> Own harassing fire continued throughout the day. At night enemy patrols were active in the Pont a'Roseaux sector. Own patrols contacted the enemy in buildings. A machine gun duel took place. Own patrol eventually withdrew and the buildings were stonked by Arty.[43]

This then, is a detailed look at the activities of 7th Royal Tank Regiment in the last months of 1944 during the Siege of Dunkirk. The Regiment was later reborn as a Crocodile flamethrowing unit in February 1945. In this role, the 7th were much in demand as the Allied armies pushed into Germany and towards victory. Lieutenant Colonel R.B.P. Wood took over command of the Regiment in late February.

Chapter 13

The Air Campaign and Epilogue

While much of this book has been devoted to the ground operations against the German defence of the Channel ports and Dunkirk in late 1944, little detail has been provided on the air campaigns that supported the operations to liberate the ports. Of course, throughout the analyses of the operations to capture the ports within this book, air attacks have been shown as being integral parts of the overall operations.

It is hoped this final chapter will provide the reader with a brief understanding of the air campaign as well as a more accurate picture of the all-arms effort it took to liberate the Channel ports and ultimately, Dunkirk. While this is not a definitive study, it should give an idea of the amount of effort, materiel and manpower needed for victory as well as the cost in blood and treasure.

Before we look into the bombing campaign over the Channel ports it is worth a brief glimpse of what the Germans felt about the Allied air campaign. General Field Marshal Otto Moritz Walter Model,[1] appointed C-in-C West in August 1944, stated on 15 September:

> By employing their air force chiefly in front of the spearheads of their attack the enemy are succeeding not only in harassing our movements, but often in completely eliminating them. Considerable losses in personnel and equipment have occurred during transport to the front, which often cannot take place at the required time. For example, six ammunition trains became casualties, and of these one train contained 128 tons of close-combat anti-tank weapons urgently required by my Army Group.[2]

Allied tactical air forces provided close support to the ground campaigns from the Battle of Normandy onwards. Indeed, we have seen throughout this book how Allied bombers and fighter-bombers, most notably the Hawker Typhoon, provided air support for the campaigns against the German garrisons in the Channel ports. 'In September (and indeed always) they provided information by reconnaissance over and forward of the Army front, supplied overhead protection for Allied troops and collaborated in attacks on enemy positions.'[3]

Let us, therefore, look at the role the Typhoons played in the trapping of the German troops in the Falaise Gap. In an earlier chapter this is reported on from the perspective of the ground operations but in this brief study we will look at it from the point of view of Typhoon operations. We must also remember that there were other dedicated fighter-bombers attacking the German ground forces during this time. The United States Air Force was flying the P-47 Thunderbolt, the P-38 Lightning and the P-51 Mustang. The RAF was flying the excellent Spitfire, Mosquito and, in some operations, the Hurricane Mk IID and even the Westland Whirlwind in fighter-bomber and rocket-firing roles. All excellent aircraft flown by highly capable pilots. However, it is the British Hawker Typhoon that seems to have had the greatest impact on the Germans at the receiving end of its might.

As the gap closed the demand for the Typhoons, the rocket-firing types and the bombing types, grew exponentially. The 'set-piece' attacks were becoming less and less prominent as this demand increased. However, let's examine one 'set-piece' attack that was mounted on 10 June when 181, 182, 245 and 247 Squadrons provided forty aircraft, rocket-firing Typhoons, for an attack on the Panzer Group West Headquarters at Chateau de la Caine. The Typhoons roared in at low level, firing off their rockets and strafing the target with 20mm cannon, and almost immediately afterwards sixty-one RAF Mitchell bombers pounded the target with 500lb bombs dropped from 12,000ft. Three hundred bombs hit the target. A large number of Germans were killed in this operation including Major General Ritter and Edler von Dawans.[4]

On several occasions the Americans also called in Typhoon support as they advanced into France and Germany. Whenever the Germans counter-attacked, the Americans would call on the Typhoons to roar in low and fast and mete out the kind of punishment they were known for. Generally, this would be against targets such as German armour and troops. 'In one attack near Saint-Lô halting a powerful column of tanks by the simple expedient of blowing off the tracks of the leading vehicle, and then of the rearmost tank, before setting about those trapped between.'[5]

198 Squadron began the practice of setting up 'cabrank' patrols that the Allies had used to great effect during 1943 in North Africa and Italy.

Essentially, this meant that that Typhoon squadrons would mount almost continuous patrols with small formations of aircraft operating over a small section of the front:

> ... their pilots in radio touch with a contact van among the leading elements of the ground forces. In the event that the advancing troops encountered enemy resistance that could not be quickly and economically overcome – be it a strongpoint or enemy armour – the contact controller would call up the patrolling fighters, passing a map reference and describing the target, while the ground forces would loose off coloured mortar bombs as target indicators.[6]

Typhoon pilots quickly built up experience to the point that they were able to accurately take out many of the targets identified by the ground forces.

Throughout July 1944, the pincers created by the advancing Allied armies of the Falaise Gap steadily closed on the Germans while overhead, the Typhoons flew patrols all over Normandy almost unopposed by the Luftwaffe, their only real danger was anti-aircraft fire. 175 Squadron, on 8 July, attacked a Hitler Youth battalion near Caen, then pounded a concentration of German self-propelled guns with their rockets and cannon fire the following day. One Typhoon was lost to flak (anti-aircraft fire) but the Typhoon pilots claimed five of the guns as destroyed.

As the Allied armies pushed on, the demand for the Typhoons was increasing so much that before July was out constant strikes on German targets were being flown by twelve Typhoon squadrons. These sorties were against sixteen German divisions, nine of which were Panzer divisions. One of the most constantly involved squadrons in action during July was 182 Squadron. In six days, the Squadron flew almost 300 missions. On 25 July, Major D.H. Barlow SAAF, 182's commanding officer, was hit by flak and had to bail out. Ground patrols had seen large numbers of German troops enter a wood and the coordinates had been passed onto the squadron who tore down at the target, plastering the trees with rockets and cannon fire. Every squadron operating over Normandy suffered casualties and 182 was no exception. Before the end of July, the squadron had lost three experienced flight officers.[7]

As the American Third Army supply lines became overstretched the Germans decided to launch a major offensive west towards the sea in order to cut the Americans off from the rest of the Allies. This offensive took place on 7 August. Perhaps if the Germans had attacked either north or south or both to break the pressure of the Allied pincer movements bearing down on them they might have had much greater success.

However, the German offensive ran into the might of seven Typhoon squadrons on that day. 'Their pilots found a concentration of 60 tanks and more than 200 support vehicles; in nine hours these squadrons flew 312 sorties, destroying about 30 tanks, a similar number of other armoured vehicles four self-propelled guns and 50 supply trucks.'[8] For a brief moment the Typhoons were diverted to the British sector where they destroyed another five German tanks in order to counter a smaller thrust by the German army.

Worse devastation for the Germans came the next day when an entire German infantry battalion took refuge in a wood south-east of Alençon, near Le Theil. The Americans called for the Typhoons to attack this small wood. Seven of them arrived overhead five minutes after receiving the call. They then proceeded to obliterate the wood first with rocket fire then, once their rockets had been expended, to roar in again and continue the attack with their 20mm cannon. Those Germans that survived this terrible ordeal by fire, as soon as the Typhoons had gone, wanted to immediately surrender, according to the Americans.[9]

While it's true that Luftwaffe sorties were not frequent during this time, it doesn't mean that there were none, as can be seen on 17 August. This is the day when the First Canadian Army reached Falaise and captured it. Typhoons from 183 Squadron had been called on for an armed reconnaissance flight over the area. Nine Typhoons roared in but quickly found themselves surrounded by more than fifty of the latest German version of the vaunted Messerschmitt Bf 109, the G variant. As they battled to extricate themselves, four Typhoons were shot down.

Retribution, however, came three days later when the Polish Armoured Brigade pushing east of Falaise near Vimoutiers found themselves up against two Panzer divisions, or what was left of them as almost 100 German tanks rolled out from a wood to face the Poles. They quickly called for air support and shortly afterwards thirty-two Typhoons attacked the German armoured tanks and armoured vehicles destroying fifty-six and damaging several others.

This is a brief look at the effectiveness of the Typhoon operations after D-Day and is designed to give the reader a glimpse of the destructive power of these aircraft and the types of tactics used in order to maximise this power. Over the years, many authors have played down the damage caused by the Typhoon attacks but perhaps the most telling point of the success of the Typhoon was its debilitating effect on the morale of the German armoured crews and infantry caught on the sharp end of this machine.

Yet as an example of its destructiveness, during the month of August 183 Squadron destroyed thirty-one tanks, damaged twenty-seven, destroyed eleven other armoured vehicles, damaging thirteen more, and flamed more than fifty trucks. That is just the tally of one Typhoon squadron. If there were twelve Typhoon squadrons or more ranging all over Normandy and the Channel ports during the months leading up to 1945 probably racking up similar scores it's little wonder the Germans hated them.

It's now time to turn our attention to the operations of the heavy bombers. Bomber operations were split between providing the Allied armies, mostly British and Canadian for the purposes of this book, air support during ground offensives and in the strategic air campaign against Germany. New advances in technology such as scientific aids for increasing bombing accuracy and new aids for navigation provided the Allied air forces with an edge. Also, the fact that the German early warning radar system had been captured by the Allies as they pushed the German armies further and further back towards Germany helped to give the Allies an edge in the air, in daylight and in darkness. The destruction of the German oil industry and fuel supplies for its fighters and fighter-bombers and lack of trained pilots meant that the German Luftwaffe was unable to stop the Allies from gaining air supremacy. In September 1944 alone, Bomber Command dropped 52,587 tons of bombs on German targets while the American Eighth Air Force unleashed 36,332 tons on the hapless enemy troops.

Indeed, 50 per cent of Bomber Command's total tonnage dropped was in support of the Army. The German oil industry felt the weight of 7 per cent of Bomber Command's total number of bombs dropped while German towns were pounded by 28 per cent of its total tonnage. Of the American total tonnage, 40 per cent went towards the bombing of communications while 19 per cent of their total tonnage dropped hit German factories and another 19 per cent pounded the German oil and gas industry.[10] For example, by looking at the bombing campaigns we can see in some cases, the bombing was very accurate and effective but in others it was the reverse.

The first meaningful campaign this book seeks to acknowledge was a raid that Bomber Command carried out of 144 aircraft attacking a concentration of German troops north of Falaise. This bomber raid was made up of ninety Lancasters, thirty-six Halifaxes, twelve Stirlings and five Mosquitoes. The reports at the time indicated that the bombing was effective and no RAF aircraft were lost during the raid.

Le Havre was bombed several times from June 1944 up to its liberation in September of 1944. The first meaningful example of this was on 14 June when aircraft from 1, 3, 5 and 8 Groups of Bomber Command attacked German defences in and around the city. In this raid, 221 Lancasters and 13 Mosquitoes took part. The main targets were German naval assets in the port area of Le Havre that had been harassing Allied troops, equipment and supplies landing on the beaches of Normandy. The beaches were only 30 miles from Le Havre port and the fast motor torpedo boats, known as E-boats, were a thorn in the side of the Allies.

The first wave of this raid took place in the evening while the second took place under the cover of darkness later that night. Most of the aircraft of the first wave came from 1 Group while those of the second wave belonged mostly to 3 Group. 'Pathfinder aircraft provided marking by their normal methods for both raids. No unexpected difficulties were encountered; the naval port area was accurately bombed by both waves with 1,230 tons of bombs and few E-boats undamaged.'[11]

Twenty-two Lancasters from 617 Squadron carried 12,000lb Tallboy bombs and these were sent ahead of the first wave along with three Mosquitoes to mark the targets. Their objective was the concrete-covered E-boat pens. 'Several hits were scored on the pens and one bomb penetrated the roof.'[12]

As this was an early operation for Bomber Command after D-Day and part of the first wave was still within daylight hours it was regarded as an experiment. The bombers in both waves were escorted by 11 Group Spitfires. One Lancaster was lost on this raid. However, there are two reports from this raid from local French press that both identify the considerable damage the Tallboy bombs caused.

> The Notre-Dame district, near the port, was devastated, but the people there had fortunately been evacuated at an earlier date. Other districts were also hit, with 700 houses and a tobacco factory being destroyed and the local gaol damaged: 76 civilians were

killed and 150 injured. These details of damage and casualties in the town area should not obscure the fact that most of the bombing fell into the harbour area and that the E-boat threat to the invasion beaches from the port was almost completely removed by this raid.[13]

On 5 September, a bombing raid took place over Le Havre when 348 aircraft attacked the German defences around the city. These aircraft were from 1, 3 and 8 Groups and were made up primarily of Lancasters (313), Mosquitoes (30) and five Stirlings. Visibility was good, and according to reports, the bombing was accurate. This raid by the RAF was particularly successful as they lost no aircraft during the entire operation.

The following day another heavy raid took place over Le Havre where more German defensive positions were pounded by bombs as were several vehicles, with 344 aircraft taking part. In this case, it was primarily Lancasters (311) supported by 30 Mosquitoes and three Stirlings. None of these aircraft were lost on this raid.

Further bombing raids took place a few days later over Le Havre. On the 8th, Bomber Command sent over 333 aircraft, mostly Lancasters but this raid was not as successful as the previous raids. To begin with, the weather was pour and visibility of the target area was difficult. Out of the total number of aircraft only 109 managed to drop their bombs with minimal damage to the Germans. Also, on this raid, two Lancasters were lost. As with the previous raid on 5 September, these aircraft were all from 1, 3 and 8 Groups.[14]

An interesting note to this raid is that for all four of the Stirling heavy bombers that took part in this attack it would be the last time that Bomber Command would employ them on bombing missions of this type. Indeed, 'It is believed that Stirling L.K. 396, piloted by Flying Officer J.J. McKee, an Australian, was the last Stirling to bomb the target.'[15]

German defences at Le Havre would be treated to another heavy bombing operation on the following day when 272 aircraft, this time predominantly made up of Halifax heavy bombers (230), were sent to hammer German targets. However, the weather was so poor and visibility so bad that the raid was called off by the Master Bomber and no bombs were dropped. No aircraft were lost either.[16]

The 10th saw a huge bombing force of almost a thousand aircraft (992) dispatched to Le Havre. Bomber Command had identified eight different

German strongpoints in the Le Havre area for special treatment and these were marked by Pathfinder aircraft then duly bombed with a high degree of accuracy. Fortunately for the bomber crews, no aircraft were lost on this operation.[17]

The next raid on German defences in and around Le Havre took place the following day on 11 September but this time with a much smaller concentration of heavy bombers. This time 218 aircraft from 4, 5, 6 and 8 Groups attacked German positions outside of the city. Visibility was excellent and so the bombing was accurate and intense, pounding the defenders, bringing up smoke, dust and debris. After 171 bombers had dropped their payloads and before the final wave went in, the Master Bomber decided to halt the bombing because the targets had become obscured by all the debris.[18] Shortly after this raid, the commander of the German garrison at Le Havre surrendered. As we have seen, this was not due to the bombing alone but to the combined ground and air assault on the garrison over several days.

Boulogne was also subjected to Allied bombing. The first big attack came on 15 June when 1, 4, 5, 6 and 8 Groups sent out 297 aircraft to attack shipping that had sailed into the harbour at Boulogne. Visibility for this raid was not as clear as it had been the night before when Le Havre had been attacked. The strategy was similar to the attack on Le Havre. According to local reports, this attack on Boulogne was described as the worst Allied attack on that city up to that point in time. Two hundred people were killed and the port infrastructure along with the surrounding areas was heavily damaged in this one raid.

The next attack on Boulogne by heavy bombers was on 17 September in support of the ground operation to liberate the city. In this case, Bomber Command dispatched 762 aircraft to pound the German defences in and around Boulogne. This raid marked the beginning of the ground offensive and, as we have seen in previous chapters, the Germans surrendered shortly after Allied ground troops entered the city. In this raid, there were 370 Lancasters, 351 Halifaxes and 41 Mosquitoes. More than 3,000 tons of explosives were dropped on German positions with the loss of only one Lancaster and one Halifax.[19]

With Le Havre, Dieppe and Boulogne in Allied hands the next job of the heavy bombers was to support the ground offensive against German positions in and around Calais. September 20th saw the first major raid with 646 heavy bombers attacking. German targets around the Calais area were earmarked for being bombed by 437 Lancasters, 169 Halifaxes and 40 Mosquitoes. Although one Lancaster was lost, the bombing was highly concentrated in the target area and accurate, according to the reports.[20]

The next raid against German positions in Calais was mounted on 24 September when 188 aircraft from Bomber Command attacked, or tried to. Visibility above 2,000ft was bad as the entire area was covered in cloud. Out of the 188 aircraft only 126 dropped their bombs. Most of these aircraft bombed 'Oboe-aimed sky-markers, but some aircraft came below cloud to bomb visually and seven Lancasters and one Halifax were shot down by light Flak, which was very accurate at such a height'.[21]

The next day, Bomber Command mounted another attack on German positions in Calais but this time it was much, much larger, with 872 aircraft involved. However, the cloud was low and made identification of the targets on the ground difficult. The number of aircraft capable of bombing through gaps in the cloud cover was 287 all told. This attack consisted of 430 Lancasters, 397 Halifaxes and 45 Mosquitoes and, fortunately for the Allies, none of these aircraft were lost.

German positions in Calais were again hit on 26 September. This time, four targets at Cap Gris Nez were pulverised by 531 Bomber Command heavy bombers, while three targets around Calais were attacked by 191 aircraft. Visibility in this raid was much better than the previous two days and on all targets the bombing was seen to be concentrated and accurate. Out of a total of 722 aircraft, two Lancasters were lost.[22]

The next raid on the Germans at Calais took place the following day, 27 September 1944, with 341 aircraft taking part. Although the entire target area was covered in cloud, the Master Bomber decided to bomb visually so he ordered the bomber force to descend below the cloud, which they did, led by the Master Bomber. This made the entire bomber force vulnerable to anti-aircraft fire from the Germans, however, the bombing was carried out successfully with only one Lancaster lost.

September 28th saw the final raid on the German positions in and around Calais before the garrison there surrendered. This attack consisted of 494 aircraft attacking six German gun batteries at Cap Gris Nez and 4 German positions at Calais. According to reports, Bomber Command had allocated roughly fifty aircraft per target but the number of aircraft that actually managed to drop their bombs were much less as the worsening cloud cover brought an early halt to the proceedings. In this case, of the targets at Calais

The Air Campaign and Epilogue 189

only sixty-eight aircraft managed to get through and drop their bombs. It was a similar story for the attacks on the six targets at Cap Gris Nez where only 198 aircraft out of 301 were able to release their bomb loads on the targets. Fortunately, no aircraft were lost on this raid.

> Calais surrendered to the Canadian Army soon after this raid and all the French Channel ports were thus in Allied hands, although most of the facilities required extensive clearance and repair. This, and the continuing presence of German troops along the River Scheldt between Antwerp and the sea, would cause the Allied ground forces serious supply difficulties for several more weeks.[23]

This is just a short overview of the air campaign that supported the various ground operations undertaken by the Allies to clear the Channel ports and get them working again. There were many more raids prior to D-Day on these same ports that one could say helped to soften up the German positions in preparation for the ground assaults to come.

***

This book illustrates the monumental effort it took for the Allies to liberate the Channel ports and use the port facilities for their war effort. As far as the Allies were concerned clearing the Channel ports of German troops was a combined arms effort, each of the arms dependent upon the other. Infantry depended on armour and both depended on artillery. The whole ground force depended upon the air campaigns and Allied air supremacy as well as the logistical efficiency of the Allies. The reason for attacking the ports and liberating them was for logistics, to shorten Allied supply lines.

However, the effort it took for the Allies to achieve their goals was huge. These were not just skirmishes, but full-blown attritional warfare. In short, the Allies had to wear down the Germans every inch of the way, until the Germans could take no more. Eighty years later, we can see the same thing played out in the war between Ukraine and Russia. At the end of the day, the Germans lost because they did not have enough fuel, oil, food and weapons; they did not have air superiority and towards the end, enough air defences to stop the Allies.

Eighty years on, it seems to this author that the lessons of the Second World War have not been learned by subsequent generations. War is not the answer to any problem, but sometimes it is the only solution to stop aggression. The cost of war is gigantic. After the Allies had liberated the ports it would take them months to get them up and running as Dieppe, Le Havre, Boulogne, Calais and Dunkirk had either been heavily damaged by Allied bombing and artillery or by the Germans blowing up port facilities as they surrendered or withdrew.

We, as humans, must find a way to ensure the destruction from all-out war is never experienced again anywhere on this planet.

Notes

Chapter 1: Overview

1. Ellis, Major L. F.; et al. (2004) [1st. pub. HMSO: 1968]. Butler, Sir James (ed.), *Victory in the West: The Defeat of Germany*. History of the Second World War, United Kingdom Military Series. Vol. II. Uckfield, UK: Naval & Military Press. ISBN 978-1-84574-059-7; cited in The Siege of Dunkirk (1944-1945), Wikipedia.
2. Ibid.
3. Hyrman, Jan (2009), 'The port of Dunkirk in WWII', *Naše Noviny*. Archived from the original on 14 July 2011. Retrieved 13 November 2009; cited in The Siege of Dunkirk (1944-1945), Wikipedia.
4. See The Siege of Dunkirk (1944-1945), Wikipedia.
5. Ibid.
6. 154 Brigade At Dunkirk, September – October 1944, https://51hd.co.uk/accounts/154_dunkirk.
7. Ibid.
8. Stacey, Colonel C. P.; Bond, Major C. C. J. (1960), *The Victory Campaign: The operations in North-West Europe 1944–1945* (PDF). Official History of the Canadian Army in the Second World War. Vol. III. The Queen's Printer and Controller of Stationery Ottawa. OCLC 606015967. Archived from the original (PDF) on 21 December 2020. Retrieved 26 January 2018.
9. This information can be found at The Siege of Dunkirk (1944-1945), Wikipedia.
10. Ibid.

Chapter 2: The Situation at 30 June 1944

1. See Report No 131, Section 77, *Operation Overlord and its Sequel:* Canadian Participation in the Operations of North-west Europe, 6 June – 31 July 44.
2. Ibid., Report No 131, Section 78.
3. *The Times*, 10 November 1944, 'Armour on the West Front', as cited in Report No 131, Section 79.
4. See Report No 131, Section 80.
5. Ibid., Report No 131.
6. First Canadian Army Int Summary No 16, Part I 'General Situation' 30 June 1944, cited in Report No 131.
7. Primarily Churchill tanks specially configured for specific tasks. AVRE stands for Armoured Vehicle Royal Engineers, although they were also referred to as Assault Vehicle Royal Engineers. These vehicles were primarily engineering-orientated – demolitions, mine clearance, providing different types of roadways and so forth.
8. See 8 Canadian Infantry Brigade, Memorandum of Interview with Major S.W. Lett By Historical Officer, 14 Jul 44, Report No 131.
9. See Report No 131.
10. Ibid.

11 See Canadian History Section File AEF/ 3 Cdn Inf Div/C/F/ Folio I, HQ 3 Cdn Inf Div 9 Jul 44 and 16 Jul 44, see also W.D. G.S. H.Q. 3 Cdn Inf Div: July 1944, as cited in Report No 131.
12 See Report No 131, Section 90.
13 Ibid.
14 Ibid., Section 93.
15 Also known as GOODWOOD MEETING, according to Report No 131, Section 94.
16 See Hist Sec File 2 Cdn Corps/C/F: Op GOODWOOD MEETING and Op ATLANTIC, 16 Jul 44; also Hist Sec File 3 Cdn Inf Div/C/F/Folio I – Summary Cdn Ops and Activities 16 Jul – 29 Jul 44; both cited in Report No 131.
17 See Report No 131, Section 94.
18 See Report No 131, Section 101.
19 See Hist Section File AEF 2 Cdn Inf Div; Summary of Operations, 17 and 18 Jul 44; Report No 131.
20 See 2 Cdn Fd Hist Sec, Appx 9, 18 July 44; See also 2 Cdn Inf Div Int Summary No 4, Jul 44; Report No 131.
21 See 3 Cdn Inf Div, Int Summary No 25: 19 Jul 44; Also 3 Cdn Inf Div Summary Of Operations, 1 Jul to 31 Jul 44, cited in Report No 131, Section 105.
22 See Report No 131, Section 107.
23 See Report No 131, Section 109.
24 This is stated in the 3 Canadian Infantry Division McLellan Report, July 1944; Report No 131.
25 See 3 Cdn Inf Div Report on Op 'Spring', 25 July 44, cited in Report No 131, Section 113.
26 See the War Diary of 5 Canadian Infantry Brigade, 25 and 27 Jul 44, cited in Report No 131.
27 Hist Sec File SHAEF Press Conference of General Dwight D. Eisenhower, 31 Aug 44 as cited in Report No 131.

Chapter 3: Operation TOTALIZE: Caen

1 See Report No 146 Canadian Military Headquarters, *Operations of First Canadian Army in North-West Europe*, 31 July-01 Oct 1944, Section 9.
2 See Report No 146 Canadian Military Headquarters, *Operations of First Canadian Army in North-West Europe*, 31 July-01 Oct 1944, Section 6.
3 See Report No 131, AEF/First Cdn Army/C/F/ First Canadian Army Lectures: The Campaign in Normandy up to the 'Break out' Battle South of Caen, 7-8 August 1944.
4 See Report No 146, *Operations of the First Canadian Army in North-West Europe*, Section 10.
5 Ibid., section 12.
6 See First Cdn Army Ops Summary No 25, 6 Aug 44; Report No 146.
7 See, Report No 146, Section 26.
8 See First Cdn Army Int Summary Nos 38 and 39, 6-7 Aug 44; Report No 146.
9 See Report No 146, Section 28.
10 The Mann Lectures, 25 Nov 44, as cited in Report No 146.
11 These were prisoners from German 85 Infantry Division; 2 Cdn Corps Int Summary No. 30, 10 Aug 44.
12 See Report No 184 Canadian Participation in the Operations in North-West Europe 1944, Part V; Clearing the Channel ports, 3 Sep 44-6 Feb 45.
13 See the Mann Lectures, as cited in Report No 146.

14. Lt Gen H.D.G. Crerar, Hist Sec file AEF/First Cdn Army, G.O.C.-in-C's remarks to Senior Officers, 05 Aug 44; Report No 146.
15. See Army Commander's Report to the Minister, 1 Sep 44; Report No 146.
16. See Report No 146, Section 36.
17. See Hist Sec File AEF/First Cdn Army; Operation TOTALIZE, Docket S, Request For Air Support; Report No 146.
18. See Report No 146, Section 51.
19. Ibid.
20. See 2 Cdn Corps immediate Report, Operation 'TOTALIZE' as cited in Report No 146.
21. See Report No 146, Section 56.
22. See 4 Cdn Armd Div, Aug 44, Appx 12, 'Outline of Instructions issues by G.O.C. 4 Cdn Armd Div 071300 B, Aug 44'; Report No 146.
23. See 22 Canadian Armoured Regiment, Aug 44, Appx 16; Report No 146.
24. See 28 Cdn Armd Regt, 9 Aug 44; Report No 146.
25. This was by 10 Cdn Inf Bde who reached the hill during the night, enabling 22 Cdn Armd Regt to gain the much needed foothold on the ridge.
26. See 28 Cdn Armd Regt, 9 Aug 44; Report No 146.
27. See W.D. G.S. H.Q. 4 Cdn Armd Div, 11 Aug 44; Report No 146.
28. See Hist Sec file Aef/First Cdn Army/C/F, Operation 'TOTALIZE'. 1 Polish Armd Div 'Order of the Attack', 8 Aug 44; Report No 146.
29. See Message Log, 2 Cdn Corps, 12 Aug 44, serials 3 and 13; Report No 146.
30. See First Cdn Army Int Summaries 9-13 Aug 44 as cited in Report No 146.

Chapter 4: Operation TRACTABLE: The Capture of Falaise

1. See Report No 146, CMH *Operations of First Canadian Army in North-West Europe*, 31 Jul – 1 Oct, Section 67.
2. See the Mann Lectures, 25 Nov 44; Report No 146.
3. W.D. H.Q. 4 Cdn Inf Bde, 13 Aug 44, cited in Report No 146.
4. Battle of the Falaise Pocket, Normandy Campaign, Wikipedia.
5. See W.D. 2 Cdn Fd Hist Sec, Aug 44: Appx 2, Lt-Gen G.G. Simonds, 'O' Group, 13 Aug 44; Report No 146.
6. See Op 'TRACTABLE' An Account of Ops by 2 Cdn Armd Bde in France, 14-16 Aug 44; Report No 146.
7. See W.D. G.S. H.Q., 2 Cdn Corps: G.O.C. letter to all Officers, 25 Aug 44; Report No 146.
8. See Report No 146, Section 75.
9. See Lt-Gen Simonds, 'Q' Group, 13 Aug 44 and Appx 'D'.
10. See First Cdn Army Op Instr No.14, Air Sp – Op TRACTABLE, 13 Aug 44, Report No 146.
11. See Msg. Go-113, 2 Cdn Corps ops Log, 14 Aug 44 as cited in Report No 146, Section 80.
12. See 2 Cdn Armd Bde Report On Operation 'TRACTABLE', Report No 146, Section 81.
13. See W.D. 21 Cdn Armd Regt, 14 Aug 44; Report No 146.
14. See 2 Cdn Corps Immediate Report, Operation 'TRACTABLE', Report No 146, Section 85.
15. Ibid.
16. See Report No 146 Section 86.
17. See Report No 146, Section 92.

18. See, 1 Brit Corps Sitrep, 17 Aug 44, Report No. 146.
19. See, 2 Cdn Corps Ops Log, 16 Aug 44, Report No. 146.
20. See W.D., G.S. Ops, H.Q., First Cdn Army, Aug 44, Appx 64; Memo, First Cdn Army Operational Intention as cited in Report No 146, Section 95.
21. See W.D. G.S., H.Q., 4 Cdn Armd Div, 16 Aug 44; Report No 146.
22. W.D., G.S., Ops, H.Q., First Cdn Army, Aug 44, Appx 85; Report No 146.
23. See Report No 146, Section 99.
24. C.M.H.Q. file, 21/Spec Awards/2 as cited in Report 146, Section 100.
25. See 2 Cdn Corps Ops Log, 19 Aug 44, Report No. 146.
26. See, W.D., G.S., H.Q., 4 Cdn Armd Div, 19 Aug Cited in Report No 146.
27. See 2 Cdn Corps Ops Log, 18 Aug 44, serial 21.
28. See W.D., H.Q., 4 Cdn Armd Div, R.C.A., 19 Aug 44; Report No 146.
29. See Hist Sec file AEF/First Cdn Army/S/F/; Report of 35 Wing, RAF, 28 Jul to 31 Aug 44; Report No 146.
30. See, Report of 35 Wing, RAF, 28 Jul to 31 Aug 44; Report No 146.
31. Ibid.
32. See W.D., G.S., Ops, H.Q., First Cdn Army, Appx 97, Attacks by Allied Aircraft on own Tps – 18 and 19 Aug 44, cited in Report No 146, Section 109.
33. These facts are set out in Report No 146, Section 110.
34. See First Canadian Army Int Summaries, 20-22 Aug 44; Report No 146.
35. See Report No 146, Section 112.
36. Ibid., Section 112.

Chapter 5: In Pursuit

1. See Report No 146.
2. See 3 Brit Inf Div, under command of First Cdn Army at the beginning of the month had reverted to Second Brit Army on 2 Aug – W.D. G.S., S.D., H.Q., First Cdn Army, Aug 44, Apx 10; Report No 146.
3. See H.Q., First Cdn Army Memo re Operational Intentions, 16 Aug 44; Report No 146.
4. Cited in 2 Cdn Corps sitrep 18 Aug 44, in Report No 146, Section 115.
5. See Report No 139, The 1st Canadian Parachute Battalion in France, 6 June–6 September 1944.
6. See Report No 146.
7. Ibid., Section 117.
8. This was made up of First and Third US Armies.
9. See Report No 146, Section 118.
10. C. in C., 21 Army Group, Personal Message to all Troops, 21 Aug 44 as cited in Report No 146.
11. This is in accordance with 2 Cdn Inf Div's Historical Officer in his Summary of Ops 20-26 Aug 44.
12. The engineers, 4 Cdn Armd Div and 2 and 3 Cdn Inf Divisions respectively, Report No 146, Section 125.
13. See Report No 146, Section 128.
14. See First Cdn Army Op Instruction No 9, 2 Aug 44, The Employment of the Dutch and Belgian Contingents.
15. See 6 Airborne Div Report on Operations in Normandy, 5 Jun – 3 Sep 44, National Archives, Kew.
16. See Report No 146, Section 131.

17 Ibid.
18 See 6 Airborne Div Report on Operations in Normandy.
19 See First Cdn Army Ops Log, 24 Aug 44, Serial 1 cited in Report No 146.

Chapter 6: Crossing the Seine

1   See AEF: 45/First Cdn Army/L/F: Special Interrogation Report, Oberstgruppenfuhrer Joseph 'Sepp' Dietrich cited in Report No 146.
2   Ibid.
3   See 3 Cdn Inf Div Hist Offr's Summary of Ops 1-31 Aug 44; Report No 146.
4   This is according to W.D. 30 Fd Coy R.C.E., 27 Aug 44, as cited in Report No 146.
5   See W.D., G.S., H.Q., 4 Cdn Armd Div, Aug 44, Appendices 56, 57; Report No 146.
6   See 2 Cdn Inf Div Hist Offr's Summary of Ops, 1 to 31 Aug cited in Report No 146.
7   See W.D., H.Q., 6 Cdn Inf Bde, 29 Aug 44; Report No 146.
8   See W.D., H.Q., 6 Cdn Inf Bde, 31 Aug 44; Report No 146.
9   See First Cdn Army Ops Log 29 Aug, Ser 79; Report No 146.
10 See First Cdn Army Ops Log, 31 Aug 44, Ser 102; Report No 146.
11 See AEF/1 Brit Corps/C/F; Operation 'ASTONIA', p.1; Report No 146.

Chapter 7: Operation ASTONIA: Liberating Le Havre

1   See G.O.C-in-C., First Cdn Army, Report to the Ministers, 8 Sep 44; Report No 146.
2   See Report No 146, Section 149.
3   See 2 Cdn Inf Div Hist Offr's Weekly Summary of Ops, 3 – 9 Sep 44; Report No 146.
4   See W.D., A/Q Branch, Adm H.Q., First Cdn Army Sep 44, Appx 8: D.A. & Q.M.G.'s file on Operations of Dieppe, Report No 146, Section 151.
5   See First Cdn Army In Summary No. 65., 2 Sep 44, cited in Report No 146.
6   This figure includes those German troops evacuated through medical channels.
7   See Report No 146 Section 155.
8   See Order of Seventh Army for Defence of the SOMME.
9   See AEF/First Cdn Army/C/F: First Canadian Army Lectures, The Campaign in North-west Europe from the 'Break Out' south of Caen 7/8 August 1944 to the 31 December 1944, Brig C.C. Mann, D.S.O., Chief of Staff, 18 May 45.
10 A more detailed account of the British entering Brussels can be found at Hist Sec file AEF/30 Corps/C/F: D.T.I, (War Office) Report, 'Advance of 30 Brit Corps across R SEINE to BRUSSELS and ANTWERP 24 Aug to 4 Sep 44'.
11 The Mann Lectures, 18 May 45; Report No 146.
12 See AEF/1 Brit Corps/C/F: Directorate of Tactical Investigation, War Office, Operation ASTONIA; Report No 146.
13 See Report No 146.
14 See AEF/First Cd Army/L/F, Docket III: Ser 15, Special Interrogation Report, Colonel Eberhard Wildermuth, cited in Report No 184, Canadian Participation in the Operations in North-West Europe 1944, Part V; *Clearing the Channel Ports*, 3 Sep 44-6 Feb 45.
15 Ibid.
16 See Report No 146.
17 Ibid.
18 See Report No 184.
19 See Special Interrogation Report – Wildermuth, cited in Report No 184.
20 Ibid.

21. Ibid.
22. See C.B. 3148, February 1945, Gunnery Review, Normandy Bombardment Experience, June September, 1944; Report No 184.
23. See Report No 146 Section 163.
24. See Special Interrogation Report – Wildermuth, cited in Report No 184.
25. Operation ASTONIA, originally planned for 9 Sep 44, was postponed 24hrs due to terrible weather that affected the reconnaissance operations and the marking of forward routes for the ground assault as shown in W.D., G.S. Ops, H.Q., First Cdn Army, September 1944, Appx 126: Tel 1 Corps to Bomber Comd, 7 Sep 44, Report No. 184.
26. See Operation 'ASTONIA', 1 Corps Op Instr No. 14, Appx 'A' 'Air Support'; Report No 184.
27. See D.T.I., Operation 'ASTONIA', R.A., 1 Corps O.O. No. 7, cited in Report No 184.
28. See D.T.I., 'Operation ASTONIA', cited in Report No. 184.
29. See *The Story of the 79th Armoured Division*, October 1942 – June 1945, Military Library Research Service, https://www.mlrsbooks.co.uk/.
30. See Operation ASTONIA, cited in Report No 184.
31. Ibid.
32. See Warhurst, Capture of Le Havre, cited in Report No 184.
33. See D.T.I., Operation 'ASTONIA', cited in Report No 184.
34. Ibid.
35. Ibid.
36. See *The Story of the 79th Armoured Division*, October 1942 – June 1945, Military Library Research Service, https://www.mlrsbooks.co.uk/.
37. These facts are from the above report, p. 95.
38. Ibid. Remember, that Crocodiles were Churchill tanks converted to flamethrowers towing a fuel bowser behind them. This was a deadly weapon against which the Germans had little defence.
39. Ibid. Kangaroos became part of the 79th Armoured Division shortly after the break out south of Caen.
40. See, Special Interrogation Report – Wildermuth; Report No 184.
41. See Report No 146.
42. See *The Story of the 79th Armoured Division*, October 1942–June 1945, Military Library Research Service, https://www.mlrsbooks.co.uk/, p. 101.
43. Ibid.
44. See Report No 184.
45. Ibid., p. 105.
46. This is taken from Report No 184.
47. See D.T.I., Operation 'ASTONIA'; Warhurst, Capture of Le Havre, p. 17, paras 54, 55; and AEF/21 Army Gp/C/F, Dockett II; fol 26, Immediate Report No. 45, R.E. Branch, 21 Army Gp, Report by ARE Troop Commander on attack on Le Havre, d/7 Oct 44; Report No 184.
48. Ibid., Section 27.
49. See the *Story of the 79th Armoured Division*, October 1942–June 1945.
50. See Report No 184, Section 28.
51. Ibid., Section 170.
52. See D.T.I. Report, Operation 'ASTONIA'.
53. Ibid.
54. Banks, Sir Donald, *Flame Over Britain, A Personal Narrative of Petroleum Warfare*, Sampson Low, Marston and Company, 1948.

55 Ibid., p. 109.
56 Ibid.
57 See Special Interrogation Report, Wildermuth; Report No 184.
58 See AEF/First Cdn Army/C/I: Minutes of Morning Joint Conference, 11 and 12 Sep 44; W.D. 1 Cdn Armd Personnel Carrier Sqn, 13 Sep 44; and W.D., H.Q. 2 Cdn A.G.R.A., September 1944: Appx No. 3, Operation WELLHIT; Report No 184.
59 See A.E.F./First Cdn Army/C/E. Docket II: G.O.C.-inC. 1-0-4, 15 Sep 44, Appendix A; Report No 184.

Chapter 8: Operation WELLHIT: Boulogne Liberated

1 Field Marshal Montgomery to General Crerar Commander First Canadian Army, Official History of the Canadian Army in the Second World War, Volume III, *The Victory Campaign, The Operations in North-West Europe 1944-1945*, Colonel C.P. Stacey, The Queen's Printer And Controller of Stationery Ottawa, 1960.
2 Ibid.
3 Ibid.
4 Ibid.
5 Ibid.
6 See W.D., H.Q. 9 Cdn Inf Bde, September 1944: Appx 5, Op Order No. 2; Report No 184.
7 See, *The Story of the 79th Armoured Division*, October 1942 – June 1945, Military Library Research Service, https://www.mlrsbooks.co.uk/.
8 See, *The Story of the 79th Armoured Division*, October 1942 – June 1945, Military Library Research Service, https://www.mlrsbooks.co.uk/.
9 See, Topographical Notes of Normandy Battlefields, made by Capt R.A. Spencer, Hist Sec, C.M.H. Q., as cited in Report No 184.
10 See AEF/3 Cdn Inf Div/C/F, Docket V: Operation 'WELLHIT', 17-22 Sep 44, cited in Report No 184.
11 Ibid.
12 Ibid., W.D., Regina Rifles Regiment, June 1944, Appx 3; Report No 184.
13 See, Special Interrogation Report, Heim, cited in Report No 184.
14 Ibid., Account by Lt Col Matheson 1st Battalion, The Regina Rifles Regiment, 1939-1946, (n.p, n.d) pp. 34–5.
15 See Special Interrogation Report, Heim, Report No 184.
16 See W.D., H.Q., 9 Cdn Inf Bde, 13 Sep 44, cited in Report No 184.
17 See Report No 184.
18 See *The Story of the 79th Armoured Division*, p. 119.
19 See Operation WELLHIT, W.D., 14 Cdn Fd Regt, 6 Sep 44, cited in Report No 184.
20 See the Official History of the Canadian Army in the Second World War, Volume III, *The Victory Campaign, The Operations in North-West Europe 1944-1945*; Maj-Gen R. E. Urquhart, with Wilfred Greatorex, Arnhem (London, 1958), 9. Cf. 21st Army Gp. Intelligence Review No 160, 18 Sep 44. United Kingdome Records.
21 See the Official History of the Canadian Army in the Second World War, Volume III, *The Victory Campaign, The Operations in North-West Europe 1944-1945*.
22 Ibid., see also *The Story of Normandy to the Baltic*, 139-7. *The Supreme Command*, pp. 284–8. Capt. The Earl of Rosse and Col E. R. Hill.
23 See Operational Research in North-west Europe, Report No 16, *Air and Ground Support in the Assault of Boulogne*, p. 24.

24 See the Official History of the Canadian Army in the Second World War, Volume III, *The Victory Campaign, The Operations in North-West Europe 1944-1945*, p. 338.
25 Ibid.
26 See W.D., H.Q. 2 Cdn A.G.R.A., September 1944: Appx 3, Notes on Planning – Op 'WELLHIT', Counter Battery Task Table No. 7, cited in Report No 184.
27 This was the German gun battery at Noires Mottes.
28 The Supreme Command, Eisenhower, Crusade in Europe, pp. 167–8, cited in Volume III, *The Victory Campaign*.
29 See W.D., H.Q. 2 Cdn A.G.R.A., September 1944: Appx 3, C.B. Intelligence Summary No. 6, Area Boulogne, cited in Report No 184.
30 See, Volume III, *The Victory Campaign*.
31 Ibid.
32 Ibid.
33 Ibid.
34 See H.Q. 3 Cdn Inf Div, September 1944: Appx 20, Op 'WELLHIT', Spectators; Report No 184.
35 See 3 Cdn Inf Div OO No 5, W.D., N.Shore Regt, 17-19 Sep 44, Account of Operations in the Boulogne Area. by Lt. Col. J.E. Anderson given to Historical Offr, 27 Sep 44, cited in Volume III, *The Victory Campaign*.
36 See *The Story of the 79th Armoured Division*.
37 See AEF 45/First Cdn Army/L/F, Docket III: Special Interrogation Report, Gen-Lt Heim; Report No 184.
38 Ibid.
39 See H.Q. 3 Cdn Inf Div, September 1944: Appx 41, Ops Log, 17 Sep 44, Ser 33; Account by Lt-Col R. Rowley, and Operational Research in North-west Europe, p. 28; Report No 184.
40 See, Account by Lt-Col. R. Rowley given to Historical Offr, 21 Sep 44, W.D., 18th Fd Coy, R.C.E., 17 Sep 44; Report No 184.
41 See, Special Interrogation Report, Heim; Report No 184.
42 See, Volume III, *The Victory Campaign*, and Account by Lt-Col D.F. Forbes given to Historical Offr, 27 Oct 44.
43 See Operation WELLHIT, p. 28; Report No 184.
44 See *The Story of the 79th Armoured Division*.
45 See S.D.&G. Highrs, 17 Sep 44; and Account by Lt-Col Rowley as cited in Report No 184.
46 See, Volume III, *The Victory Campaign*.
47 See H.Q. 2 Cdn A.G.R.A., September 1944: Appx 3, Op 'WELLHIT', C.B. Intelligence Summary No. 6, Area Boulogne, 18 Sep 44; Report No 184.
48 This was a shoulder-mounted weapon based on the spigot mortar system that launched a shaped charge with a cartridge in the tail of the projectile. They were early versions of today's anti-armour shoulder-mounted weapons.
49 See History of H.Q. R.C.A., 3 Cdn Inf Div, p. 11.
50 See Operational Research in North-West Europe, p. 29, cited in Report No 184.
51 See *The Story of the 79th Armoured Division*, p. 121.
52 See *Vanguard, The Fort Garry Horse in the Second World War*, p. 72.
53 W.D., 18 Cdn Fd Coy, September 1944: Appx 3, War History, 1700 hrs 16 Sep 44 – 1700hrs 23 Sep 44; Report No 184.
54 Ibid., Section 123.
55 Ibid.
56 Ibid., Section 125.

57 This was commanded by Lieutenant J.C. Ramsey RE.
58 See *The Story of the 79th Armoured Division*, October 1942 – June 1945, Military Library Research Service, https://www.mlrsbooks.co.uk/ page 125.
59 W.D., 18th Fd. Coy, R.C.E., September 1944, Appx I; Report No 184.
60 Ibid., and W.D., H.L.I. of C., 19 Sep 44, Casualty statistics from Director of War Services, D.V.A., November 1958, Also, this information comes from the account by Lt-Col, Rowley as cited in Report No 184.
61 See G.S., H.Q. 3 Cdn Inf Div, September 1944: Appx 41, Ops Log, 19 Sep 44, Ser 78, and 54 Account by Lt-Col Rowley; Report No 184.
62 See, W.D., Cameron Highrs of Ottawa, September 1944, Appx 8, Account by Lt-Col Forbes, 10th Armd. Regt., The Story of the Battle of Boulogne, United Kingdom records, W.D. H.Q., 9th Inf. Bde., 21 Sep 1944, Appx 5; Report No 184.
63 See AEF/8 Cdn Inf Bde/C/D, Docket IV: Account by Lt-Col J.E. Anderson, cited in Report No 184.
64 See *The Story of the 79th Armoured Division*.
65 Ibid., p. 127.
66 See W.D., H.Q. 9 Cdn Inf Bde, September, 1944: Appx 17; and W.D., S.D.&G. Highrs, 22 Sep 44 as in Report No 184.
67 See, Volume III, *The Victory Campaign* also W.D., H.Q. 9th Inf Bde, 22 Sep 44. Ops Log, H.Q., 3rd Inf Div, 22 Sep 44, various serials.
68 See Volume III, *The Victory Campaign*.
69 See 2nd Corps Counter-Battery Intelligence Summary No 6, Area Boulogne, 18 Sep 44, cited in Volume III, *The Victory Campaign*.
70 AEF 45/First Cdn Army/L/F, Docket III: Special Interrogation Report, Gen-Lt Heim; Report No 184.
71 Ibid.
72 Ibid.
73 See Volume III, *The Victory Campaign*.

Chapter 9: Operation UNDERGO: Calais Liberated

1 See G.O.C.-in-C., 1-0, fol 84, Message M.203; and Mann Lectures, 18 May 45; Report No 184.
2 W.D., 7 Cdn Recce Regt, September 1944,; Appx 7: Report on Operations – Advance from Falaise to Calais, page 4; Report No 184.
3 This information comes from *The Story of the 79th Armoured Division*, October 1942 – June 1945, Military Library Research Service, https://www.mlrsbooks.co.uk/bookstore/product/item334.html p. 133.
4 See H.Q. 3 Cdn Inf Bde, September 1944; Appx 8, 3 Cdn Inf Div OO No 2 cited in Report No 184.
5 Noires Mottes is about 6km west of Calais according to reports.
6 See H.Q. 3 Cdn Inf Bde, September 1944; Appx 8, 3 Cdn Inf Div OO No 2; Report No 184.
7 See H.Q. 3 Cdn Inf Bde, 12 Sep 44; H.Q. 7 Cdn Inf Bde, September 1944; Entry for 12 Sep 44 and Appx 9, 7 Cdn Inf Bde Operation Order No 1: Report No 184.
8 See H.Q. 7 Cdn Inf Bde, 12, 13 Sep 44; Report No 184.
9 Ibid. The facts in this instance are part of *The Story of the 79th Armoured Division* which was written by many of the officers who served.
10 See H.Q. 7 Cdn Inf Bde, 17 Sep 44.
11 See H.Q. 3 Cdn Inf Div, September 1944: Appx 27, Int Summary No. 43; Report No 184.

12 Ibid.
13 See H.Q. 3 Cdn Inf Div, September 1944: Appx 27, Int Summary No. 43; France 1:25000, sheet 38NE, Defence overprint edition 12 Sep 44; Report No 184.
14 Ibid.
15 See AEF/First Cdn Army/L/F Docket III: fol 14 Special Interrogation Report, Lt-Col Ludwig Schroeder as cited in report No 184.
16 Ibid.
17 See H.Q. 3 Cdn Inf Div, September 1944: Appx 31, Op UNDERGO, Hy Bomber Effort; Report No 184.
18 Ibid.
19 See HQ R.C.A. 3 Cdn Inf Div, September 1944: Appx 6, Trace and Adm Instr No. 1; and W.D., H.Q., 2 Cdn A.G.R.A., September 1944: Appx 4 as cited in Report No. 184.
20 This ratio is specified in Report No 184.
21 See H.Q. 2 Cdn A.G.R.A., September 1944:Appx 4, Operation UNDERGO, 2 Cdn Corps C.B. Int Summary No. 12, 26 Sep 44; Report No 184.
22 See Report No 184, Section 107.
23 See G.S., H.Q. 3 Cdn Inf Div, September 1944: Appx 34, 3 Cdn Inf Div, Operation Order No. 7, Op UNDERGO, Appx A, Order of Battle; Report No 184.
24 See G.S., H.Q. 3 Cdn Inf Div, September 1944: Appx 41, Ops Log 24 Sep, Ser 43; Report No 184.
25 See H.Q. 7 Cdn Inf Bde, 24 Sep 44, as cited in Report No 184.
26 Official name of the operation to capture and clear Calais and all the surrounding areas.
27 See H.Q. 2 Cdn Corps September 1944: Appx 15, Op 'UNDERGO'. Hy Bombing Effort; and 3 Cdn Inf Div Ops Log 24 Sep 44, Ser 40, and 25 Sep 44 Ser 10 cited in Report No 184.
28 See Report No 184, Section 111.
29 See *The Story of the 79th Armoured Division*, p. 136.
30 Ibid.
31 Ibid.
32 Ibid.
33 Ibid., p. 137.
34 See AEF/21 Army Gp/C/F, Docket II: fol 19, Immediate Report No 53 cited in Report No 184.
35 See *The Story of the 79th Armoured Division*, October 1942 – June 1945, Military Library Research Service.
36 See H.Q. 8 Cdn Inf Bde, 26 Sep 44: and W.D., G.S., H.Q. 2 Cdn Corps September 1944; Appx 3, Ops Log 26 Sep 44; Sers 14, 25, and W.D., G.X., H.Q. 3 Cdn Inf Div, September 1944: Appx 41, Ops Log 26 Sep 44, Ser 48; Report No 184.
37 See Report No 184.
38 This information comes from H.Q. 2 Cdn Corps, September 1944: Appx 3, Ops Log 27 Sep 44, Ser 1: Report No 184.
39 The information in this paragraph, while cited in Report No 184, comes from H.Q. 3 Cdn Inf Div, September 1944: Appx 41, Ops Log 26 Sep 44, Ser 80.
40 See *The Story of the 79th Armoured Division*.
41 See Report No 184 Section 117 taken from W.D., R.Wpg Rif, 27 Sep 44.
42 See W.D., 1 C. Scot R. 28 Sep 44; W.D. G.S., H.Q. 3 Cdn Inf Div, September 1944: Appx 41, Ops Log 28 Sep 44, Ser 57; Report No 184.
43 See W.D., G.S., H.Q. 3 Cdn Inf Div, September 1944: Appx 38, 3 Cdn Inf Div Operation Order No. 8, Op UNDERGO; Report No 184.

44   See W.D., G.S., H.Q. 3 Cdn Inf Div, September 1944: Appx 38, 3 Cdn Inf Div OO No. 8, Op UNDERGO.
45   Report No 184, Mann Lectures, 18 May 45; Report No 184.
46   See G.S. Int, H.Q. First Cdn Army, September 1944: Appx 31, Int Summary No. 91, 29 Sep 44; Report No 184.
47   See the *History of the Brigadier's Royal Artillery*, Branch of Headquarters, First Canadian Army of Second Great War.
48   See Report No 184; Historical Section, R.C.A.F; W.D., Nth N.S. Highrs, 26 Sep 44
49   See H.L.I. of C., September 1944, Appx 4: Patrol Reports and W.D., Nth N.S. Highrs, September 1944, Appx 6: Patrols; Report No 184.
50   See Account of the Attack on Cap Gris Nez given by Lt-Col D.F. Forbes, Officer Commanding Nth N.S. Highrs, 27 Octo 44 to Historical Officer; Report No 184.
51   See *The Story of the 79th Armoured Division*.
52   See First Canadian Army, Int Summary No. 92, 30 Sep 44; Other reports indicate that the actual number of prisoners taken was closer to 65 officers and 1,600 other ranks.
53   See *The Story of the 79th Armoured Division*.
54   Ibid., p. 139.
55   Ibid. This entire excerpt comes from the report by officers of the 79th Armoured Division involved in the attack on German forces at Calais, late 1944.
56   See H.Q. 3 Cdn Inf Div, 30 Sep 44; and W.D., C.H. of O. (M.G.), 30 Sep 44; Report No 184.
57   See Report No 184 Section 133.
58   See H.Q. 3 Cdn Inf Div, September 1944: Appx Ops Log 30 Sep 44, Sers 98 and 101; Report No 184.
59   See *The Story of the 79th Armoured Division*, p. 140.
60   Ibid.

Chapter 10: The Siege of Dunkirk Begins

1   G.O.C.-in-C./1-0, fol 79, Letter, Field Marshal Montgomery to Lt-Gen Crerar, 13 Sep 44, cited in Report No 184, Canadian Involvement in Operations in North-west Europe.
2   Ibid., folio 84.
3   Ibid., fol 87, Directive M.525, Report No 184.
4   See AEF/First Cdn Army/C/E, Docket II; fol 36, Directive Army Comd to Corps Comds. 15 Sep 44; Report No 184.
5   See AEF: 45/First Cdn Army/L/F, Docket II: Vol 2, Special Interrogation Report, General Otto Sponheimer; Report No 184.
6   See W.D., G.S., H.Q., 2 Cdn Inf Div, September 1944, Appx 27, Sitrep 180215 and Appx 28, Int Summary No. 49, cited in Report No 184.
7   See Report No 183, Canadian Military Headquarters, Canadian Participation in the Operations in North-west Europe, 1944, Part IV: First Canadian Army in the Pursuit, 23 Aug – 30 Sep.
8   See W.D., G.S., H.Q. 2 Cdn Inf Div, 5 Sep 44; Report No 183.
9   See, Report No 183, W.D., H.Q., 5 Cdn Inf Bde, 6 Sep 44: Report No 183.
10 Also known as The Black Watch of Canada; Report No 183.
11 See W.D., R de Mais, 7, 8 Sep 44; AEF/5 Cdn Inf Bde/C/D: Account of R. de Mais at Bourbourgville by Capt. Fafard; Report No 183.
12 See, W.D., Calg Highrs, 6, 7 Sep 44, Report No 183.

13 There is no indication of what these tracked vehicles could be. The author of the report refers to them as T.C.Vs which might mean M29 Weasels.
14 See W.D., H.Q. 5 Cdn Inf Bde, 8 Sep 44; Report No 183.
15 Ibid.; section 204.
16 Ibid.
17 See W.D., Calg Highrs, 8, 9 Sep 44, Report No 183.
18 See W.D., H.Q. 5 Cdn Inf Bde, 17 Sep 44; Report No 183.
19 See A.E.F/5 Cdn Inf Bde/C/D, Docket IV: Account by Major Pinkham, 'C' Coy, R.H.C., of the Attack on Coopenaxfort; Report No 183.
20 This was a little south-west of the town of Berques. See AEF/5 Cdn Inf Bde/C/D, Docket IV: Account of a Two-Coy Attack on Spycker by 'B' and 'C' Coys R.H.C; W.D., R.De Mais, 11, 12 Sep 44, Report No 183.
21 These were members of the Belgian White Brigade who had cleared Nieuport of German defenders in order to make way for the advancing Canadians. See Report No 183, Section 206.
22 See W.D., S. Sask R., 8 Sep 44, Report No 183.
23 Queen's Own Cameron Highlanders of Canada.
24 See W.D., Camerons of C., 9 Sep 44.
25 From 2 Cdn Inf Div Sitrep GO-2, 10 Sep 44, Report No 183, Section 207.
26 See W.D., S. Sask R., 10 Sep 44, Report No 183, Section 208.
27 See AEF/First Cdn Army/C/E, Docket II: Directive to Individual Commanders, 12 Sep 44; Report No 183.
28 See W.D., H.Q. 6 Cdn Inf Bde, 12 Sep 44; W.D., S. Sask R., 12, 13 Sep 44; Report No 183.
29 See W.D., Camerons of C., 12 Sep 44, 13 Sep 44; and Appx 6, Battle of Bray Dune, 'D' Coy, Camerons of C., Report No 183.
30 See W.D., H.Q. 6 Cdn Inf Bde, 14 Sep 44; Report No 183.
31 See W.D., Camerons of C., 14, 15 Sep 44; W.D., S. Sask R., 13-15 Sep 44; Report No 183.
32 Ibid.
33 See W.D., H.Q. 6 Cdn Inf Bde, 14, 15 Sep 44; Report No 183.
34 Ibid., 15 Sep 1944, Section 212.
35 Ibid., 16 Sep 1944.
36 See W.D., H.Q. 4 Cdn Inf Bde, 9 Sep 44; Report No 183.
37 This is sited in Report No 183, Section 213.
38 See Wikipedia Page – *4th Canadian Infantry Brigade*, History Section, https://en.wikipedia.org/wiki/4th_Canadian_Infantry_Brigade
39 See W.D., R. Regt C., 10 Sep 44, Report No 183, Section 214.
40 Ibid., 11 Sep 44.
41 See W.D., G.S., H.Q. 2 Cdn Inf Div, Sep 1944: Appx 30, Ops Log, Serial 7899, 12 Sep 44: and W.D., 18 Cdn Armd C. Regt, 12 Sep 44; Report No 184.
42 See W.D., Essex Scot, September 1944: Letter Lt-Col P.W. Bennett to Col Prince, 13 Sep 44; Report No 184.
43 Ibid.
44 See W.D., R. Regt C., 14 Sep 44; Report No 184.
45 See W.D., H.Q. 4 Cdn Inf Bde, 15 Sep 44: W.D., R.H.L.I., 15 Sep 44; Report No 184.
46 See W.D., H.Q. 4 Cdn Inf Bde, 15 Sep 44; Report No 184.
47 See Report No 184, Section 140.
48 See W.D., G.S., H.Q., 2 Cdn Inf Div, 18 Sep 44, cited in Report No 184.
49 See AEF/First Cdn Army/C/E/, Docket II: Message C110, Simonds from Crerar, 15 Sep 44; Report No 184.

50   See W.D., G.S., H.Q. 2 Cdn Corps, September 1944; Appx 3, Ops Log, 26 Sep 44, Ser 19.
51   See Report No 184 Section 141.
52   See W.D. 2 Cdn HAA Regt, October 1944 Appx 24, W.D., 11 Cdn HAA Bty, cited in Report No 184.
53   From the battery diarist 2 Cdn HAA Regt, 3 Oct 44, cited in Report No 184.
54   Ibid.
55   Ibid.
56   Ibid.
57   As cited in W.D., 12 Cdn HAA Regt, 3 Oct 44; Report No 184.
58   See W.D., Civil Affairs, H.Q. First Cdn Army, October 1944; Appx 9, Semi-Monthly Report No 6, Part III, Detailed Report No. 4.
59   Ibid.
60   Ibid.
61   See the Mann Lectures, 18 May 1945, cited in Report No 184, Section 147.
62   See W.D., 2 Cdn HAA Regt, October 44: Appx 11: Memorandum, Meeting of C.O.'s, H.Q. R.A., Dunkirk, 6 Oct 44; Report No 184.
63   According to reports the crew of the stolen tank were out on infantry duties at the time.
64   See *A History of 2 Cdn HAA Regt*, p. 43. A detailed account of this action was published on the front page of *La Voix Du Nord*, dated Lille, 12 October 1944.
65   German Panzerfausts were also included in this mix of equipment. The horse-drawn carriage was referred to by the Germans as puppchen.
66   See W.D., 2 Cdn HAA Regt, October 1944: Appx 23 & 25, 8 Cdn HAA Bty, October 1944: Appx V, 2 Cdn HAA Regt Sitrep, Appx IV; Report No 184.
67   See W.D., 2 Cdn HAA Regt, 24 Oct 44; Report No 184.
68   See W.D., 2 Cdn HAA Regt, October 1944: Appx 23, War Diary 8 Cdn HAA Bty Appx II, 2 Cdn HAA Regt, Streb 290900A, No 9; Report No 184.
69   See W.D., 8 Cdn HAA Sty, November 1944; Appx VI, 2 Cdn HAA Regt, Special Int Summary 1-5 Nov 44; Report No 184.
70   Ibid.
71   See 2 Cdn HAA Regt, 5 Nov 44, cited in Report No 184, section 154.
72   See W.D., No 22 Liaison H.Q. 31 Oct 44 cited in Report No 184.
73   Ibid.
74   *A History of 2 Cdn HAA Regt*, p. 40.
75   Ibid.
76   See AEF/1 Czsk Armd Bde/C/I, Docket 1; Historical Note on the Operations of 1 Czechoslovak Independent Armoured Brigade Group in North-west Europe, Sep 44 – May 45, cited in Report No 184.
77   First Cdn Army Int Summary No. 298, Part II, 24 Apr 45; Report No 184.
78   See W.D., G.S., Ops, H.Q. First Cdn Army May 1945: Appx 14, Ops Log, 4 May 45, Ser 93; Report No 184
79   See AEF: 45/First Cdn Army/C/E. Docket I, fol 3: G.O.C.-in-C's Report to the Minister of National Defence upon Operations 2 Sep – 30 Sep, dated 8 Nov 44.

Chapter 11: The Siege of Dunkirk: 1st Czech Independent Armoured Brigade Group

1   This number is an estimate only and, depending upon which source used, varies in numbers, anywhere from 12,000 upwards.
2   See Bleacker, Brigadier H.C., Commander 22nd Liaison HQ, *Outline of the Activities of CZSK INDEP ARMD BDE GP at Dunkirk 1944-1945*, National Archives.

3   See Townley, Chris, *The 1st Czechoslovak Independent Armoured Brigade Group (CIABG)*, Live Launch, https://launch.battlefront.co.nz
4   See Bleacker, Brigadier H.C.
5   See Townley, Chris.
6   Ibid.
7   Ibid.
8   Ibid.
9   Ibid.
10 Ibid.
11 Ibid.
12 Ibid.
13 Ibid.
14 Ibid.
15 See Bleacker, H.C., p. 2.
16 See Townley, Chris.
17 Ibid.
18 Note, the report I used here does not state if the dates were in 1944 or 1945 as the siege went on until the Germans surrendered in May 1945.
19 See Bleacker, H.C., p. 2.
20 Ibid.
21 Ibid.
22 Ibid.
23 Ibid., p. 4.
24 Ibid.
25 This is a term coined by the author of the Report from which this information was taken.
26 See Bleacker, H.C.
27 Ibid.
28 Ibid., p. 5
29 Ibid.
30 Ibid.
31 Ibid., p. 6.
32 Ibid.
33 See Townley, Chris.
34 Ibid.
35 Ibid.
36 Ibid.
37 Ibid.

Chapter 12: The Siege of Dunkirk: 7th Royal Tank Regiment War Diary

1   See Normandy War Guide, *War Diary: 7th Battalion Royal Tank Regiment*, December 1944 at: https://www.normandywarguide.com/war-diaries/7-royal-tank-regiment-december-1944
2   Ibid.
3   Ibid.: this information comes from the *War Diary of 7th Royal Tanks*.
4   Ibid.
5   Ibid.

6   This is according to the author of 7th Royal Tank's war diary, however, little is known about the diarist.
7   No further information on Veals has yet been found.
8   Ibid., this move completely bypassed Abbeville due to the heavy traffic there.
9   See Normandy War Guide, *War Diary: 7th Battalion Royal Tank Regiment*, December 1944 at: https://www.normandywarguide.com/war-diaries/7-royal-tank-regiment-december-1944
10 Ibid.
11 Ibid.
12 Ibid.
13 Ibid.
14 This is according to the diarist who detailed this account in the Regiment's war diary.
15 Ibid.
16 See Normandy War Guide, War Diary: 7th Battalion Royal Tank Regiment, December 1944 at: https://www.normandywarguide.com/war-diaries/7-royal-tank-regiment-december-1944
17 Ibid., as told by the unit diarist.
18 Ibid.
19 Ibid.
20 Ibid., although there is a little confusion with this entry. The diarist does not clarify if the FOO was stationed with the Heavy Anti-Aircraft Regiment or with Regimental Headquarters of 7th Royal Tank Regiment.
21 Ibid.
22 Ibid.
23 Ibid.
24 Ibid.
25 This is according to the regimental diarist.
26 Ibid.
27 This may or may not have been a Mustang. The diarist does not go into more detail than this quote so it is difficult to be sure.
28 See Normandy War Guide, *War Diary: 7th Battalion Royal Tank Regiment*, December 1944 at: https://www.normandywarguide.com/war-diaries/7-royal-tank-regiment-december-1944
29 Ibid.
30 See Normandy War Guide, *War Diary: 7th Battalion Royal Tank Regiment*, December 1944 at: https://www.normandywarguide.com/war-diaries/7-royal-tank-regiment-december-1944
31 Ibid.
32 Ibid.
33 Ibid.
34 Ibid.
35 This is according to the diarist of the 7th Battalion Royal Tank Regiment.
36 From the war diary of the 7th Battalion Royal Tank Regiment.
37 Ibid.
38 Ibid.
39 This quote is the entry for the 17 September 1944 in the war diary of the 7th Battalion Royal Tank Regiment.
40 See Normandy War Guide, *War Diary: 7th Battalion Royal Tank Regiment*, December 1944.

41 Ibid.
42 Ibid.
43 Ibid.

Chapter 13: The Air Campaign and Epilogue

1 See Wikipedia article 'Walter Model', https://en.wikipedia.org/wiki/Walter_Model
2 See, Ellis, Major L.F., and Warhurst, Lieut-Colonel A.E., *The History of the Second World War, United Kingdom Series, Victory in the West Volume II, The Defeat of Germany*, London, HM Stationery Office, 1968.
3 Ibid.
4 See Mason, Francis K., *The Hawker Typhoon and Tempest*, 1988, Aston Publications, Bourne End, Bucks UK, 1988.
5 Ibid., p. 87.
6 Ibid.
7 See Mason, Francis K. These were Flight Commander Captain G.H. Kaufmann, Flight Lieutenant A.C. Flood and Flight Sergeant H.C. B. Talalla.
8 Ibid, p. 89
9 This can be found in Mason, Francis K., p. 89.
10 Ibid.
11 Middlebrook, Martin and Everitt, Chris, *The Bomber Command War Diaries, An Operational Reference Book, 1939-1945*, Midland Publishing Ltd., 1996.
12 Ibid.
13 Ibid., p. 528.
14 Ibid.
15 Ibid., p. 578.
16 Ibid. This raid was by aircraft from 4, 6 and 8 Groups, made up of 230 Halifaxes, 22 Lancasters and 20 Mosquitoes.
17 The specifics of this raid are: 521 Lancasters, 426 Halifaxes and 45 Mosquitoes; Middlebrook and Everitt, p. 579
18 See Middlebrook and Everitt, p. 579.
19 Ibid., p. 585.
20 Ibid., p. 587.
21 Ibid., this raid consisted of 101 Lancasters, 62 Halifax bombers and 25 Mosquitoes. See Middlebrook and Everitt, p. 588.
22 Indeed, Middlebrook and Everitt state that 388 Lancasters, 289 Halifaxes and 45 Mosquitoes took part in this raid.
23 See Middlebrook and Everitt, p. 591

Bibliography

Books

Ellis, Major L.F., *Victory In The West, Volume II: The Defeat of Germany*, History of the Second World War, United Kingdom Military Series, Naval & Military Press Limited, Uckfield, 2004.

Mason, Francis K., *The Hawker Typhoon and Tempest*, Aston Publications Limited, Bourne End, 1988.

Middlebrook, Martin and Everitt, Chris, *The Bomber Command War Diaries, An Operational Reference Book 1939-1945*, Midland Publishing Ltd., Leicester, 1996.

Shores, Christopher and Thomas, Chris, *2nd Tactical Air Force, Volume Two, Breakout to Bodenplatte, July 1944 to January 1945*, Classic Publications, Hersham, Surrey, 2005.

Shulman, Martin, *Defeat in the West*, E.P. Dutton & Company, USA, 2017.

Thomas, Chris, *Low-Level Typhoon and Tempest Aces of World War 2*, Delprado Publishers, Madrid, 2001.

Reports

Hyrman, Jan (2009), The port of Dunkirk in WWII, *Naše Noviny*. Archived from the original on 14 July 2011. Retrieved 13 November 2009; cited in The Siege of Dunkirk (1944-1945), Wikipedia

Stacey, Colonel C. P.; Bond, Major C. C. J. (1960). *The Victory Campaign: The operations in North-West Europe 1944–1945* (PDF). Official History of the Canadian Army in the Second World War. Vol. III. The Queen's Printer and Controller of Stationery Ottawa. OCLC 606015967.

Report No 131, Section 77, *Operation Overlord and its Sequel: Canadian Participation in the Operations of North-west Europe*, 6 June – 31 July 44

Report No 146 Canadian Military Headquarters, Operations of First Canadian Army in North-West Europe, 31 July -01 Oct 1944

Report No 139, The 1st Canadian Parachute Battalion in France, 6 June – 6 September, 1944

Report No 184, Canadian Participation in the Operations in North-West Europe 1944, Part V; Clearing the Channel ports, 3 Sep 44-6 Feb 45

The Story of the 79th Armoured Division, October 1942 – June 1945, Military Library Research Service, https://www.mlrsbooks.co.uk/

Banks, Donald Sir, *Flame Over Britain*, A Personal Narrative of Petroleum Warfare, Sampson Low, Marston and Company, 1948

The Official History of the Canadian Army in the Second World War, Volume III, *The Victory Campaign*, The Operations in North-West Europe 1944-1945; Maj-Gen R. E. Urquhart, with Wilfred Greatorex, Arnhem (London, 1958)

Report No 183, Canadian Military Headquarters, Canadian Participation in the Operations in North-west Europe, 1944, Part IV: First Canadian Army in the Pursuit, 23 Aug – 30 Sep

Wikipedia Page – *4th Canadian Infantry Brigade*, History Section, https://en.wikipedia.org/wiki/4th_Canadian_Infantry_Brigade

Bleacker, Brigadier H.C., Commander 22nd Liaison HQ, *Outline of the Activities of CZSK INDEP ARMD BDE GP at Dunkirk 1944-1945*, National Archives

Townley, Chris, *The 1st Czechoslovak Independent Armoured Brigade Group (CIABG)*, Live Launch, https://launch.battlefront.co.nz

Normandy War Guide, *War Diary: 7th Battalion Royal Tank Regiment*, December 1944 at: https://www.normandywarguide.com/war-diaries/7-royal-tank-regiment-december-1944

Wikipedia article 'Walter Model', https://en.wikipedia.org/wiki/Walter_Model 154 Brigade At Dunkirk, September – October 1944, https://51hd.co.uk/accounts/154_dunkirk

Index

British Units
1st British Corps 11, 14, 19, 20, 29, 37, 42, 44, 46, 48, 50, 51, 54, 55, 58
1 Saint-Lothian & Border Yeomanry 81, 84, 91, 100
3rd British Division 11, 12, 17
3rd British Infantry Division 15, 16, 19
4th Special Service Brigade 3, 4, 6, 46, 134, 135
6th Airborne Division 19, 37, 42, 43, 44, 45, 46
6th Assault Regiment, RE 84, 104
7th Armoured Division 16, 17, 42, 43, 44, 46, 52
7th Royal Tank Regiment 139, 155, 156, 157, 158, 159, 160, 171, 204
8th Corps 8, 13, 14, 15, 16
11th Armoured Division 8, 15, 54
21st Army Group 2, 18, 20, 31, 37, 45, 52, 53, 54, 71, 78, 113, 120, 142, 143, 197
22nd Liaison HQ 144, 203, 208
30th Corps 13, 14, 195
31st Armoured Brigade 76, 100
34th Tank Brigade vii, 54, 172
43rd Division 11, 12, 13, 14
49th (WR) Infantry Division 6, 19, 37, 42, 43, 44, 46, 50, 54, 55, 57, 60, 64, 65, 66, 122
51st Infantry Division 19, 28, 29, 63, 156
56th Infantry Brigade 155, 156, 157
79th Armoured Division vii, viii, ix, 34, 58, 60, 68, 75, 76, 81, 88, 96, 98, 100, 119, 196, 197, 198, 199, 200, 201, 207
141st RAC 60, 61, 64, 89, 90, 100, 106, 107, 108, 117
154th Infantry Brigade 3, 4, 6, 26, 67, 135, 138, 144, 159

Canadian Units
2nd Canadian Armoured Brigade 19, 34, 35, 36
2nd Canadian Corps 11, 13, 14, 16, 18, 19, 29, 32, 36, 37, 39, 43, 44, 51, 69, 75, 76, 110, 111
2nd Canadian HAA 136, 138, 140, 141, 142, 170

2nd Canadian Infantry Division 1, 2, 4, 11, 14, 15, 16, 17, 19, 25, 28, 31, 32, 33, 36, 39, 48, 49, 51, 52, 99, 122, 128, 130, 134, 135
3rd Anti-Tank Regiment 93
3rd Canadian Infantry Division 11, 12, 14, 16, 19, 26, 32, 33, 35, 39, 47, 48, 50, 69, 72, 98, 104, 122
4th Canadian Armoured Division 11, 19, 27, 32, 35, 37, 40, 41, 47, 48, 52, 132
4th Canadian Infantry Brigade 44, 49, 50, 122, 131, 132, 133, 134, 202, 208
5th Canadian Infantry Brigade 3, 5, 6, 28, 50, 122, 124, 126, 135
6th Canadian Infantry Brigade 25, 36, 122, 124, 127, 128, 135
7th Canadian Infantry Brigade 12, 14, 28, 35, 48, 50, 99, 103, 104, 105, 107, 109, 112, 118
7th Canadian Recce Regiment 12, 14, 98, 99, 101, 112, 113
8th Canadian Infantry Brigade 10, 11, 15, 49, 50, 103, 104, 105, 109, 199, 200
8th Canadian Recce Regiment 51, 125, 126, 134
9th Canadian Infantry Brigade 11, 12, 15, 85, 86, 94, 103, 112, 113
10th Canadian Armoured Regiment 83, 99, 104
10th Canadian Infantry Brigade 10, 35, 37, 48, 52, 83, 99, 104

German Units
1st SS Panzer Division (Adolf Hitler) 8, 30, 47
2nd SS Panzer 30, 37, 41
10th SS Panzer 30
12th SS Panzer Division 11, 20, 32, 36, 37, 41
89th Infantry Division (German) 21, 26
116th Panzer Division 30, 37
226th Infantry Division 6, 121, 122
708th Infantry Division (German) 41, 53

Miscellaneous Units
1st Belgian Group 45
1st Czechoslovak Armoured Brigade 2, 3, 4, 6

1st Polish Armoured Division 27, 31, 35, 37, 39, 40, 41, 47, 52
2nd Czech Armoured Regiment 140, 141
12th US Army Group 31, 43
No 84 Group, RAF 33, 40, 77

A
Abbeville 22, 52, 158, 205
AGRA (Arny Group Royal Artillery) 35, 44, 58, 69, 149, 153, 200
Alençon 20, 30, 31, 183
Ambleteuse 100, 115
Antwerp 1, 2, 3, 4, 54, 68, 70, 71, 72, 98, 116, 120, 130, 134, 135, 172, 189, 195
Argentan 20, 31, 32, 36, 40, 43
Auster aircraft 79, 104, 153
Avranches 18, 20, 30
Avro Lancaster 35, 79, 105, 185, 186, 187, 188, 206

B
Bazookas (Panzerschreck) 165, 167
Belle Vue 102, 106, 108
Berques 3, 4, 123, 124, 125, 131, 133, 134, 202
Bofors guns 24, 25, 63, 133, 138, 139, 146, 174
Bomber Command ix, 56, 57, 66, 69, 72, 77, 95, 184, 185, 186, 187, 188, 206, 207
Boulogne v, vii, xiv, 1, 21, 54, 68, 69, 70, 71, 72, 73, 74, 75, 76, 77, 78, 79, 80, 81, 82, 83, 84, 85, 86, 87, 88, 89, 91, 93, 94, 95, 96, 97, 98, 99, 101, 102, 103, 104, 113, 116, 120, 121, 143, 145, 187, 197, 198, 199
Bourbourg 3, 122, 123, 124, 126, 167, 173, 201
Bourbourgville 122, 123, 126, 201
Bourguébus 16, 17, 19, 42
Bradley, General Omar 30, 43
Bray-Dunes 3, 4, 129, 130
Brest 20, 30
Brittany 20, 30, 43, 53
Brussels 52, 54, 71, 195

C
Calais v, xv, 1, 3, 8, 71, 77, 78, 85, 97, 98, 99, 101, 102, 103, 104, 105, 107, 108, 109, 110, 111, 112, 113, 115, 117, 118, 119, 120, 121, 122, 143, 145, 187, 188, 189, 190, 199, 200, 201
Calgary Highlanders 3, 5, 123, 125
Cameron Highlanders of Ottawa 50, 92, 112, 124, 127, 128, 129, 130, 131, 202
Cap Gris Nez ix, xvii, 3, 73, 98, 99, 100, 103, 107, 112, 113, 114, 116, 188, 189, 201

Carpiquet 9, 10, 11, 12
Coquelle 102, 103, 108, 109
Chemin Vert, Le 87, 89
Cherbourg 8, 10, 19, 20, 30
Churchill Infantry Tank vii, viii, 10, 61, 63, 88, 90, 108, 110, 146, 154, 191, 196
Colombelles 15
Coppenaxfort 4, 123, 125, 126
Crocodile AVRE (flamethrower) vii, 10, 26, 58, 60, 61, 62, 63, 65, 66, 67, 68, 75, 76, 82, 84, 89, 90, 91, 93, 94, 100, 104, 105, 106, 107, 108, 109, 110, 112, 113, 115, 116, 118, 149, 179, 196
Crerar, General Henry 3, 23, 46, 51, 69, 71, 77, 118, 120, 121, 135, 193, 197, 201, 202
Criquebeuf 48
Cromwell tank 144, 145, 146
Czech Independent Armoured Bde Gp v, 138, 145, 147, 149, 151, 153, 203

D
Dieppe xi, 51, 52, 70, 71, 122, 124, 127, 145, 187, 190, 195
Dives River 20, 35, 36, 37, 38, 39, 40, 42, 43, 44, 45
Douglas Dakota 145, 165
Dunkerque 134, 136, 137, 148, 149, 152, 153

E
Eisenhower, General Dwight D. 3, 71, 72, 192, 198
Elbeuf 47, 48, 49, 50
Elfeld, Lieutenant General 41
Entrees 28
Erebus, HMS 57, 59
Escalles 102, 103, 105, 108, 109
Essex Scot 129, 131, 132, 133, 134, 202
Evrency 12, 13, 20

F
Falaise v, ix, 10, 16, 22, 27, 28, 29, 30, 31, 32, 33, 35, 36, 37, 39, 40, 41, 42, 43, 47, 52, 53, 144, 181, 182, 183, 185, 193, 199
First Canadian Army 2, 3, 19, 20, 22, 23, 31, 34, 37, 41, 4243, 44, 46, 52, 53, 54, 69, 71, 85, 120, 138, 142, 183, 191, 192, 193, 194, 195, 197, 201, 207, 208
First US Army 20, 31, 43, 44, 54
Fontenay-le-Marmion 16, 17, 24, 25
Forêt De La Londe 49
Forêt De Montegeon 57, 65, 157
Fort de la Crèche 73, 75, 86, 93, 94
Fort Lapin 110, 111
Fort Nieulay 109, 110
Fort Sanvic 56, 66

French Forces of the Interior (FFI) 6, 46, 47, 75, 138, 139, 146, 161, 164, 165, 167, 169, 173
Frisius, Vice Admiral Frederick 2, 121
Furnes 124, 127, 134
Fusiliers Mont-Royal 127, 128

G
Ghent 71, 159
Ghyvelde 4, 130
Grand Mille Brugghe 126
Grande-Synthe 162, 164, 165, 166, 168, 174, 176, 178, 179
Gravelines 102, 123, 124, 171
Gravier 49, 50

H
Handley Page Halifax 79, 185, 186, 187, 188, 206
Haringzelles 98, 100, 113, 116
Haut Mensil 24, 26, 27, 35
Hawker Typhoon vii, viii, ix, 9, 66, 78, 104, 109, 110, 112, 114, 128, 129, 147, 161, 168, 171, 180, 181, 182, 183, 206, 207
Heim, Lieutenant General Ferdinand 74, 83, 89, 94, 95, 96, 198, 199, 201
Herquelingue 72, 74, 75, 92
Highland Light Infantry (HLI) Canada 17, 24, 25, 62, 64, 88, 91, 95, 113, 114, 115, 116, 131, 132, 134, 136, 139
Hobart, Major General Sir Percy 68, 75
Honriville 90, 91
Hubert La Folie 15, 16, 17

K
Kluge, Field Marshal von 21, 121, 134, 135

L
La Hogue 15, 26
Le Portel 89, 91, 93, 94, 95,
Lezarde, River 55, 56, 59, 60, 65
Liane, River 73, 75, 83, 84, 85, 88, 91
Liska, Brigadier General 2, 138, 140, 143, 145, 159
Lisieux 37, 42, 43, 44, 46,
Loon-Plage 3, 125, 139, 159, 160, 161, 162, 165, 167, 168, 169, 170, 171, 173, 176
Louviers 44, 154

M
M7 Priest/Kangaroo 4, 33, 34, 62, 82, 83, 104, 108, 117, 196
Marcyck 3, 4, 125, 162, 165, 166, 167, 168, 169, 170, 171, 172, 173, 174, 175, 176, 177, 178

Marquise 98, 100, 111
May-sur-Orne 14, 17, 25
Menny, Lt-General Erwin 41
Mezidon 19, 20, 37, 42, 43
Mitchell medium bomber 151, 176, 181
Mont Lambert 72, 73, 74, 75, 79, 81, 82, 83, 86, 87, 89
Montgomery, Field Marshal 2, 3, 5, 22, 31, 37, 53, 71, 77, 98, 120, 121, 147, 197, 201

N
Nebelwerfer 162, 174, 177, 178
Nieuport 122, 124, 127, 128, 129, 202
Nieuwpoort, Belgium 4
Nocquet 75, 93
Noires Mottes 99, 101, 102, 103, 106, 198, 199
North Nova Scotia Highlanders 17, 80, 83, 86, 87, 92, 93, 113
North Shore (New Brunswick) Regt 15, 81, 85, 93, 105, 108

O
Octeville 55, 57, 66, 67
Onglevert 98, 100, 115, 117
Oostende (Ostend) 4, 131, 132
Operations:
    ASTONIA v, xiii, 51, 54, 55, 57, 59, 61, 62, 63, 65, 67, 69, 72, 156, 195, 196
    ATLANTIC 13, 14, 192
    CHARNWOOD 11
    SPRING 16, 17, 18, 26
    TOTALIZE v, 19, 21, 22, 23, 24, 25, 26, 27, 28, 29, 34, 42, 53, 192, 193
    TRACTABLE v, 30, 31, 32, 33, 35, 36, 37, 39, 41, 42, 193
    UNDERGO v, ix, xv, xvi, xvii, 3, 98, 99, 101, 103, 105, 107, 109, 111, 113, 115, 117, 118, 119, 199, 200, 201
    WADDLE 140, 141
    WELLHIT v, xiv, 70, 71, 72, 73, 75, 77, 78, 79, 80, 81, 83, 85, 87, 89, 91, 92, 93, 95, 97, 197, 198
    WINDSOR 10, 12
Orne River ix, 6, 9, 11, 12, 13, 14, 15, 16, 17, 18, 19, 20, 25, 28, 30, 37, 42, 43, 44, 45, 46, 63, 131, 150, 194, 195
Outreau 75, 90, 91, 92, 93, 95

P
Patton, General George S. 30, 43
PIAT (Projector Infantry Anti-Tank) 86, 135
Pont a'Roseaux 169, 170, 171, 173, 174, 176, 178
Pont-Audemer 45, 46

Pont De L'Arche 348, 155
Pont L'Eveque 42, 43, 45
Potigny 27, 32, 33
Predembourg, Grande and Petite 140, 164, 165, 166, 167, 169, 173, 174, 175, 177, 179

Q
Quesnay Wood 27, 28, 33, 35

R
R. de Mais 123, 201
R. Regt of C. 131, 132, 134
Regina Rifles 15, 99, 107, 108, 109, 111, 197
Roquancourt 16, 17, 25
Rouen 47, 48, 49, 50, 51, 54,
Royal Hamilton Light Infantry Canada 88, 91, 95, 113, 115, 116, 131, 132, 134
Royal Highland Regiment (RHC) 123, 125, 126
Royal Navy 1, 56, 57, 67
Royal Netherlands Brigade 45, 50
Royal Winnipeg Rifles 10, 11, 15, 101, 108, 109, 110

S
Sangatte 9, 101, 103, 108, 109
Scheldt Estuary xi, 3, 54, 68, 70, 71, 135, 189
Schroeder, Lieutenant Colonel Ludwig 102, 103, 111, 112, 117, 118, 200
Second British Army 8, 13, 14, 19, 20, 22, 30, 31, 43, 44, 47, 36, 52
Second Tactical Air Force 40, 51
Spry, General 111, 112, 118
Spycker 3, 125, 126, 202
St Aignan-de-Cramesnil 26, 28
St Andre-sur-Orne 17, 18, 19
St Etienne 75, 93

St Omer 102, 122, 131, 159
St Pierre-sur-Dives 36, 37, 42, 43
St Sylvain 24, 26, 28, 37
Saint-Lô 10, 18, 81, 84, 89, 90, 91, 100, 116, 181
Sherman Crab tanks vii, 58, 60, 61, 65, 68, 90
Simonds, Lieutenant General 33, 75, 76, 77, 135, 193, 202
South Saskatchewan Regiment 25, 50, 124, 128
Stormont, Dundas & Glengarry Hlndrs 12, 80, 82, 85, 86, 91, 198, 199

T
Tardinghen 101, 117
Third US Army 20, 36, 43, 47, 54
Tilly-la-Campagne 17, 29
Touques River 44, 45
Tourneham 122, 124
Tourville 8, 47, 48, 50
Troarn 16, 19, 21, 37
Trun viii, 35, 36, 37, 38, 39, 40, 41, 42, 43, 52

V
Verrières 14, 17, 18
Vernon 43, 47
Veurne 4
Vieux Coquelles 102
Vimoutiers 44, 183

W
Warspite, HMS 57, 59
Westende 129, 132
Wildermuth, Colonel Eberhard 55, 56, 57, 62, 63, 67, 68, 195, 196, 197
Wimereux 73, 93, 94
Wimille 80, 93
Wissant 99, 113